Essay Index

Eleanor Flexner

American Playwrights:

1918-1938

THE THEATRE RETREATS FROM REALITY

Essay Index

With a Preface by John Gassner
and a new Preface to This Edition
by Eleanor Flexner

Essay Index Reprint Series

 BOOKS FOR LIBRARIES PRESS
FREEPORT, NEW YORK

Reprinted 1969 by arrangement with
Simon & Schuster, Inc.

INTERNATIONAL STANDARD BOOK NUMBER:
0-8369-1412-0

LIBRARY OF CONGRESS CATALOG CARD NUMBER:
77-99634

PRINTED IN THE UNITED STATES OF AMERICA
BY
NEW WORLD BOOK MANUFACTURING CO., INC.
HALLANDALE, FLORIDA 33009

TO MY FATHER AND MOTHER

Contents

Preface to the BOOKS FOR LIBRARIES Edition

When this book was first published, the world thought it had escaped a second great war by the agreement at Munich which recognized Adolph Hitler's conquest of Czechoslovakia. The last Spanish Republican resistance to Franco was crumbling, and the Japanese had only recently invaded China.

But the gap between that time and today is even wider and deeper than these news items might suggest. My generation spent its early adult years looking for work when there were no jobs — quite simply no jobs at all, either for them or their elders. Millions of people who had known ten or twenty years of security were suddenly reduced to joblessness. Nor were there any cushions against acute need, such as unemployment insurance or social security. Collective bargaining was unknown; unions were organized at the risk of losing one's job if one still had one, or bodily harm, sometimes even death. Establishing such minimal bulwarks against hunger and homelessness as trade unions and social insurance were the elemental concerns of a generation of American workers, and many professionals and intellectuals, during the Great Depression. A passion for security became the hang-up, the identifying scar which our generation carried over into better times, and the relative affluence of today.

In addition to presenting an evelution of the plays of another era, this book may serve a second purpose, by reminding readers, many of them hopefully students, that social protest and dissent have had a longer history in the United States than merely their own lifetime. Social concern was one of the principal yardsticks against which I measured the work of the leading playwrights of the twenties and thirties, and found iv

them severely wanting. (My publishers invited the late John Gassner to contribute a Preface which would in some degree blunt what they felt were my too radical strictures!)

Some of my hopeful prophecies were not realized. Today it seems strange ever to have thought that the C.I.O. might patronize the arts and trade unions foster drama companies. But the dream of a Federal Theatre in some form is not one to be lightly relinquished. The proliferation of permanent theatres outside New York, and the reception accorded an adventurous project like New York's Shakespeare-in-the-Park, confirm the continuing existence of a mass audience for live theatre.

I would also hazard another prophecy: that however wide the arc of convention may swing (the "theatre of encounter", of "participation", and of – total "revelation"? –), there will continue to be an audience and writers for the play of ideas. To those I singled out for special notice within the two decades covered by this book, I would now add such works as the late Lorraine Hansberry's *Raisin in the Sun*, Arthur Miller's *Death of a Salesman* and *The Crucible*, and Lillian Hellman's *The Little Foxes* and *Another Part of the Forest*. I would also reiterate the prediction that despite all forecasts and vagaries, nothing will kill the theatre, not even TV, or the featherbedding still practiced by theatrical unions (their memories haunted by those appalling years of breadlines, joblessness, and stranded, payless road companies).

Until very recently, the greatest failure of our theatre (as with the rest of our culture) has been its treatment of the American Negro experience. By omission, our playwrights denied the very existence of black Americans, as well as their segregation and oppression. The theatrical structure as a whole had no place for drama that dealt with the black heritage and expressed its culture. As I reread this book I am aware of my own shortcomings, for while I tried to point out the prejudice inherent in the few plays which dealt with black Americans, I fell into the common trap of speaking in terms of "southern" prejudice, as if this was the sum total of white America's sins of neglect and distortion.

We need to remember our failures when we evaluate the work of black artists today or fault them for what we feel to be undue bitterness. Like every other institution of our society, the theatre practiced discrimination and exclusion — until black militancy forced it to begin slowly making room for black writers, actors, directors, and producers. More pliant than either film-making or television because it lends itself to small-scale production, the theatre today can play a unique role in presenting the issues and helping in the development of black artists. This is its heavy responsibility, but also a priceless challenge and opportunity.

Eleanor Flexner

Northampton, Massachusetts
June, 1969

Preface by John Gassner

It is one of the commonplaces of contemporary American criticism that we have been in possession of the best drama in the world since 1918. Except for the isolated phenomena of a Shaw in England and an O'Casey in Ireland, we see in postwar (or is it now to be "prewar"?) Europe, England's theatre bogged in polite sentiment, the French stage still largely devoted to adultery, and Russia as poor for the time being in drama as its theatre is rich in acting, production technique, and organization. The Spanish stage was tepid even before the present civil war, Italian drama was at best only cerebral until fascism destroyed the intellectual integrity of Pirandello, and the German theatre was far richer in experimental forms than in solid accomplishment even before Hitler made accomplishment a crime. Glancing at our own stage during the same years, we are comforted by the dramatic output of O'Neill, Anderson, Howard, Behrman, Kaufman, and a host of

other playwrights; we note the rise of institutional or
"art" theatres like the Provincetown, Theatre Guild,
Group, and Mercury; and many of us glow with pride
that our stage should have room for all techniques and
shades of opinion. Nothing, we say, is too outspoken or
revolutionary for us; where else can one satirize the
head of a government as in *I'd Rather Be Right* or challenge the prevailing social order with the vigor of *Waiting for Lefty* and *The Cradle Will Rock?* A poor year
may draw harsh words from us, and there are always
enough exceptions to deflate our vaunt, but the appearance of a handful of striking plays in any season easily
restores our optimism. We do not even wonder at our
supremacy, but take it as the rightful heritage of our
democratic institutions and national energies.

Side by side with this allegedly glorious state of
affairs, however, we can descry a situation that provides
scant reason for optimism, and may puzzle us no end.
For more than a decade the American stage has been
retreating into a corner, until today (if we except the
Federal Theatre Project) it is mainly confined to about
fourteen square blocks in the heart of Manhattan. The
doldrums that have descended upon theatre business
and affect the quality of the drama furnish the subject
of a good many books, articles, and public speeches.
Sometimes it is perhaps necessary to discount the pet-
tishness of a bankrupt producer who strives to make his
exit properly eloquent and exemplary. But it is never
possible to neglect the fundamental truth of the situation which serves Miss Flexner as a springboard for
her evaluation of the American drama.

There is, in fact, a portentous anomaly—is there not?
—in our having a national drama which is said to be

the most vital in the world and a theatre which (without the Federal Theatre Project of recent years) is so picayune in comparison with other forms of entertainment in this country. How is it possible that such an undersized Jack Horner should be pulling out so many plums from such a minute Christmas pie? Those who believe that our best plays have really been so good must explain this miracle; probably they will resort to an analogy with the Elizabethan theatre which was largely confined to one bank of the Thames on the outskirts of London.

Miss Flexner, however, owes us no such explanations, since it is her contention that the miracle does not really exist. According to her diagnosis, much of our drama has declined with our theatre, and our favorably received plays have been for the most part grossly over-estimated. As a charter member of the new "younger" generation, the author of this book has of course the inalienable right, and the ability, to upset the apple-cart of established reputations. It seems almost pre-ordained that the estimates of one generation should be revised by its children.

Still Miss Flexner, who has been variously active in the theatre and was one of the able editors of *New Theatre* magazine, has a discipline and point of view many degrees above the fashionable apple-spilling game. The vigorous writers who comprise the group to which she belongs have a respect for the drama which does not encourage skittish irreverence. Their disgust with the Broadway theatre arises from a desire to make it over into a genuine people's theatre that would reach and express the great mass of the American people; and their dissatisfaction with the established playwrights springs from faith in the drama as a medium for the most forceful projection of the problems and aspirations of our time. I shall not anticipate the author by specifying her charges against Messrs. O'Neill, Anderson, Howard, and company beyond the general contention that they have failed to grapple with present realities or have done so fumblingly. The reader will of course determine for himself whether there is sufficient ground for Miss Flexner's indictment, but it would be beyond the realm of probability that writers who are plagued by contradictions in their thought should not reflect them in their plays to the detriment of structure, clarity, and force. In the work of each of our established playwrights the author traces a distressing falling off of power, dramatic logic, and significance; and throughout Miss Flexner's diagnosis locates the source of failure in the author's system of ideas or in an uncertain response to the time spirit.

The yardstick of so-called social criticism, which was generally employed in *New Theatre* and is here applied to the whole body of modern American drama, may prove an irritant to the many who surround the arts with a picket fence to secure them against profanation by economics. And it must be, I fear, conceded that this type of criticism may err by going to the opposite extreme of allowing no limits to its application. But incisive criticism always has a way of excising certain aspects of the larger problem of creative activity and subjecting it to analysis. Any other method either proves too confusing or demands extended studies which would fill several volumes. The clarifications supplied by Miss Flexner have validity even when it is possible to feel that she is not telling the whole story.

It is not too difficult, of course, to set down some qualifications with respect to the method adopted in this book, and it does not weaken the force of Miss Flexner's criticism to do so. For example, I fear that critics of the school are too fond of requiring playwrights to follow some blueprint of social analysis. One sometimes demands more attention to social causation than is perhaps necessary in a play; for example, the social background of the mother in *The Silver Cord* seems to me sufficiently implicit and her abnormal possessiveness can be safely left to the realms of emotion and psychology, without bothering to say that some aspect of capitalism is at the bottom of it all. A comedy which describes the futilities of upper-class individuals is intrinsically social criticism even if it does not declare explicitly that the social order produces the disease and is the seed of all corruption. Something, after all, must be left to the intelligence of playgoers and readers. It is likewise unnecessary to insist that the hero of a play should be clearly oriented toward the problem which he is facing and supposedly solving. Life is not like that, as every great playwright has realized. Dramatic characters are necessarily flawed like Hamlet and Lear, and if the exile in *Rain from Heaven* goes to join the underground movement in Germany with an extremely vague notion of how he is to function he is perhaps only behaving in accordance with his nature. Miss Flexner moves cautiously in her analysis, but she cannot avoid the emphases inherent in the prevailing sociological approach.

I am also troubled by the whole question of "confusion" as it applies to writers. Contemporary criticism is sometimes relentless in ferreting out the confusions of our authors, and there is much to be said for the procedure when it illuminates the dynamics of their creative processes. But at the risk of being set down as an obscurantist, I should like to say a kind word for confusion. . . . The writer who is absolutely clear in his point of view, and knows all the answers without fear or hesitation will most likely write tracts for the times; or if it is plays that he composes they may easily remain superficial. The fact remains that life is "confused" and confusing, and the great writer who is perhaps the most sensitive film for recording the conflict of principles in the surrounding world is himself a battleground for them. One wonders whether the beauty, depth, and fidelity to life in the work of such masters as Euripides, Dante, Shakespeare, Racine, Goethe, Balzac, Tolstoi, Dostoevsky, and Shaw do not spring in part from the confusions which be-devilled them. If they had succeeded in settling all problems for themselves would they have been so restless, complex, and human? Finally, the cynic might well ask whether we can be so sure that the confusion does not exist in ourselves rather than in the object of our criticism; isn't it always the other person who strikes us as being confused? One cannot help wondering whether it is not sometimes a trifle dangerous to settle a writer's hash simply because his outlook strikes us as inconsistent.

At the same time, of course, criticism cannot neglect a writer's system of ideas and reactions without becoming invertebrate and largely pointless. Perhaps there are actually two kinds of confusions which although they cannot always be distinguished manifest themselves differently even within the same piece of writing—those which deepen and intensify an author's work, and those which weaken it. I take it that Miss Flexner is thinking of the second kind when she finds our playwrights wanting, and to the degree to which there is truth in her indictment it is provocative and valuable. And even if we should feel that this critic is asking too much when she contends that Anderson and his colleagues should have risen above private and class limitations, her book is important precisely because it is just this demand that is being voiced by the new generation of writers. The group for which Miss Flexner is speaking calls for a body of drama greater than any seen on this continent, thus perhaps paying our cultural resources the greatest compliment of all. Nor are such critics content with wishful thinking. They descry significant social changes on the American horizon which may provide the theatre with the mass basis so important to its vitality. With high resolve and great tenacity, they went to work, and established "New Theatre League" groups, the Theatre Union, the Group Theatre, the Mercury, the Actors' Repertory Company, and trade-union theatres; they fought for the Federal Theatre Project and remain its staunchest supporters; they influenced older playwrights and producers, and gave rise to new authors, directors, and scene designers. Pessimism is foreign to these theatre workers; so is lassitude and carping from the side lines. It will be seen then that Miss Flexner's animadversions against our playwrights are written not to bury the theatre but to give it more life.

The history of our theatre, as I see it, is one of complex development in response to broad social and cultural forces. In the first postwar decade, the energies of a middle class that gained momentum from the artificial stimulus of war profits and financial speculation flowed, in part, into the theatre. No luxury of culture was too good for this class, which toured Europe, bought its masterpieces, tried to ape its manners and sophistication, and demanded as mature a theatre as any that the mother continent could provide. Our playwrights met this demand with plays that championed individual liberty, freedom from sexual and religious taboos generally described by the opprobrious term "puritanism," and tolerance for human passion. The understanding and freedom of spirit in work like *Anna Christie, Holiday, In Abraham's Bosom,* and *They Knew What They Wanted* were products of this liberation. But at the same time, in sharing the *malaise* of our middle-class life, our writers made excursions into abnormal psychology and tragic bedevilment that gave depth, even as they sometimes brought confusion, to work like *The Silver Cord, Hotel Universe, Desire Under the Elms, The Great God Brown,* and *Strange Interlude.* Being sensitive rebels, like all artists, they also revolted against the shortcomings of the society in which they lived, and so wrote a host of spirited critiques of commercialism, injustice, and folly—without, of course, wholly freeing themselves from inherent hesitations and contradictions. In this spirit were written such notable plays as *The Hairy Ape, Marco Millions, The Adding Machine, Street Scene, Processional, Beggar on Horseback,* and *Dodsworth.* It is not difficult to see where and how little Jack Horner got his plums.

Then, as the environment in the second decade began to sicken too gravely, the same writers became so troubled in spirit and so bewildered that generally their energies declined and their dramatic logic was weakened. Most of them became stalemated like Philip

Barry or began, as Miss Flexner would say, "a retreat
from reality." They retreated to mysticism or romanticism, or they evaded the very issues which they raised in
their work. But all was not lost, and plums continued
to come to the surface—partly from the perverse power
of these writers, and partly from the fresh resources of
their successors, who brought a new exaltation and passion into the theatre. The latter arose to condemn the
old order or demand modifications in it. They envisaged
a new world, voiced new aspirations or sounded a deeper
note of pity. They were not without limitations of
their own; but they galvanized the theatre into new life
with such works as Stevedore, Waiting for Lefty, Bury
the Dead, The Cradle Will Rock, The Living Newspaper,
and Of Mice and Men. And with the work of the New
Theatre League, the Theatre Union, Labor Stage, and
the Federal Theatre Project arose an effort to build a
mass basis for the drama that will not be satisfied until
Jack Horner grows up and leaves his corner; until America becomes the home of a great people's theatre. In
other words, despite serious difficulties, American society
has revealed a remarkable capacity for producing important theatre, and the one real quarrel with it is that
it has merely scratched the surface of its potentialities.

What the immediate future will bring cannot, of
course, be predicted, since we have not yet resolved our
basic social problems; and it is always possible that the
catastrophes that have befallen Europe may also become
our lot. But if one may resort to an ancient bromide,
while there is life there is hope, and there is certainly
life in us yet. The very fact that Miss Flexner, who is
in the vanguard of the progressive theatre movement,
can write a book like the present one indicates that

at least one generation has not given up the struggle in art or in society and has not retreated to Hindu fatalism. Moreover, if the catastrophe should come (a necessity which we in America cannot admit without being basely false to our heritage), there will be some crumb of comfort to the artist and humanist in the fact that out of our travail came plays that attest the power of the human spirit. Catastrophes marked the conclusion of the great Attic and Elizabethan periods in the theatre; but the tragedies and comedies written while the evil was brewing—the plays of Sophocles, Euripides, Aristophanes, and Shakespeare (none of them incidentally, free from much perturbation, which is the life of art)—testify to the one thing we are sure of, that the desire for a sane life is strong in us. Perhaps it may even conquer in the end. It is possible, of course, that such consolation is mere pap, but even so a hungry man will not lightly reject it, and that it should never be needed at all is the chief reason why the younger generation in the theatre addresses itself so persistently to the larger problems of our day. That these should intrude themselves into a discussion of the drama is moreover no inconsiderable evidence of the vitality of the theatre as a social force. If Miss Flexner did not believe this she would probably not have gone to the trouble of writing her book.

Foreword

This book makes no pretense at being a comprehensive survey of the American drama during the past twenty years. It deliberately confines itself to evaluating and questioning the achievements of those writers who have won not only audience but unbounded critical acclaim. (In doing so, it inevitably takes up conditions and developments in the theatre itself as well as in such a closely related sphere as the moving pictures. In addition, it goes at some length into the work of more recent and less orthodox dramatists in order to indicate more clearly the extent of their predecessors' failure.)

In such a scheme much that is worthwhile is inevitably omitted. In particular I regret that I have been unable to go into the plays of Paul Green, John Howard Lawson, Elmer Rice, and a few others in more detail. Undoubtedly their contribution to our theatre is a more significant and lasting one than that of some of the playwrights whom I have included. I did not set out to put every dramatist who has written, well or ill, for our stage in the past two decades, in his proper place. It is time that someone better suited to so large a task than myself, did so; a thorough re-evaluation of our drama is long overdue.

Since the passages on the Hollywood motion-picture industry in Chapters I and VIII were written, an event of far-reaching importance has occurred. The stranglehold of a few large corporations on the making and distribution of motion pictures has been threatened by a United States government antitrust action against eight of the major producing companies, numerous subsidiary corporations, and one hundred and thirty-two executives in the film industry. If the government wins the equity decree it is seeking, forcing the defendants to release control of distribution and exhibition, the big corporations will have to relinquish their huge chains of theatres and "block-booking," and other vicious practices crippling the independent producer and exhibitor will be curtailed. The results will be incalculable. There will be a real opportunity for the independent producer with courage, taste, and enterprise to make, and successfully market, forthright and artistic pictures. At present box-office and fan-mail indications are that such a development will be heartily supported by a public which has been staying away from the picture theatres recently in direct proportion to the declining quality of the films shown.

I wish to make acknowledgment to the following playwrights and publishers for permission to quote from plays written and published by them:

To Maxwell Anderson and Harold Hickerson for permission to quote from *Gods of the Lightning*, published by Longmans, Green and Co.; to Mr. Anderson for permission to quote from *Mary of Scotland*, published by Doubleday, Doran and Co., *Elizabeth the Queen*, published by Longmans, Green and Co., and *Valley Forge*, *Winterset*, *The Wingless Victory*, and *The Masque of Kings*, published by Anderson House.

To Eugene O'Neill and Random House, Inc., New York, for permission to reprint passages from *Strange Interlude*, *Dynamo*, *Lazarus Laughed*, *The Great God Brown*, *The Hairy Ape*, *All God's Chillun Got Wings*, *Desire Under the Elms*, *Mourning Becomes Electra*, *Days Without End*; to Mr. O'Neill for permission to use excerpts from an article on *The Great God Brown*, and from a letter to Arthur Hobson Quinn, which appears in the latter's *History of the American Drama*, F. S. Crofts and Co., revised edition, 1936.

To Clifford Odets and to Random House, Inc., for passages from *Waiting for Lefty*.

To George S. Kaufman and Marc Connelly and to Random House, Inc., for passages from *Beggar on Horseback*; to Mr. Kaufman and Moss Hart, and Random House, Inc., for passages from *Merrily We Roll Along* and *Once in a Lifetime*.

To Philip Barry, for passages from *Holiday* and *Hotel Universe*, published by Samuel French.

To Robert E. Sherwood for passages from *The Petrified Forest*, *Idiot's Delight*, and the introduction to *Reunion in Vienna*, published by Charles Scribner's Sons.

To George Sklar and Paul Peters, for passages from *Stevedore*, published by Covici, Friede, Inc.

To George Kelly, for passages from *Craig's Wife*, published by Little, Brown and Co.

To Rachel Crothers, for permission to quote from *Nice People*.

To Random House, Inc., for permission to quote from the text and introduction to *Rain from Heaven*, by S. N. Behrman, and from Harold Clurman's introduction to *Golden Boy*, by Clifford Odets.

To Harcourt, Brace and Co., for permission to quote an excerpt from Carl Sandburg's *The People, Yes*.

E. F.

American Playwrights:
1918-1938

The books of man have begun only a short stammering memoranda of the toil, resources and stamina of man,

Of the required errands, the dramatic impulses, the irresistible songs of this given moment, this eyeblink now.

Every day the people of the city haul it away, take it apart and put it together again.

The how and the why of the people so doing is the saga not yet written.

Carl Sandburg, *The People, Yes*

I Introduction

Since the days when it was weaned from religion on the
one hand, and lost the patronage of kings and courts on
the other, the theatre has suffered from a split personality. An art admirably suited to the portrayal and illumination of life, it could survive only by combining or
subordinating this function to the purveying of entertainment on a strictly profitable basis. That the two
occasionally coincided was no more than luck. With
culture limited, under a profit system, to a microscopic
proportion of the population, the demand for theatre of
a high artistic level has never been sufficient to make it
more than a luxury commodity. The theatre in modern
times has flourished only by virtue of its ability and
willingness to amuse, titillate, excite, mock, and afford
vicarious enjoyment of pleasures not always counte-
nanced by society. Its ability to communicate an understanding and a vision of life has become incidental.

Today it is a complex economic organism, suffering

3

from conditions in the business world, victim of developments in other fields—moving pictures, radio, television. It can no longer claim exclusive rights over the men and women who work for it. In an age of machines and corporations the theatre, essentially individualistic and small-scale, is no longer its own master.

Prophecies of the theatre's decay and demise are as old as the institution itself. Nevertheless, the advent of motion pictures is a menace of unprecedented seriousness. Because its product is capable of mechanical reproduction, the cinema has, in America particularly, lent itself to mass production and to the control of huge trusts who have made it their business to cripple the theatre as a competitor, and have very nearly succeeded in doing so.

Parallel to this attack has gone the transformation of the theatre in line with the whole trend of social and economic development. In an era of increasing consolidation of capital, heightened competition and recurring crises, it has become indistinguishable from any other business, as the revealing epithet, "show business," implies. The margin of profit has decreased, risks have increased, labor conditions and organizations (because of those risks) have come to bulk as large in theatrical enterprise as in the manufacture of automobiles. Those who cry out that the trade unions are strangling a noble art are blind to the whole set-up of the modern theatre, which is predominantly financial rather than aesthetic. Against a background of the transformation of an entire society three factors have operated, themselves alternately cause and effect, to make the American theatre what it is today: the centralization of the theatre in New

York, the change in the nature of financial backing, and the rise of the motion picture industry.

1

In the opening decade of the century the United States was still dotted with stock companies; in addition numerous traveling companies went out from New York to cover the entire country. There was hardly a small city which did not have its fair share of legitimate drama during the year. "The road," in other words, flourished. A number of factors contributed to its decline: railway fare increases, the stringency of theatrical union regulations (due to the unreliability of a certain class of managers, and the risk attendant on their enterprises), the declining quality of touring companies, which not only drove away critical audiences but reacted upon the better players, who became unwilling to associate themselves with inferior companies, and, most important of all, the advent and growth of motion pictures. The latter's influence was two-fold. Not only did they make available inferior entertainment at low prices, thus attracting the theatre audience and ruining its taste, but the picture companies inaugurated a deliberate policy of buying up available theatres, thereby excluding legitimate companies from a town that only boasted one or two playhouses suitable for speaking drama.

By 1920 the American theatre had come to mean New York and the small number of nearby cities where plays opened before their New York premieres. In New York itself the boom nineteen-twenties introduced a period of cut-throat competition and insensate speculation on theatre profits. Rents and production costs shot up, the public showed its willingness to buy tickets at any price, profits and losses alike ran into fantastic figures. A theatre shortage led to an orgy of theatre building, often by the producers themselves. By 1926, almost seventy theatres were playing simultaneously, most of them within an area of twenty city blocks. Even before the big slump it was clear that there had been considerable over-building. When the depression came in 1929 and the men who had been underwriting theatrical production lost everything on the stock market, production was drastically curtailed and theatre real estate values crashed. Firm after firm went into bankruptcy.

Meanwhile the figure of the producer who owned his own theatre and financed his productions from his own earnings had passed into mythology. The "backer," drawn by tales of immense profits (less was bruited about concerning possible losses), because of a surplus of capital he had nothing else to do with, because of the aura which has always surrounded the theatre, entered the picture. He might be anyone from a Wall Street magnate to a cloak and suit manufacturer or a night club proprietor and he might be the sole backer or one of ten others, each with an equal share in the venture. The problem of suiting the script to the taste of half a dozen people who knew nothing of the theatre except what they had witnessed from second row aisle seats, but who had a stake in the production and therefore a right to dictate came to be a major one in the writing and staging of good plays.

Even more significant was the appearance of the motion picture companies in a new role. Anxious to foster the type of play which would make good picture material and sell to their distributors throughout the country by virtue of its previous incarnation as a Broadway "hit,"

the film companies began to contribute towards the production of promising scripts. With a few exceptions,
their patronage has been limited to the type of material
which they so firmly believe is the only thing the public
wants; romance and adventure, realism distorted into
the American dream "success story" Cinderella formula.

Even the producer who is not backed by picture
money relies heavily on the sale of his motion picture
rights for profit or as a cushion for his losses. The market for new plays which might by a stretch of managerial
courage and imagination appeal to a New York audience
but which cannot possibly sell to the picture producers,
because they are too "intellectual" or too "radical" or
too "sad," is infinitesimal. By and large it boils down to
the Theatre Guild, whose subscription audience insures
it for a limited run at small loss, the Group Theatre,
which canvasses for backers sympathetic to its social
ideas, and Guthrie McClintic and Katharine Cornell,
who are reputed to enjoy the support of permanent backers. These are the only producing organizations which
can afford with any degree of consistency to set merit
above profit and ignore Hollywood (and even they cannot afford to be too disinterested). Other producers
may make an occasional beau geste for art's sake, an
Alex Yokel offers *Bury the Dead*, Herman Shumlin presents *The Children's Hour*. If they succeed, well and
good; but one failure, and they draw in their horns or
return to the common currency of entertainment. In
an era of growing demand for serious novels and nonfiction concerned with the economic, political and
social problems of our times, the theatre, with a few exceptions, remains devoted to stock comedy or roman-

tic dramas, farce and musicals. Hollywood is not the
only factor in bringing about this state of affairs, but
it is a major one.

While depressing the level of play quality, the films
have also taught audiences to look in the theatre for the
same kind of shoddy entertainment which they themselves purvey. Lastly they have drawn away from the
theatre a large proportion of its talent: actors, directors
and writers. That they have been able to do so is due,
not only to the fantastic salaries they offer, but to the
prevailing insecurity of theatrical employment; this condition however, as we have seen, the pictures have done
their fair share to bring about. Loss of talent has low-
ered the level of writing and acting still further, and
driven away from the theatre even more of that audience
which looks for something superior to motion picture
fare behind the footlights.

The champions of the cinema, and the theatre as it
exists today, are fond of pointing to the striking difference, in intellectual and artistic content, between the
best plays of today and of twenty years ago. The superiority of the present-day product shows, they say, that the
moving pictures have not harmed the theatre, that the
theatre itself is intellectually sound and progressive. The
fallacy of this reasoning becomes apparent when one
considers both the theatre and the motion pictures
against the background of our social and intellectual development during the intervening period. A growing
number of people who go to the theatre and who buy
books are interested in something more than entertainment. In response to this demand there has been a flood
of histories, biographies, serious books on economics and
politics, and novels far above the general war-time level.

The rise of standards in the theatre has been nowhere near as great, because too many factors operate to keep the theatre on a purely entertainment basis, and to affect adversely the work of the talented dramatist.

2

The cost of production and the speculative condition of the New York theatre necessitate immediate success if a play is to run. Very few producers have the patience or the capital to carry a weekly loss until such time as a play which receives adverse notices can surmount them by word-of-mouth advertising. The cut-rate agencies, which occasionally take over such plays, have provided a limited remedy, but they are not interested in productions that either operate at a high cost or do not have the elements of extreme popular appeal. Such instances of survival as *Tobacco Road*, *Abie's Irish Rose*, and *The Old Maid*, are only exceptions that prove the rule.

The influence of the New York newspaper critics who view the play on its opening night is therefore enormous. Quite literally theirs is a power of life and death. It must be constantly borne in mind that what takes place in the New York theatre governs what plays shall be seen outside of New York. The past five years have seen the road revive to the point where twenty-five odd companies go out from New York during the year, stopping for a week in the larger centers, and making one- and two-night stands elsewhere. But very few plays go on tour unless they have been successful on Broadway first. Thus the critics are invested with an even more abnormal responsibility than they would otherwise have. Without questioning their sense of responsibility and conscientiousness one may yet draw attention to several striking facts. This group of men who can make or break a play (and the fortunes of the people involved in it) work under terrific pressure. They sometimes go to the theatre six nights a week (and a succession of five bad plays is not always conducive to a sympathetic impression of the sixth, which may happen to be good). They write their reviews immediately after the performance under the shadow of a deadline.[1] Some have come to dramatic criticism via the sports page or feature writing. They are required by their employers to be journalists as well as critics, and a good "story" is not necessarily a good piece of criticism, since the two must emphasize different values. Occasionally, therefore, the dramatic reviewers write with a casualness or flippancy, or even brutality, hardly consonant with detachment, fairness, and good judgment.

The cost of production requires that a producer sell the majority of his high-priced ($3.30) seats in order to keep a play running. The approval of the class of patron who can only pay $1.65 or $2.20 is not enough. A small section of the society of our largest city therefore shares with its critics and the taste arbiters of Hollywood the responsibility of choosing what plays the remaining proportion of our population shall see, who see any plays at all. This audience is by no means as cosmopolitan and broad-minded as it is supposed or as it fancies itself to be. It prefers the entertaining to the grave or disturbing. It wants comic or romantic relief after the routine and tension of a business day. It is apt to rebuff

[1] For years the critic of the American was forced to leave at the close of the second act because his paper went to press early; this meant that he had to attend a dress rehearsal for his view of the entire play.

drama with a social tinge as propaganda, tragedy as too depressing, art as highbrow. It has occasionally less discernment than the critics; it vetoed *Waiting For Lefty* and *Bury the Dead*, which received unanimous critical acclaim, and which played to packed balconies throughout their runs. It exercises far too much power in proportion to its size and intellectual displacement, and yet this is the audience for which the less than ultraradical dramatist writes his plays. Consciously or subconsciously he dilutes his thinking to the level of its members, indulges them with clever dialogue, and limits his material to what will not too greatly brusque their sensibilities.

A large proportion of theatregoers with the price of orchestra seats (plus the commission charged by agencies which control the better seats for all shows of the hit class) are from out of town: buyers, sightseers, traveling businessmen who pack a year's entertainment into a week's intensive theatregoing. But they follow the recommendations of the ticket brokers whose "buy" has been guided by the reviews and the demand immediately following them or by word-of-mouth recommendation. Their taste is no guide to that of the potential out-of-town theatre audience (the road as it exists today hardly scratches the surface) any more than the preferences of the New York carriage trade correspond with those of the balcony and galleries.

This has been strikingly proved in the past three years by the Federal Theatre Project. Starting with the idea of keeping actors and technicians out of the bread lines, the project soon developed the additional aim of providing a section of the population with the theatre of which it had so long been deprived. (What was true of the rest

of the country was true of New York as well, where, because of high prices and concentration in the narrow
Broadway area, people are movie- rather than theatre-
minded.)   Where within the memory of younger people no speaking theatre company had come, the Federal
Theatre proved, to the amazement of some producers
and the disquiet of all the picture companies, that hundreds of thousands of people *like* the theatre, and what
is more, like *serious* theatre. It proved that, given prices
equal to, or slightly higher than movie prices, they will
pay to get it. That many of the Federal Theatre productions were inferior in quality only proves that if people
will go in droves to see not very good plays, not very well
acted and produced, their hunger for the first-rate must
be immense!

3

It is obvious that the dramatist is faced with an entirely different problem from, let us say, the novelist.
The latter can have his work simultaneously on sale all
over the United States. It can go on selling for as long as
there is any demand for it. To place him on the same
footing as a playwright would mean withdrawing his
book if a certain number of copies were not sold in the
first week in New York alone.

Nor is the novelist so dependent on the Hollywood
market. With lower production costs, a publisher can
afford to regard motion-picture sale as pure velvet.
Lastly, his work, once he has found a publisher, sells
largely on the appeal of its writing alone. But the merit
of a play depends not only on the quality of the script
as the playwright wrote it, but on the contribution made
by the director, the scene designer, and the actors. In

addition, its success may be crucially affected by whether it opens in New York on the same night as another play which may draw the first-string critics and thus secure a greater measure of publicity and interest, or by whether it rains every night during the first week, or by the income tax, Lent, the World Series, and intense heat or cold. People get sick or travel or have birthdays all year round; and on such occasions receive books as gifts. But they only go to the theatre in considerable numbers— because the theatre is New York—from October to April. A play that opens after Christmas can only do business (significant word!) for the remaining winter months, except in those half a dozen instances when a smash hit runs through torrid summer heat on the attendance of out-of-town visitors.

But it is when we go into the detail of how a play is actually sold and produced that the discrepancy between the playwright and other literary craftsmen becomes most evident. To anyone familiar with the day-by-day procedure of the "commercial theatre" the wonder is not that there are so few well-written, coherently thought-out plays, but that any of them make any sense at all.

To begin with, a particular manager's schedule is very much more limited than that of a publishing house; hence competition for his interest is the more intense. For this reason most playwrights, whether beginners or old-timers, make use of an agent. The number of successful and reputable agents is extremely small and of these the top flight, who naturally attract the ambitious young writer, have little time to give him even if they undertake to handle his work. In fact, the better the agent the less he can do for the young writer, and the more his successful clients get in each other's way. The ridiculous spectacle of an agent handling the work of three or four of our better-known writers, and trying to sell a play by each of them to one manager with backing, time, and taste for only a single production, is by no means unknown.

Nowadays it is not only necessary for a producer to like a script, but for a legion of advisers, ranging from his favorite director to his business manager, his publicity agent, and his office boy, to approve of it. Having received this endorsement, the manager must procure backing, and this often involves hawking the script about for months until the requisite thirty or forty-five thousand dollars have been raised. The less the shareholder knows about the theatre the more eager he is to participate in revisions and rewriting, even in casting and staging. Naturally this is less apt to be the case with the successful dramatist, who is moreover apt to sell his play to a solid producer with assured backing. But when production is once under way, he will find himself battling with the same forces of chaos as his less prosperous colleagues.

As rehearsals proceed and the date of opening draws near, tension mounts and doubts increase. The result is endless rewriting, recasting, redirecting. In an effort to approximate the vagaries, the high and low of public taste, everybody's opinion is asked and everyone offers advice. Because, "If it doesn't go over with a bang, it won't go at all." The critics hang over the proceedings like a pall. Such remarks as, "Cut that line—so-and-so won't like it," or "Halfway through that scene Mr. X will be out on Forty-fourth Street," are frequent. During the out-of-town tryout, which may last several weeks,

or the invitation dress rehearsals which take its place if
a play "opens cold" in New York, writer, producer, director, backers, and friends sit up all night worrying,
prognosticating, and arguing. Additional scenes are
written at 3 A.M., rehearsed the following morning, in-
serted at an afternoon "run through," and played that
night. The result, not surprisingly, is unsatisfactory, so
the scenes are "yanked" and others substituted the following evening after the process has been repeated.
Whole acts, characters, situations, appear and disappear.
Supplementary writers, new actors, another director, are
injected into the situation.

Occasionally a critic, if he is a good friend of the
author's or producer's, will journey unofficially to Boston
or Philadelphia and either reassure the frantic participants or plunge them into fresh apprehension. Frequently the playwright or the producer may be dividing
his time and attention between two plays, one rehears-
ing in New York, the other opening in Pittsburgh, or
Washington.[2] If the playwright of today is a frail and
sensitive artist he is doomed not only to failure but to
ulcers of the stomach; he must be capable of going
without sleep, have nerves of steel and a cast-iron diges-
tion, and be able to do good work in the midst of utter
turmoil and against an inexorable deadline. There is
this difference, and only this, between having a play
produced and childbirth: at no moment during the
former can the principal figure resort to anaesthesia.

What other art worthy of the name is pursued under
such conditions? The methods of Hollywood are fre-

[2] Joseph Verner Reed has described the "gentle art" of the
theatre under the "stagger system" in inimitable fashion in his
book, *The Curtain Falls.*

quently cited, in contrast to those of the legitimate theatre, as the reason why its pictures are so often disjointed and inane. But, while a single writer is usually enough for a play, and the theatrical producer has less scope for disastrous interference than in the picture studios, and while the stage director is not subject to the cutting-room scissors as is his cinematic colleague, the theatre's overweening pretensions to order and sanity are unjustified. The thought and contrivance that go into a well-written play cannot be arbitrarily raveled out, patched up, and amended without organic injury. When a writer is forced to tear his play apart and rebuild it at the last minute, with the opening looming unavoidably ahead because a postponement means a conflict with some other *première*, or additional rehearsal and production expenses, no good can come of so arbitrary and hectic a process.

Is improvement within the framework of the theatre as it exists today within the realm of possibility? Something could certainly be achieved with a little common sense, but for the most part the trouble lies in a contradiction of values: the role of art in a system geared to profit as the sole means of survival. In the Soviet Union today, by contrast, a play does not open until it is ready. The critics attend final rehearsals in a friendly, consultative capacity. If, after deliberate discussion between director, author, and critics, the play is adjudged unready, the *première* is postponed—for six months, if necessary. This does not mean that Russian plays are necessarily better than American plays or, if they are, that it is for these reasons alone. It serves to show that other methods are practiced, but only under a completely different system of life, and it throws some light on the folly of pursuing an art under conditions which have evolved, not to assist the creative process, but because of economic chaos. The nightmare of theatrical production is due to the uneconomic organization of something that cannot be treated as a business, and yet cannot exist unless it is.

4

Paramount among the influences that shape the playwright is that of Hollywood, not only because it is a secondary market for his plays, but because it employs him directly, in his capacity as a writer. The successful dramatist today is almost always a screen writer as well. Sooner or later he signs a contract with a picture company, usually over a term of years; the only outstanding exception so far has been O'Neill. Of the writers who have gone West, some have done so in more ways than one. Hollywood has been called the graveyard of Broadway. A good many playwrights have stayed there; others have tried to make of screen writing a dual career, dividing their time between plays and pictures. A few, having sampled the work and found it not worth the fantastic remuneration, have abandoned it completely.

Why has Hollywood so often held the touch of death for the creative writer? In what way has its influence been evident where he continued to write for the stage? It is necessary at the outset to draw a sharp distinction between the two crafts from the creative point of view. A play may suffer considerable emasculation at the hands of a producer, director, actors, and other unwanted collaborators in the commercial theatre, but the chances that it will reach the stage bearing some resemblance to what its author originally intended are much greater than those of a Hollywood picture script. This question of a writer's control over his material is a moot point between screen writers and producers, on the one hand, and dramatists and the film companies in the role of Broadway backers and producers, on the other. Thanks to the provisions of the Dramatists' Guild's minimum basic agreement, which is the standard contract for the sale of a play, the dramatist has titulary control over his material (though his exercise of that control depends on his own ability or strength of character or on that of his agent). The screen writer has no contractual protection for his work whatsoever. Often he is only one of half a dozen writers assigned to work on a picture in the various stages of its development—original, adaptation, screen play—as "story man," "gag man," "dialogue man," or rewriter, and his contribution may be completely eliminated by the time the picture reaches the screen.

Because of the nature of the medium, with the tremendous scope it affords director and cameraman, the writer's creative share in the picture is secondary. Conception, treatment, emphasis, may change completely during the process of photographing, and later of cutting, the picture. The well-known names in moving picture history are those of directors: Eisenstein, Dovjenko, Lang, Pabst, Hitchcock, Clair, Griffith, Ince, von Stroheim, Capra, Leroy, Dieterle, Ford.

There are, of course, instances in which writers have been largely responsible for a good Hollywood screen play. One thinks of Lillian Hellman's versions of *These Three* and *Dead End*, Sidney Howard's *Dodsworth*, and the treatment he prepared of *It Can't Happen Here*, reputedly a splendidly imaginative piece of work. But in every such case the writer is at best functioning as an *adaptor*. It is impossible to put such work in the same class with writing a first-rate play, and in no sense of the word are the writers so employed making the most of their talents. By comparison it is hack work, yet the salaries paid are lavish, and the temptation is to abandon a less remunerative medium or try to pursue both simultaneously.

In the case of the latter, a dramatist's technique is apt to be affected, usually for the worse. The grind of screen writing may be intense, as few authors who have gone to Hollywood have failed to let us know, but its discipline is far less stringent than that of playwriting. The freedom and flexibility which are the very essence of the cinematic form are demoralizing to the dramatist. Writers confess to difficulty in handling a plot with the concentration and unity demanded by the stage, after a bout with the films. "I find myself writing all over the place; the story keeps running away from me" is a typical complaint.

Hollywood being what it is, emphasis is laid, not on character or the careful development of a situation, but on smart, snappy dialogue, on "laughs" and sudden melodramatic twists with "surprise value." The influence of this technique on a play like George Kaufman's *Merrily We Roll Along* is unmistakable. Naturally writing for pictures is not the only influence operating on the playwright; the slick, fast-moving play has its origin in seeing as well as in working for the films. But the individual who is practicing as well as observing a technique is doubly its victim.

The psychology of the Hollywood producer, who has enormous investments to safeguard and dares not limit his market by offending any section of society overtly, has produced a code of what is proper and improper in motion pictures which is probably the strangest conglomeration of values in the world. The get-rich-quick fairy tale, the Robin Hood gangster and desperado, seduction (by implication), fraud and violence are not only permissible—they are the industry's stock in trade. On the other hand, certain words, phrases, gestures, and poses are barred with the utmost rigidity by the industry's self-imposed censorship, exercised by the Will Hays office. Intellectual censorship is even more stringent.Hollywood has one word which serves to damn anything that may lead people to think in a manner displeasing to the men who control the industry: labor questions, politics, racial prejudice, social injustice, and inequality are "controversial." They must either be avoided completely or subjected to reactionary distortion and caricature. Thus, Negro characters are invariably burlesqued or ridiculed, strikes and trade-union militancy ("outside agitators") are grossly misinterpreted and a poor boy's search for opportunity is given a happy ending. The writer who tries to transcend these formulas soon finds himself up against a stone wall of prejudice or ignorance. He chafes at his bonds, alternately ridicules and blasphemes them, but conform he must and does. Such a compromise, pursued over a period of years, does not make for candor and honesty when he comes to treat such problems for the stage.

American movies are the product of a mass industry. Simultaneous releases in every city and village in the country make for low admission prices; consequently the demand for pictures is inexhaustible. Production is geared to a terriffic pace; all grades of talent are used to turn out a supply that will be at least quantitatively sufficient. And the most vicious thing, from the point of view of the writer of distinction, is that the third- and fourth-rate writer is better suited than he is to this kind of work, and competition thus becomes a matter, not of merit, but of debasement. The writer who has any standards must override them and deliberately aim at mediocrity if he wishes to achieve success in his new medium. Even if he is fortunate enough to work for a producer whose taste and intelligence are above the general level, he is working and living in an atmosphere of intellectual dishonesty and mechanical inventiveness, of device and trickery. His imagination and sensivity cannot but grow sluggish from disuse, his ideas be corrupted, his mind lose its penetration and discipline.

To some of the younger dramatists, an early division of their energies is apt to prove even more dangerous than to their elders. Long before they have learned the rudiments of their craft they troop out to the Coast. It is not surprising, of course; they are either afraid of insecurity or tired of it. The commercial theatre is about as reliable a livelihood as roulette; it treats young talent with shortsighted shabbiness and deserves nothing from it. There are signs that leaders in the field are uncomfortably aware of this contradiction: talk is rife of "scholarships" and "tryouts." But a year or two of grace is of little value. Once over, the young writer, like the young actor, would be cast adrift with his fellows in a maelstrom, in which Hollywood or that chance in a thousand—a Broadway hit—appears the only holdfast.

Small wonder, therefore, that as new talent crops up

—the past few years have witnessed the emergence of Sidney Kingsley, Leopold Atlas, Clifford Odets, Lillian Hellman, Irwin Shaw, Victor Wolfson—it is immediately diverted westward. Some of these young writers have shown more stamina than their elders. A brief taste of screen writing has sent them fleeing back to New York, or else they have secured contracts which give them a substantial proportion of each year at liberty. This arrangement may turn out to be the most practical solution for the writer who has been able to get a Broadway production but must still eke out his living by other means. (It does not, of course, solve that other contradiction—the Broadway theatre itself.)

So much for necessity. But what of the men and women who, no longer under such compulsion, continue to divide their time between the two mediums? Theirs is a story by no means limited to the playwrights. Where an art cannot provide a safe livelihood, the necessity for supplementing it leads insensibly to the pursuit of wealth for its own sake rather than for a minimum of security. The novelist who writes for the "slicks," the musician who traffics with the radio, the painter who resorts to commercial advertising—will, when the real need for such additional revenue has passed, (like their theatre colleagues) tell you in all sincerity that they "must make a living." But what *kind* of a living? That is the question that lies at the bottom of many a compromise, and its answer is, in the last analysis, rooted in an individual's personal and artistic integrity, and in his philosophy of life.

Those who make such a compromise in the belief that they can get away with it, reap the rewards, and avoid the penalties are wrong. In the case of the dramatist "gone Hollywood," not only do his technique and standards of craftsmanship suffer. But work that is primarily creative (which screen writing, at least in Hollywood, is not) requires a kind of abstinence, spiritual as well as material, incompatible with too comfortable an existence and too many compromises. Security in which to work in peace and freedom is divided by a tenuous but none the less palpable barrier from that degree of immunity which isolates instead of protecting, which threatens to cut the artist off from that direct experience of life as most people enjoy or endure it which is the wellspring of first-rate work, particularly for the writer. There is no possible substitute for this experience; books, newspapers, and hearsay furnish not the thing itself, but other people's interpretations of it. Without the ever-renewed stimulus afforded by his own immediate perception of the forces, the circumstances which hedge about or impel human beings, the writer loses perspective, direction, sensitivity, the ability, in short, to create *life* in the full complexity of its conflicts and relationships, to evaluate and interpret it.

Mention has been made of the hectic state of competition which pervades the Broadway theatre. The playwright who goes from New York to Hollywood is only exchanging one set of artificial standards for another. Despite such healthy trends as the rise of the film trade unions, an increasing consciousness of the world outside the studios, as indicated by the formation and growth of the Anti-Nazi League, and the aid for political prisoners, for the California labor movement, and for Spanish democracy, Hollywood is still a world apart. Its more prosperous members lead a special existence, unreal because immune, highly organized and encumbered with publicity and business trivia, geared to a purely material set of values—hardly a stimulating alternative for the dramatist who in New York is drawn into equally limited and artificial relationships.

Meanwhile the pressure of two conflicting sets of commitments keeps him on a kind of double shift, from which he only occasionally escapes to Europe or to the country. It is the worst possible existence for a creative writer whose time away from his desk should be spent in acquiring experience and background for a new piece of work, in re-establishing contact with people of every social level, every category and activity, at work and at leisure. He might even well spend some of his time in just thinking. Without the understanding which springs not only from perception but reflection his work will lack penetration. And time—in which to reflect—is the one thing the writer living on a transcontinental shuttle does not possess.

5

Picture money of course is not the only insulator, nor is Hollywood the only snare. In taking refuge from its meretriciousness or from the distractions and detail which are apt to beset the successful writer in New York, some, like Maxwell Anderson and Eugene O'Neill, have fled to the country, to the Georgia coast, to the Riviera. Thereby they have also escaped from the more essential aspects of life. Flight from the superficial concomitants of success has isolated them and intensified the unrealistic, mystical strain present in their work.

Both tendencies show the extent to which our playwrights lose sight of the essentials of their craft. In

resisting such dangers they get little help from the theatre as it operates today, with its uncertainties, its consequent premium on quick success, its limited audience
whose approval must be courted. And the theatre, as
we have seen, is but one aspect of a profound disorgani-
zation, a mass of contradictions which pervades every
phase of our existence. Nevertheless the writer, be he
dramatist, novelist, poet, or critic, cannot plead absolu-
tion. His very gift places him under a social obligation,
to be a teacher and a guide. If he relinquishes his position, if he suffers himself to be led rather than to lead,
to be molded into something flabby and mediocre instead of coming to grips with the forces of chaos at
work in our midst, then little blame can attach to others
who succumb.

Dramatists and critics alike have invoked the axiom
that "art and propaganda do not mix." It has become
an excuse for avoiding any clear-cut political or social
point of view, anything resembling an honest or realistic
statement of life. One reason why so many plays which
attempt to deal with such questions as war and peace,
democracy and dictatorship, labor and capital, are bad
plays is because their authors, under the pretext of
avoiding all isms in the name of tolerance and liberalism,
eschew a basic philosophy from which they may regard,
understand, and interpret life. They confront a world
in travail with a handful of words—democracy, freedom, tolerance. Detached from basic concepts, what
meaning can they have? Democracy—how, and for
whom? Tolerance—of what? Freedom—what kind, and
at whose cost?

"Art cannot be created out of shreds and patches of

beliefs and sentiments. One cannot interpret a living social process without a living social philosophy." [3] A false code of conduct, a scale of values lacking in dignity or discernment, ignorance of the fundamental roots of character and behavior, are all manifestations which go back to the absence of such a philosophy, and they take their toll in shoddy and impoverished dramaturgy. "When artists close their eyes to the most important social currents of their time, the intrinsic value of their work is greatly lessened, and as a result, their work suffers." [4] For the writer to ignore the sharpening contradictions in our society, to overlook the gathering resistance to the forces of anarchy at work, is to turn his back on some of the richest dramatic material available to him today. Yet turn away from it is what our foremost successful dramatists have done, from reasons ranging from a heritage of "artistic detachment" to a philosophy of personal success.

The result is apparent in the disintegration which has without exception overtaken them, in their progressive loss of imagination, originality, craftsmanship, and honesty of thought, whether they were attempting to write explicitly social plays or not. It has led Eugene O'Neill into religious beatitude, Maxwell Anderson into the glorification of despair, and S. N. Behrman into the position that the enemy of civilization today is socialism. Look back to their earlier work, to the promise of *Anna Christie* and *S. S. Glencairn*, and Howard's *They Knew What They Wanted*, to the vigorous protest against fascism in *Rain From Heaven*, and then consider

---

[3] John Howard Lawson: "Lillian Hellman," *New Theatre and Film*, March, 1937.
[4] George V. Plekhanov: *Art and Society*, Critics Group, No. 3.

the ineptitude of these men's most recent plays: *Days Without End*, *The Ghost of Yankee Doodle*, *Wine of Choice*. What went wrong—and why?

6

The American drama first came to maturity at the turn of the century with the plays of Clyde Fitch. Fitch assimilated all the advances made during the previous decade by James A. Herne and William Gillette and Augustus Thomas, in play structure and naturalness of dialogue and realism of characterization, and passed beyond them with his comedy of New York society life, *The Climbers*, in 1900.

The chief claim to distinction of *The Climbers* and, after it, of *The Truth* and *The City*, is not their technical excellence but the fact that they were the first full-fledged examples in this country of the drama of ideas, specifically of social comedy. In 1893, in France, Brieux had written *Blanquette*, and Arthur Wing Pinero had shocked London with *The Second Mrs. Tanqueray*. But in America, despite the very real interest of James A. Herne in the social currents of his time and the infiltration of such interests into his plays (notably the protest against land-boom profiteering in *Shore Acres* and against the double standard in *Margaret Fleming*), the theatre had resolutely maintained its remoteness from anything suggesting criticism of life until suddenly with *The Climbers* it emerged into full-fledged comedy of manners.

Fitch's thinking, with its inconsistencies and shortcomings, was that of the more advanced progressive of his time. In play after play he satirized the climbers after wealth and position but he saw them, characteristically, as traitors, through weakness of character, to their class. His men and women of distinction and integrity are almost always those of established position, "to the manner born." In other words, Fitch was something of a snob, a believer in the mission and superior merit of the dominant social class. Nevertheless, he demanded of it that it measure up to a high standard of behavior, and his wit and perception pierced distinctions of caste to the essentials of character beneath. He could declare, in addition, that women as well as men should work for their living, a startling heresy at the time particularly in the milieu to which he was referring, and that dishonesty is a vice fostered by a society which puts a premium on showy appearances.

Fitch laid down what was to be the predominant pattern for writers of social comedy and tragedy for the next twenty-five years: beyond drama of character and the more striking and superficial influences of mores on character, he could not and did not go, and neither did the majority of his successors. They demonstrated that American drama was to make its most significant contribution in the critical study of character against a native background. This tradition gave us the finest and most enduring plays of the first dozen years of the century: *The Truth, The City, The Great Divide, The Easiest Way* (despite its melodramatic twists a provocative study of character deterioration *and its causes*), *A Man's World, The Faith Healer, As A Man Thinks, Milestones,* and *Within the Law* (in whose first act Bayard Veiller in 1912 heralded the stringent arraignment of society as the breeder of crime twenty years later).

In general, with a few isolated exceptions, the war years coincided with a period of sentimental stagnation, into which O'Neill's one-act plays of the sea and Jesse Lynch William's brilliantly sophisticated comedy *Why Marry?* fell like bombshells during 1917–18. The theatrical renascence of the twenties took up where the earlier development had left off, and the story of our native playwrights since then has been the attempt to develop the tradition of realism along the lines of developing thought *outside* the theatre, just as Fitch and Moody and Rachel Crothers had carried over into the theatre the progressive and growing thought of their day. What these had been to their generation, Sidney Howard and Eugene O'Neill and their contemporaries gave every promise of being to theirs. But the promise was not realized. Taking up where their predecessors left off, they went hardly any further in their understanding and interpretation of life. They gave us the realism of *The Silver Cord* and *Anna Christie*, the penetration of *Beggar on Horseback*—and stopped, or turned back in their own footsteps.

What the critics of the so-called propaganda dramatists who have grown up in the last five years have failed to realize is that the latter are the logical development of our finest and most fruitful dramatic tradition, carried a step further as their predecessors should have done and were unable to do, to an understanding of life and character as the product of social forces and social relationships in perpetual conflict and dynamic evolution.

II Sidney Howard

A curious dualism runs through the work of Sidney Howard. Undoubtedly his forte is character portrayal. His finest creations along this line are the simpler types —sterling, vivid, individual, and solidly human—which people our heterogeneous American scene. Be they immigrants, like Tony in *They Knew What They Wanted*, or deeply rooted native stock, like the McCobbs in *Ned McCobb's Daughter*, they have a raciness, a quality of forthrightness, independence, and integrity which epitomizes what is best and most typical in our American tradition. They are Sidney Howard's most valuable contribution to our theatre, for as characters they have a greater importance than the plays in which they appear.

Yet the creator of such distinctive American types has devoted a large proportion of his energies as a playwright to the adaptation of superficial Continental comedies, of the type of *Ode to Liberty*. This is due to two things: first, to Howard's undoubted mastery of stagecraft, in which he ranks second only to George S. Kaufman and which makes him greatly in demand among theatrical producers for work that requires such mechanical deftness and inventiveness; second, and more important to his work as a whole, to a superficiality of mind which manifests itself, on the one hand, in his concern with such potboilers (there is no kinder word which is at the same time honest, where a talent such as that of the author of *Yellow Jack* is concerned) and, on the other, seriously affects even his best work.

For while Sidney Howard is gifted with genuine insight into human character, he persistently ignores the conditions under which human character is obliged to exist and function. Thus he never probes the essentials of any dramatic situation. When he encounters a dramatic conflict such as that in *The Silver Cord* or *Dodsworth* he does not ask why, with the result that he never discovers in just what the conflict really consists.

Modern science has clearly established that character is not an accident. It can be definitely related, in great part, to certain factors of environment, heredity, opportunity, and acquired processes of thought. Yet the leading playwrights of the past two decades have patently ignored this fundamental concept of modern knowledge. Their conception of character is of a separate and absolute entity, unrelated to social or economic causation, and its importance lies in the fact that it absolves them from the necessity of examining the basic social forces and conditions of modern life. It limits them to a comedy treatment of their material or seriously vitiates their attempts at serious drama.

This disregard is nowhere more apparent than in the plays of Sidney Howard; it has caused his gift for characterization and comedy, for a richly human idiom of language, to dwindle away into platitudes. There is something radically wrong when the author of *They Knew What They Wanted* and *Ned McCobb's Daughter* writes *The Ghost of Yankee Doodle* a dozen or so years later.

1

Howard's first play to reach production was *Swords*, a romantic verse drama. But the adaptation of *S. S. Tenacity*, a simple and touching genre study of French types, showed what was to be his real medium—the study of character—a fact which became even more apparent with *They Knew What They Wanted*, which won the Pulitzer prize for 1924–25.

"No story is older than its applicability to life," wrote Howard, defending himself against the charges that his plot was as old as the story of Tristram and Iseult, or Paolo and Francesca. The situation is certainly not novel: the sixty-year-old fruit grower, Tony, lacks the courage to send Amy, whom he is wooing by mail, his own picture; instead, he sends that of the young and handsome overseer, Joe. On his helter-skelter way to the station to meet his bride Tony overturns his Ford and breaks both his legs. His incapacity, and Amy's shattering disillusionment, when she first sees the man she is marrying, precipitate a brief affair between Joe and Amy. Tony's common sense and sound domestic instincts preserve him from murdering his rival; he sends Joe away, and keeps Amy, and the baby that is on its way. The vintage of the plot is irrelevant because Howard has animated it with living people. He never surpassed, and rarely enough equaled, the authenticity and perfect pitch of human psychology he achieved here. The result is effective theatre, character comedy at its best, and dialogue warm with life and salty with Tony's inimitable dialect and irreverencies.

Technically Howard never wrote anything better than the first act of *They Knew What They Wanted*, which is a model of deftness in its exposition, character portrayal, and development. It has tension and pace. Thereafter the play sags, during the second act in which action is practically at a standstill, and the playwright is forced to draw heavily on the color and life of the *festa* with which Tony's neighbors celebrate his wedding. The third act also begins slowly, and it is not until a third of the way through that we learn the fact towards which the play has built—that Amy is going to have Joe's child. Because this revelation is placed so late in the play, and in the act itself, the dramatist is obliged to crowd the principal problem of his drama—the effect of Joe's and Amy's casual and fortuitous affair upon a lasting relationship between Amy and Tony—into one tightly written scene. A situation rich in implications and dramatic possibilities is broached, discussed, and resolved in one scene. The dramatic action of *They Knew What They Wanted* is confined to the first act, one scene in the second, and one in the third. The rest is padding. For all its human validity, technically the play is an immature piece of work.

They Knew What They Wanted was followed, within two years, by three plays varying in quality, but all of them solid achievements: *Lucky Sam McCarver*, an experiment in dramatic biography; *The Silver Cord*, probably the most widely known of any of Howard's plays;

and *Ned McCobb's Daughter*. It was an extraordinary body of work, the more so when one remembers that during the same period he produced three adaptations; for productivity, success, and quality Howard has never equalled this period in his career.

In *Lucky Sam McCarver* he drew a portrait of the prohibition era self-made success man, sharply contrasted with a woman who embodied the standards and point of view of established wealth. The play was an avowed experiment, consisting of four detached episodes in the lives of the two protagonists, with no more interconnection than their own personalities gave them. In the first, McCarver, a combination of naïveté and careerism, puts Carlotta Ashe so deeply in his debt that she marries him; in the second Carlotta, who has fallen in love with the man circumstance forced her to marry, discovers that he married her to forward his own self-advancement, and begins to hate him; in the third Sam, who has forced Carlotta to introduce him to her social world as a step in his rise in the world, vents his disgust with it and her, and breaks with her; in the fourth Carlotta and Sam are brought together after the lapse of a year only to demonstrate anew their complete dissimilarity and antipathy.

Just what the author set out to establish by this sequence of events is difficult to ascertain. This vagueness on his part accounts for the play's rambling structure. In form it is less a play than a series of one-acters; transitions are sudden and baffling, not only because the dialogue is often elliptical to the point of obscurity but because they are totally unprepared for. New characters are introduced, old ones drop out, as desultorily as in real life; the result is a quality of haphazardness out of place in the theatre. And the author's complete renunciation of any aim beyond that of putting two characters on the stage and letting them work out their relationship to its disastrous conclusion, robs the play of a badly needed point.

There are no rules as to what constitutes a play. In the main, however, it has proved a valid axiom that in order to satisfy an audience it should follow some logic of its own to a satisfactory conclusion, satisfactory as distinguished from *happy*. And whereas a *happy* conclusion has always been sufficient justification for itself (provided that it follows logically from the premises and circumstances of the play), an *unhappy* conclusion must, in addition to being the reasonable outcome to what has taken place on the stage, have some meaning which gives it significance above and beyond its own tragedy. To have human beings suffer for nothing in the theatre, *unless* the author draws some conclusion from that suffering which criticizes the circumstances that caused it, has never been acceptable to an audience. In *Lucky Sam McCarver*, Sam and Carlotta cause each other anguish because of their temperamental incompatability. There is no point in what we have witnessed. The author does not indicate that Sam is a cad; he takes great pains to exculpate and justify him. Sam is simply that kind of human being. And Carlotta's death serves no purpose whatever except to bring the action to a stop.

An attitude of social criticism, which would do much to lend validity to *Lucky Sam McCarver* as drama, is completely absent. It is not even implicit because there is no scale of values present. A point of view, if not embodied in one or other of the characters, must be implicit in the organization of the play, in the conclusion to which it moves. But as already stated, the conclusion of *Lucky Sam McCarver* indicates nothing, except that Sam is a certain kind of person, which we have known all along, and that Carlotta had a weak heart.

In *The Silver Cord* Howard swung to the opposite pole. While *Lucky Sam McCarver* is without theatrical direction, is life rather than contrived drama, *The Silver Cord* is life so highly organized in terms of theatre as to suggest special pleading. Whereas, in *Lucky Sam McCarver*, the author held no point of view towards his characters, in *The Silver Cord* he belabors them to the point of incredibility. Howard himself admitted his indebtedness, as dramatist, to the superb performance Laura Hope Crews gave in the role of Mrs. Phelps. He had good cause for gratitude. What must not the actress provide in the way of subtlety, plausibility, and variety, to overcome the exaggeration and reiteration, the extraordinary monotony of Mrs. Phelps' attack on Christina, who, she believes, is robbing her of her son Dave. We all know a Mrs. Phelps and have witnessed the havoc she wreaks. But knowing that such people exist is not the same thing as believing in them on the stage. Howard does not make us believe in the possibility of such a person from evidence presented by him on the stage and unsupported by our experience; the reasons for his failure lie deep in his approach to his material.

Mechanically the weakest link is the second act which takes place in Dave's bedroom, connected with his mother's by a communicating door. On the one hand Dave, who has already been shown as deeply in love with his wife and repeatedly hostile to his mother's de-

monstrativeness and possessiveness, nevertheless capitu-
lates to her with inacceptable celerity: on the mechanical side we witness Mrs. Phelps' entrance into Dave's
room from her own no less than four times. The result
is that her last appearance, which should come like a
bombshell in the middle of a tense scene between Christina and Dave, partakes of the ridiculous. Fortunately
for the play she has an antagonist who is not merely the
author's forceful mouthpiece, but a well-rounded character in her own right. Christina is deeply in love with
her husband; she has a telling gift of irony; and she is
not too rational to lose her self-control and her temper
when goaded past endurance. She does much to save
The Silver Cord from the unreality which the quality
of caricature in Mrs. Phelps occasionally gives it.

The play would carry even more weight if Howard
had examined to any degree the forces, the pattern of
life, which account for the Mrs. Phelps we all know.
The whole point of *The Silver Cord* would seem to be
that she is not unique. If this is the case, then she represents some fundamental quality of human nature
gone awry. Why? The author has Christina sum matters up by saying: "You're not really bad people, you
know. You're just wrong, terribly, pitifully wrong, and
you're trapped—" Later she calls Mrs. Phelps "a son-
devouring tigress." If this is true, then, as John Howard
Lawson points out in his *Theory and Technique of
Playwriting*, "We can hardly excuse her on the ground
that she is not bad, but only pitifully wrong. She has
become bad and we must investigate the causes. Middle-
class family life does not turn all mothers into 'son-
devouring tigresses.' Then there must be differences of
character and environment which determine the actions

of Mrs. Phelps." In other words, unless the author analyzes his characters in terms of social forces, unless he states clearly whether these people are *consciously* what they are, which in this case he never does, the play loses much of the impact and universality it might otherwise have. The same is true of Sam McCarver and Carlotta Ashe, or of Sam and Fran Dodsworth. These characters are representative of certain aspects of social and economic organization, yet they are examined without any definite relation to that structure; they are drawn in a vacuum, due to the playwright's inability, as Lawson shows, to consider character in terms of cause and effect, as anything but a static and fortuitous aggregation of personal qualities.

The pitfalls into which this point of view can lead the dramatist are again apparent in *Ned McCobb's Daughter* —in many respects Howard's best play. In it he demonstrates his undeniable flair for the creation of simple straightforward types, for the American character in its most native terms. His McCobbs, like Tony and Amy, are head and shoulders above Carlotta Ashe or Mrs. Phelps as character portrayals. They are never exaggerated; they are completely unself-conscious, profoundly human, and at the same time perfect examples of local individuality.

Ned McCobb's Daughter is a better constructed play than *They Knew What They Wanted.* The plot is more complex, the situations more completely developed, the "build" is carefully prepared and sustained throughout the play; the minor characters are integrated in the plot, the final denouement is logical and yet unexpected. The story of Carrie McCobb's victory, first over her wastrel husband, and then over his brother

Babe Callahan, who only helped her against George to have a hold over her for his own schemes, never sags and never diverges. And the triangular contrast between the delinquent Federal Prohibition agents, the salty inhabitants of Maine, and the alien Babe from New York's East Side not only furnishes abundant color and humor, but basic motivation.

But no play is better than the system of ideas it expresses. Inevitably, excepting in the case of pure farce or melodrama, if the underlying philosophy is ramshackle or false, the play loses, perhaps not in sheer entertainment value, certainly in enduring literary merit. And *Ned McCobb's Daughter*, for all its veracity of characterization and all its knowledge of human nature as expressed in some of Howard's pithiest dialogue, is a fairy tale in the best American tradition. When the weakling George cries out, in a short-lived moment of self-accusation, "I'll do the right thing if it kills me," Carrie McCobb answers, "Doin' right kills fewer 'n doin' wrong does. Bein' strong's mebbe harder 'n bein' weak but it's a sight safer." This may be a laudable axiom of conduct, but it is hardly substantiated by the facts of present-day life. There is little evidence in newspapers, in prison records, in social workers' reports on slum and housing conditions, that the good prosper and the evil get their due or that being strong and being good are at all synonymous. In the America of the gangster and the racketeer, the strong man is the one with the fewest scruples, as Howard himself took pains to show in *Lucky Sam McCarver*.

Ned McCobb's Daughter is a fable of the pioneer code of living: the square deal, the rewards of enterprise, of thrift, of rugged honesty. But the fable ignores any present-day phenomena which do not fit into its precepts. There is Jennie—product of a Saco mill—weak in flesh and spirit—Jennie, who begs Carrie not to send her away because she can only go back to the mill, to a way of life she abhors, and cannot resist. The forces which drive her inexorably to prostitution—her associations in the mill, an insufficient wage, the deadening routine of mill work over long hours—these are ignored, presumably as having no place in the fable. George, the villain of the piece, at one time a taxi driver, served a term in prison which was commuted for good behavior; George is "weak," a visitation on the family who is finally hurled into outer darkness. "Seems like lookin' after the weak must be the price a real man has to pay for bein' able to look after himself," Carrie remarks. Lastly there is Babe Callahan, as appealing a romantic swashbuckler as ever swaggered across Sabatini's pages. "You're no better in your way than George is in his," the incensed Carrie finally admits. George and Babe are brothers not only in blood. But George's pilferings are on a small scale and the work of an amateur; Babe is brilliantly creative and professional in his transgressions, and he has public opinion behind him. We are as proud and fond of the bootlegger as any Elizabethan was of the freebooters of the Spanish Main. So romanticism cloaks social cause and effect. Courage and integrity triump—"Doin' right kills fewer 'n doin' wrong does." Essentially the fable is the same as that which flickers at us from every moving picture screen. It arises from the dramatist's fundamental premise that character is fortuitous and that being as we are, we can be no otherwise.

2

The Silver Cord and Ned McCobb's Daughter were
produced in the winter of 1925–26. Since then Howard
has had a hand in a dozen plays, of which only three
have been his own original work. None of the latter
measure up to the best of the others in quality, and of
the former, only three stand out as possessing real
merit. Yellow Jack, although derived in subject matter
and outline from Paul De Kruif's Microbe Hunters,
owes far more to the dramatist's creative treatment than
to its original sources. The Late Christopher Bean
was originally an undistinguished French farce which
Howard, thanks to his aptitude for dialogue and characterization, transformed into genuine comedy. Dodsworth was a dramatization of the Sinclair Lewis novel,
concerning which Howard wrote in the introduction to
the published version, "It remains far less than the
novel, and therein lies my dissatisfaction with it and my
reason for saying that I shall hardly attempt another
dramatization. Works of art are best left in the form
their creators selected for them." He was thus clearly
aware that no matter how much the adaptor may contribute, his role is a secondary one; he is superimposing
his own work on the outcome of another man's inspira-
tion, effort, and artistry. When we remember, therefore, that Yellow Jack, which of the three owes the
most to Howard as a creative artist, was written back
in 1928, we realize that the past ten years represent,
not the development which might have been expected
from a steadily maturing writer of Howard's endowment,
but a decline in quality and a dominant interest in
secondhand material.

The theme of *Alien Corn* is significant and provocative. Through the necessity of supporting her crippled father, Elsa Brandt, talented young pianist, is trapped in the mediocre environment of a Midwestern college, where she gives piano lessons. Academic prejudices, hidebound mechanical restrictions, petty jealousies, rob her of the opportunity to win a scholarship which will let her try out and develop her talent abroad. Conway College, born of the vanity of a wealthy and conventional businessman, is the grave of talent, ambition and youthful hopes.

Unfortunately we never know just what it is that "traps" Elsa Brandt: the need of supporting her father or her insufficient courage and initiative. If it is the former, then Elsa's dilemma is a tragedy of circumstance—if the latter, it is a tragedy of character. This confusion explains why there is no real progression in the play. Elsa makes several abortive attempts to break away and go to Vienna, symbol of her artistic fulfillment. She tries to earn money by joint recitals with Mrs. Conway, and then by herself. Both methods fail. Then her father, suddenly alive to the fact that it is he who is the cause of Elsa's clinging to her job (we may well ask why such a possibility never occurred to him before if his daughter's career is his sole preoccupation, as we are repeatedly told), demands that she go ahead anyway: "I have a *right* to starve—you have no right to betray my hopes in you!" The logic of the play demands that at this point Elsa justify his sacrifices by making the plunge into insecurity. When she refuses and the situation becomes exactly what it was at the rise of the curtain, the play falters irretrievably: there has been no development. An emotional reaction to the ups and downs she has undergone throws Elsa into Conway's arms, and it is only Julian's suicide which, fortuitously and providentially, jars her into an awareness of the falseness of her relationship to Conway and a sense of true values. She once more recognizes that she must break away, and the dramatist would have us believe that her realization is definite and final, the prelude to action. The curtain falls on the question, "Is this her home?" and Elsa's cry of affirmation: "No—Vienna!" But we are not convinced because we know that none of the conditions which had a share in imprisoning her (the presence of her father, for instance) have been altered, and because we have only witnessed what John Howard Lawson calls "recognition as a substitute for action." [1]

Throughout the play the academic world and the college professor are contrasted with real life as if there were something integral to college life which prevented it from being anything but a sheltered travesty of "real life outside." Actually there is no reason why college life should be any more unreal than any other kind of life. The scholar has become identified with second-hand book learning; this state of affairs is not an inevitable concomitant of scholarship or teaching. It is possible that Elsa, if she had broken away from Conway College, would have lived an existence as isolated from the main currents of her time as do the professors and instructors at Conway. Many artists, writers, and even businessmen are as aloof from "real life" as is the college professor who has become the epitome for "unworldliness"; many professors, on the other hand, are alert and active participants in "real life." This was al-

[1] *New Theatre & Film*, March, 1937.

ready true in 1931, when *Alien Corn* was written. Howard draws a false distinction between the isolated academic world and the world outside, instead of distinguishing between people who live in ivory towers,
on college campuses and elsewhere, and people who
do not.

In the preface to *Dodsworth*, Howard wrote, "A
love scene is either Juliet's balcony or a painful embar-
rassment." Too often in his own plays it is the latter.
Despite his earlier excursions into the romantic and
lyric mood, he has generally avoided—it seems almost
consciously—dealing with the emotional and passionate
elements in men's lives. When he does touch on them
it is from an essentially rational point of view, as in
The Silver Cord. The scenes between Dave and Christina, for all Christina's suppressed emotion, are an intellectual examination of the basis of their relationship.
When, as in *Alien Corn*, Howard tries to make sexual
attraction between a man and a woman an essential part
of his plot development, he fails completely. Elsa's attraction to Conway is never believable. We know that
human beings fall in love irrationally, but Sidney Howard as a playwright never convinces us of Harry Conway's power over Elsa. Nor is the love which leads Julian
to commit suicide any more successfully expressed in
terms of theatre. Howard has only once been eminently
successful in portraying an overmastering emotional
drive on the stage, and that was not in a love story; it
was in *Yellow Jack*. Ordinarily he is at his best when his
approach can be rational or humorous; when he tries
to write about the most instinctive of all human emotions, he is proportionately unsuccessful, and this short-

coming is one of his most serious limitations as a dramatist.

Yellow Jack, though written in 1928, was not produced until 1934 because of the vicissitudes of Broadway show business. Technically it probably belongs in the category of collaboration; De Kruif's name appears on the title page of the published play, and Howard undoubtedly drew heavily for the continuity of his play on the latter's account of the fight against yellow fever in Cuba. Creatively, however, it is Howard's work, and and as such it ranks as his most considerable achievement. The action centers around the work of the Yellow Fever Commission, sent to Cuba at the conclusion of the Spanish-American War to ascertain the cause of yellow fever, which was decimating the army and the civilian population. Unable to discover the agent of the disease through microscopic work, the commission turned to an investigation of the transmission of yellow fever, a line of research which came to a successful conclusion with a controlled experiment on four volunteer privates. Short episodes in yellow-fever research in recent years serve as prologue and epilogue to the main action, and establish it as only one incident in the march of science against ignorance and disease.

In *Yellow Jack* Howard made no concessions to convention in subject matter or treatment, and eschewed sentimental interest and ordinary plot machinations. He set out to depict the drama inherent in man's struggle against an obscure disease which menaced thousands of lives, including those of the men who were combating it. The real antagonists are a mosquito and an unknown quantity on a microscopic slide. For the most part, Howard adhered to known historic and scientific facts and limited his characters, with few exceptions, to the persons who had actually participated in the events he related. The writing throughout is on a level with Howard's best: terse, forthright, and literate.

The result was a play concerning whose merit controversy raged. Very few denied its originality or its integrity of purpose; whether the play came alive as theatre was the real point at issue. Its appeal proved to be limited; few experiments in form as well as subject matter are commercially successful. The fact that in retrospect it has already assumed the proportions of a landmark bears better witness to its real significance than the duration of the original production.

That Burns Mantle failed to include *Yellow Jack* in the 1933-34 edition of his yearly anthology of the *Best Plays* merits some comment in this connection. Mr. Mantle's compilation has a wide circulation, and exerts undoubted influence among writers and other theatre professionals, and in the large realm of the amateur and semiprofessional theatre. The more seems the pity that he saw fit to exclude *Yellow Jack* (which he described as "a really fine play—an outstanding novelty in its staging, sincerely and strongly-written") because "it must be classed as laboratory drama in the sense that it represents a definite departure from conventional play forms and is dependent upon a special and expensive production which will probably confine its showing to New York playgoers alone. — The yearbook of the American drama, I feel, should be principally concerned with those plays that represent the whole theatre rather than with laboratory experiments of special types in which the larger playgoing public is seldom interested. — It seems to me the duty of a yearbook is to report trends rather than to

direct them." Mr. Mantle is entitled to his own conception of the function of the work to which he has so notably devoted himself; nevertheless it seems an unduly
passive one, more likely to perpetuate the accepted and
commercially successful types of drama than to infuse
the theatre with new and vital ideas. The substitution of
Yellow Jack for *Her Master's Voice* or *No More Ladies*
or *The Shining Hour*, all of which duplicate representa-
tion of "existing trends" in the volume, would have enlarged the sphere of influence of an enterprising and
arresting experiment.

Consideration of *Yellow Jack* is inextricably bound up
with the notable production which Guthrie McClintic
gave the play. Just as the dramatist dispensed with a conventional plot, so the designer and director abstained
from conventionally realistic settings. On a unit set consisting of two levels connected with a curving flight of
steps, Mr. McClintic staged a production which ebbed
and flowed from one level to the other, and back and
forth across a spacious stage, without once dropping the
curtain for an intermission. Only in this way, he felt,
could the requisite illusion and absorption in so novel
a theme be maintained. Let an audience, however highly
keyed, into the lobbies for ten minutes' chatter, and it
would be difficult to recreate the same tension over
events taking place in a laboratory, the spectators would
have to be completely recaptured. As it happened, the
uninterrupted tension made for an exhausting evening,
which probably accounted in part for the play's lack of
popular appeal.

The continuous action was broken up into scenes by
lighting; one section of the stage would be "spotted,"
then the lights would fade, there would be a complete

"blackout," and the lights would come up on another section. There was no attempt at "scenery" with the exception of a small screened enclosure on the upper level, which represented, realistically enough, the Yellow Fever Commission's laboratory, with sinks and test tubes and microscopes, and two movable platforms which rolled onto the forestage just above the footlights from either side for brief scenes, carrying soldiers' tents or hospital cots, and were then whisked out of sight again during blackouts. A sparing and effective musical background was furnished by the use of army bugles, and a male quartet singing such songs of the period as "There'll be a Hot Time in the Old Town Tonight" and "Good-by, Dolly, I Must Leave You." And perhaps the most tense moments in the play came when, after a gripping scene in the laboratory or at the bedside of a man struck down by yellow fever, all the lights went out except those illuminating the cyclorama draped at the back, and against the glow of a southern sky a silhouetted frieze of soldiers passed across the stage carrying stretchers laden with blanket-shrouded figures, while a bugle in the distance played "The Last Post."

For characters Howard confined himself largely to the known figures in the events portrayed. However, although his characterization of known persons was so true to life as to win praise from the widow of Dr. Lazear and others who had known the members of the commission, he wisely permitted himself some leeway in creating the secondary incidents and detail needed to carry the play along. These arose naturally, and without any falsification of essential facts, from the nature of the commission's work, which involved enormous exactitude

of detail and experiments on human beings, and consequently bred strain and tension. It also developed from
a careful characterization and individualization of the
four privates who, from a kind of chorus in the earlier
scenes of the play which reveal the fear and uneasiness
that pervade the army, become the central figures in the
experiment that scientifically determines the carrier of
yellow fever, once and for all.

It is interesting to note that the only points at which
the credibility, and hence the illusion, of the play falters
are where Howard—and De Kruif before him—departs
from the known continuity of scientific events. At the
opening of the main action, the members of the commission, having failed to discover the actual germ which
causes yellow fever, are shown as ready to give up and
go home. Then Dr. Carroll, one of them, arrives from
a nearby camp with a curious incident of a soldier who
has become infected, though completely isolated under
arrest for a considerable period of time before he was
taken ill. This suddenly suggests a new approach to the
problem to Walter Reed, head of the commission; in
the following scene, Reed declares that he suspects
the fatal carrier is a mosquito. Lazear thereupon calls to
mind the crank scientist Finlay who has held this same
mosquito theory for twenty years; and when Colonel
Tory pooh-poohs the possibility, Lazear recites the list
of scientific discoveries during the past few years which
lend support to such an hypothesis:

> Where have you been at? Never heard of Texas
> Smith's fever-tick? How about Bruce and the tse-
> tse fly in Africa? Haven't Ross and Grassi just
> nailed malaria to a mosquito? I confirmed that my-

self!—Read Carter on the epidemic in Alabama! He came so near this!

Obviously if Lazear were so well acquainted with the progress of research in related fields (as all the members of the commission, being outstanding scientists, would naturally be), it would not take a sudden brain storm to start them off on a new tack of investigation. Actually, scientific accounts show that the members of the commission not only were familiar with other lines of research but had been working on yellow fever prior to their appointment to the commission. When one approach to the problem proved unsuccessful they quite naturally and inevitably took up another: the question of prevention.[2] The important point at issue here is not so much that Howard tampered with reality in the interests of dramatic structure (he needed a compact climactic scene which would project the almost insuperable difficulties the commission was facing, and its new line of attack) as that in taking liberties with actual facts he did not take sufficiently into account the way men's minds really work: his dramatic motivation and his psychology are at fault, and account for the lack of plausibility.

By contrast, the scenes where the tense and jaded Carroll and Lazear all but fly at each other's throats are theatre of the most gripping kind. These men may not actually have lost their self-control to such a point; but everything in our experience of people working under a terrific strain for the highest possible stake—life itself— and themselves in immediate personal danger—confirms the possibility that these men might have behaved in just such a manner.

[2] *Walter Reed and Yellow Fever*, Howard A. Kelly, McClure, Philips & Co., 1906.

The ultimate test of a play is its validity on the stage. While the original production of *Yellow Jack* impressed some as an unsuccessful tour de force, it stirred others to an intense pitch of emotional excitement. Certainly, *Yellow Jack* is of enormous significance in its attempt to enlarge the boundaries of the present-day theatre and recall it to the more spacious vision of the Greeks and the Elizabethans.

The dramatization of Sinclair Lewis' *Dodsworth* affords excellent evidence of Howard's technical skill. The prefaces which he and Lewis wrote to the published version of the play are required reading for any dramatist. In the novel Lewis portrayed in vast and colorful detail, not only the moderately wealthy middle-class American woman, as epitomized by Fran Dodsworth, and the successful businessman of the same category, immortalized in Sam Dodsworth, but the entire strata of life from which they came and against whose standards and habits of life they both, in their several ways, rebelled. Since the theatre was manifestly no place for such a survey, the play had to be limited to the story of Fran and Sam.

But in transferring their wanderings and growing estrangement and self-realization to the stage, Howard could not limit himself to the incidents and even the characters which Lewis had supplied. And while he condensed with one hand, he had to amplify with the other. The novel was crowded with characters with whom he could dispense and did; but Lewis had barely mentioned in passing two figures who were largely responsible for the break between the Dodsworths, and Howard had to bring the audience face to face with them: Arnold Israel and the Baroness von Obersdorf. The novel is extremely repetitious, and cumbered with descriptive detail; it is lacking in scenes which compactly present a situation at the same time that they forward the action to a fresh situation. Howard therefore wrote two scenes which took the place of fifty pages of descriptive detail and anecdote, without actually duplicating anything that happened in the book—a process he described as "dramatization by equivalent"—showing Sam's return to Zenith while Fran was at Montreux. The events of the book are seen entirely through Sam's eyes, and therefore some of the most important occurrences, from the dramatist's point of view, are only mentioned in Fran's letters; but a play is fatally weakened when crucial events take place off stage, and so Howard wrote two more scenes in which Sam does not even appear and in which the leading figures were precisely those characters which he had had to create in default of the novelist: a scene showing Fran's budding affair with Arnold Israel, and another in which the Baroness von Obersdorf breaks up Fran's proposed marriage with her son Kurt.

There was another difficulty. Lewis first introduced Edith Cortwright on page 222: there he gave her one page. Then he dropped her until page 332, where she suddenly emerged as Sam's savior and Fran's victorious antagonist. But you cannot in the theatre, as Howard remarked, "summon a pinch hitter into the last act to give the play a happy ending and not be called up to face charges of dirty work." He therefore introduced Mrs. Cortwright to the Dodsworths as a fellow passenger on the boat that took them abroad, where her genuine distinction was immediately contrasted with Fran's triviality; she reappeared briefly, but again, in telling contrast to Fran's newly acquired friends and her scrambling

social careerism, at a Paris dinner party. When Sam
encountered her in his hour of need in the Naples office
of the American Express Company, in the third act, the
audience was able to accept their friendship as dramatically valid.

But while he was forced to supplement the material
the novel furnished him at numerous points, Howard
ruthlessly eliminated everything which did not contribute to the main line of action or which repeated anything
that had already been established. He cut down the
Dodsworths' European acquaintances to Israel, Madame
Penable, and Kurt von Obersdorf. Of the people who
helped Sam Dodsworth to preserve some shreds of self-
esteem, or fight loneliness and desolation, he kept only
A. B. Hurd and Mrs. Cortwright, and dispensed with
Ross Ireland, Minna von Escher, and Nande Azeredo.
Young Brent Dodsworth went by the board, leaving Sam
and Fran only a daughter; the Pearsons—Tubby and
Matey—remained intact, but the rest of Sam's American
friends and business associates were merged in the new
character of Henry Hazzard. Lastly, almost all the dialogue in the play, even in scenes which are taken straight
from the novel, is not the novelist's, but the dramatist's.

The result was a living dramatization and eminently
successful theatre. For the character of Dodsworth, the
kernel of the play, credit must naturally go to Lewis,
and to Walter Huston, who created the role. But Howard's theatrical craftsmanship is nowhere more evident
than in the manner in which he met the technical problems incident to transferring *Dodsworth*, or even a
fragment of it, to the stage. Few dramatizations can
approach it.

The weaknesses of the play are largely those of the

novel, and they are inherent in Lewis' fundamental approach to his material which Howard took over, rather than in the technical handling of that material. As in *The Silver Cord*, we have characters whose behavior cannot be disassociated from social and economic causes. What are the factors in American life which have reduced Fran to a state of boredom and tension that inevitably results in an explosion under the circumstances of her freer, more colorful life abroad? What has made Sam Dodsworth a self-conscious puritan, limited his vision to the walls of his automobile factory, kept him a child about everything but automobiles? *Dodsworth* is a carefully documented survey that never rises to real analysis and stops short of any conclusions. "Criticism and satire imply a conception of a better way of life," wrote Granville Hicks.[3] "Lewis knows what he would like to destroy—provincialism, complacency, hypocrisy, intellectual timidity, and similar faults—but he has only the vaguest idea of what kind of society he would like to see in existence." In *Dodsworth* he would seem to be making a plea for individual sincerity and honesty, for realism and courage; there is no hint that a problem exists which the simpler virtues cannot solve. All-encompassing in detail, the novel narrows down in the last analysis to a Sam Dodsworth who was lucky enough to meet the right woman, a conclusion which may be emotionally satisfying but which intellectually is nothing less than a tragic anticlimax. And while the play never attains the scope of the novel, it suffers from the same failure to follow the facts of the case through to a conclusion.

Paths of Glory was far less successful as a dramatiza-

[3] *The Great Tradition*, Granville Hicks, Macmillan, p. 235.

tion than *Dodsworth*. The first half of Humphrey
Cobb's novel of the Great War is devoted to building
up a background of horror and brutality for the story of
the execution of three French privates for cowardice of
which they were not guilty; but there could be no theatrical equivalent for Cobb's harrowing descriptions of
battle, slaughter, and despair. If there is one thing it is
impossible to create on the stage (in striking contrast to
the film), it is the audible and visual illusion of war.
But *Paths of Glory* called for a heavily shelled stretch of
open road and the parapet of a front-line trench during
a major attack! It asked too much from the theatre.

Howard unfortunately chose to follow the outline of
the novel so closely as to limit his first act to establishing
atmosphere and character, with proportionately unfortunate results. It is a succession of desultory scenes, with
no progressive dramatic action whatsoever between the
second scene, in which General Assolant decides to
sacrifice his regiment for the sake of a general's epaulettes
and the attack itself, *six* scenes later. By contrast, the
second and briefer act, which is concerned with the fate
of the three soldiers who pay with their lives for the
general's vanity, builds with unremitting tension to a
terrific climax, because it deals, not with the physical
manifestations of war but with its spiritual attributes—
egoism, hypocrisy, stupidity, terror, and brutality. But
for all its power, the play lacks the significance implicit
in its subject matter. In his foreword to the published
play, Howard stated, "It is unlikely that any war play or
novel could be written without some element of mis-
sionary motive. . . . In *Paths of Glory* Arthur Hopkins
and I saw something for which we had both been waiting: namely, an indictment of war so direct as to exclude

any possibility of confusion . . . a demonstration of the ruthless workings out of wartime logic." Actually, the tremendous tragic background to the incident of the three soldiers practically obliterates it. The case is admittedly an unusual one. But the attack in which they had participated was not unusual in that it had killed thousands. The war killed ten million men. The three shot for cowardice of which they were innocent were no more the victims of Assolant's vanity and ambition than the uncounted victims of the attack itself. On the stage, robbed of the novelist's psychological analysis which lends universality to the emotions of the condemned men irrespective of the circumstances in which they find themselves, their fate is in itself harrowing, but trivial as an indictment of war. The words of Langlois, one of the victims, "If a man's got to be killed it doesn't much matter how," best sum up the comparative irrelevance of the episode.

Neither Cobb nor Howard ever attempts to show that the real protagonist is not Assolant, or even military bureaucracy in general, but the society which wages war. Howard does put into the soldiers' mouths the reiterated question, "Why are we here? Why do we stand for it?" But the argument is not pursued further. As in *Dodsworth*, as in *Ned McCobb's Daughter* and *The Silver Cord*, the question "Why?" assumes enormous proportions precisely because it is so patently ignored. Today an antiwar play which ignores the economic basis of war lacks any impact, dwindles to a *Snow-White and the Seven Dwarfs* in which a witch is the cause of all evil.

At long last such myopia leads the author into the theatrical and intellectual morass of *The Ghost of Yankee Doodle*, also an antiwar play. A family of liberal ideals and high integrity confronts the contradictions of a social system it cannot reject. The Garrisons are staunch democrats and pacifists, and they have the courage of their convictions to the point where they refuse to buy security at the cost of manufacturing armaments. Society today being organized as it is, the price of American neutrality and the Garrisons' high-mindedness, as Howard shows, is mass unemployment and untold suffering, which are dispelled only when we plunge into war to redeem our "national honor," and factory wheels, once more in motion, indiscriminately provide jobs and death together.

In his portrait of Jim Clevenger as an irresponsible, all-powerful, and viciously stupid newspaper mogul, Howard does very well. He is considerably less successful in making Clevenger's warmed-over passion for Sara Garrison the mainspring of his foreign policy; the Hearsts of this world move in response to more cogent forces. Sara's emotional lapse, since Clevenger stands for everything she claims to despise, is palpably unbelievable, and the whole hit-or-miss aggregation of characters, incidents, and opinions which make up the plot are arresting evidence of Howard's deterioration as a dramatist.

The statement has been made that Howard, while interested in human beings, persistently ignores the circumstances under which they exist. We have here another aspect of this tendency, since he is considering the dilemma, the advantages, and disadvantages of being a liberal, without very careful reference to the world outside of that belabored figure. He shows that a society in which liberals still exist has certain aspects. Its economic organization is such that millions of men depend for their jobs on the prospering of private enterprise.

One man, owning many newspapers and owing responsibility to no one, can plunge a country into war.
Howard also shows that the dilemma confronting the
kindhearted Garrisons is absolute: American neutrality
forces them to close down their factory, war permits them
to reopen it. Yet he persists in considering the question:
"To be or not to be a liberal?" on a plane of moral conviction, much as to say, "To be or not to be polite"?
To him liberalism represents such virtues as tolerance
and enlightenment, freedom from dogma of any kind.
But the question implicit in the play—is there no alternative to a system which carries want for a vast number
of human beings in one hand and death by battle for
many in the other?—goes not only unanswered, but un-
asked! Thus the Garrisons in reality are not so much
tolerant and enlightened as self-centered and strangely
content that a grisly price should be paid by others for
their privilege of remaining liberals. If Howard had seen
his Garrisons in perspective, if he had looked beyond
individual human beings to the larger world in which
they live along with a good many other people, he might
have achieved a more realistic view of them. They would
have lost their aura of nostalgia and become symbols of
a profound conflict in modern life. *The Ghost of Yankee Doodle* might have been an exciting play of the
American spirit embodying itself in new forms, new out-
looks, applying a tradition of integrity and enterprise
and courage to the realization of old ideals in new ways.

III S. N. Behrman

For the past ten years S. N. Behrman has been a leading
figure in the field of sophisticated comedy. With little
regard for plotting or theatrical devices of storytelling
and highly paced drama, he is usually content to fill his
stage with literate and articulate people and set them
talking. Mostly we are aware, not of recreated human
beings beyond the footlights, but of the mind of the
dramatist, examining and displaying different facets of
life and thought today through a class whose advantages
have fostered articulateness and an ironic sense of
humor.

The quality for which he has come to be known most
widely is detachment or tolerance, shown in his willingness to examine and express every point of view. Such
an attitude is admirably suited to the technique of intellectual comedy. But an increasingly sharp contradiction has manifested itself between the lightness of his
style and the weightiness of the topics which engage his

interest, and little by little he has been drawn into a position which, as manifested in his most recent play, is far from either tolerant or detached.

Behrman has developed a curious obsession for a character whom he employs again and again—the "radical" tempted by, and yet inimical to, "bourgeois" ideas and surroundings. He never succeeds in creating anything more real than his own idea of such a figure. One suspects that real radicals lie outside Mr. Behrman's beat, and that the figure which haunts him is a subjective image of his own perplexities and conflict. For while he is profoundly disquieted by some of the phenomena he observes around him he is unable to break the emotional and intellectual ties which bind him, in despite of his smarting conscience, to existing society. The outcome of his struggles has taken the form, in the recent *Wine of Choice*, of dissociating himself from the radical, who becomes a composite of everything which repels the dramatist. It is an apparently sudden *volte-face*, the origins of which can be traced back to his first play.

1

When *The Second Man* was produced in 1927, critics and audiences alike were astounded at the spectacular emergence of a mature comedy talent. With brilliant wit and deft stagecraft Behrman juggled only four characters for three acts (a feat in itself) to the accompaniment of an uninterrupted flow of urbane and amusing epigrams. The play deals with those members of the leisure class who combine great charm with an ingratiating sense of their own inadequacies. None of the characters are very profoundly analyzed; the author's touch throughout is lighter than thistledown. This need not in itself rob the play of significance. What prevents it from becoming genuine comedy of manners is the author's own lack of a point of view. Despite their many shortcomings, of which they themselves are almost too incessantly aware, the characters charm not only themselves and each other but the playwright; with all his perception of their essential worthlessness he would have them accepted as agreeable ornaments of an otherwise graceless world.

Clark Storey, worldly-wise, cynical, and a little shopworn, used to be "different":

> I went through the idealistic stage. I used to sit in a garret and believe in Socialism——It didn't take me long to find out how easy it is to starve on idealism. I had facility, and there is a ready market for facility. I got $5,000 for writing a whitewashed biography of a million-dollar sweatshop owner.

Blame, if any, for this metamorphosis, is put on a second nature which has dominated his better self: "There's someone inside of me—a second man—grinning, sophisticated, horrid." At times Storey resents this second self; most of the time he lives with him without protest and even with enjoyment. It is the old theory of dual personality, of demoniac possession and domination, which absolves its unfortunate victims of all social responsibility for their natures and their acts. According to the theory of the second man, which recurs again and again in Behrman's thinking, we are the helpless victims of such aggregations of strength and weakness, prejudice and loyalties, as fate has bestowed on us in the guise of character.

There is another respect in which *The Second Man*

first makes use of a pattern which Behrman is to repeat in his later plays. Again and again he uses the same formula: a man and a woman love each other, but are parted by some deep-seated opposition within themselves. Sometimes they bridge the gap and draw together, but never with any assurance of permanence. In *The Second Man* the idea is only slightly developed: Monica adores Storey; he is attracted by her youth and devotion, but the cynical "second man" prevents him from accepting her love or returning it. This is a formula which is repeated, with variations and complications, in *Meteor, Brief Moment, Biography, Rain From Heaven,* and *Wine of Choice,* and its recurrence cannot be without significance.

In some respects *Meteor* is Behrman's best play qua play. It is structurally more compact and closely knit, less given to conversational digressions, than his other work; as always, it is extraordinarily literate and well-written. The character of Raphael Lord is Behrman's finest imaginative creation (with the possible exception of Hugo Willens in *Rain from Heaven*). Lord is the febrile incarnation of American enterprise and irresponsible individualism. He combines all the qualities of the superentrepreneur: Showmanship, charlatanry, versatility, arrogance, ruthlessness, will-to-power, and complete lack of direction, of *real purpose*. His craze for power for its own sake, his ability to predict coming events and its sudden inexplicable failure, are extraordinarily prophetic of American finance capital's conviction of its manifest destiny, and its appalling collapse. (Although it was produced in December 1929, *Meteor* was written before the October crash.)

On the other hand, *Meteor* clearly suffers from several

fundamental weaknesses. It lacks theatrical interest and variety because it is built around the development of one character, and that a genius. It is always difficult to make a genius convincing on the stage, witness the many unsuccessful dramas about great generals, musicians, and writers. Moreover, in this case the genius is a sublime egotist who is shown only revolving around himself, never in conflict with other characters on the stage. It is no wonder Behrman never makes clear (because he himself does not know) whether Lord is the product of economic forces or an inexplicable psychological freak. Everything in the circumstances of the play demands that Lord be analyzed in relation to the social organism as a whole. Instead his power to foretell coming events and read other minds derails the play because it takes Lord out of the class of the ordinary rapacious financier into that of the superman. Immediately he is exempted from ordinary ethical standards; his gift is made a curse. "Why was this given to me? Where does it come from? Why was I chosen?" he asks. Lord is not guilty of the harm he does. It is the theory of the "second man," in a new guise.

Because of this unrealistic conception the author is not required to show Lord in actual relationship to any of the other men whom he overthrows (except the football player Sherman Maxwell, in the first act). We never learn anything about his opponents; we never see him in actual collision with them. We hear him making telephone calls, the newspapers are quoted, but there is no real conflict which could be resolved in a climax— only the ever-continuing growth of Lord's power which finally breaks of its own weight.

It is Lord's "evil genius" which comes irrevocably be-

tween him and his wife, Ann. She leaves him because he
has become too immersed in his mania for power and
manipulation to exist as a human being whom she can
love. She herself never comes to life as a character,
largely because the man in whom she is absorbed the
whole time we see her is himself so unreal. The other
characters are hardly less shadowy. Dr. Avery, for all his
mellow wit and wisdom, is curiously blind to the inequity
and menace of an untrammeled power such as Lord's.
Such qualms as he has are easily silenced by a first-edition
Sir Thomas Browne ("This makes up for everything").
Perhaps Behrman meant him to symbolize the academic world's shockingly unquestioning acceptance of
boom-America's ethics and standards; if so, he has failed
to make this purpose clear.

Because the author's approach to a problem of in-
escapably social significance—on an enormous scale—is
purely personal and psychological, *Meteor* is a fragment
of the play it might have been. The inner mental strain
and anguish of a financial titan whose power has run
away with him offers rich dramatic possibilities, *if* it is
studied in context. The fate of the millions of human
beings whose lives and fortunes Lord juggles in his business dealings—his investors, the native population of
Ariandos—are what lend real importance to the vertigo
that overtakes the financier. But the author's conception of Lord as an unaccountable phenomenon of the
human spirit absolves him from any necessity of probing
into the structure and logic of an economic system which
produces men of his temper and ethics.

Nevertheless, coming after *The Second Man* and
Serena Blandish, *Meteor* showed an undeniable trend
towards the consideration of serious problems. It is less

of a comedy than any of his other plays. In *Brief Moment* the playwright returned to a lighter vein. Practically every other line is an epigram. But the shadow of present-day problems and confusions hangs over the denizens of the luxurious Deane penthouse and over the quipping author. *Brief Moment* deals with the self-questionings of a rich young man, Roderick Deane, who is conscious that he is, to use his own words, "spiritually unemployed and highly dispensable." He falls in love with a clear-cut, hardheaded night-club singer who is not troubled by Roderick's neuroses. She marries him, and they quarrel (it is never clear just why). As in *The Second Man*, the emotional combinations shift and change, there are endless reconciliations, and fresh quarrels. At one point Deane announces his intention of giving away all his money and going to Russia, in search of a creative, positive life. He abandons the scheme and he and Abby are reconciled, but we are left with the feeling that the settlement is only temporary and that the pattern of doubt and friction will be repeated ad infinitum.

Once again, not content with aphorisms alone, Behrman hints at more serious comment. Roderick asks his friend Sig:

> Don't you get a sense, somehow, especially lately, of things disintegrating, crumbling—some enormous transition—the final flicker of civilization— *après nous le déluge?*

But Sig's answer is a flippancy, and the isolated remark is lost. *Brief Moment* remains diffuse and inconclusive, never becoming the penetrating study of wealthy demoralization it might have been. Behrman is tolerantly amused at his characters; he is also not a little disquieted by a sense of their inadequacy, and the meaninglessness of their existence. But he likes them too well, he enjoys their urbanity and sophistication too much to arraign them at all sharply or probe too deeply into the dynamics of a social structure of which they are—presumably—the apex, the last word in refinement and articulate self-consciousness.

As is so often the case with Behrman's plays, the plot of *Biography* is slight. Marion Froude—warmhearted, witty, above all tolerant—falls in love with an intractable young radical, and he with her. They have an affair. He persuades her to write her autobiography, which threatens to involve an earlier friend, now a would-be senator from Tennessee. Because of the complications that would ensue, Marion finally destroys the manuscript, despite the fact that her lover had staked everything on its publication. They realize how far apart they are in temperament and beliefs, and separate.

Biography is Behrman's most human play. For one thing it has comedy of character (as opposed to that of phrase). It possesses real emotion; for once the author succeeds in establishing genuinely moving relationships between his characters. One feels that Marion and Richard Kurt represent a conflict which he feels to be deeply tragic. Behrman has never written with more delicacy and poignancy than in the scene where Marion questions Kurt about his early life and unintentionally wrings from him the avowal of his love. In addition, there is the inimitable Bunny Nolan, an excellent caricature of political naïveté on the make, and the figure of the shrewd and benevolent Viennese composer Feydak.

Fundamentally, however, the two principal characters

lack real stature. Kurt is supposed to be a radical: Marion, speaking of him to Feydak, says, "He's some kind of a fanatic—social." His father, an innocent bystander, was shot down and killed before his eyes during a coal-mine strike, when Kurt was a child. Yet his ambition, as he himself states, is no more concrete than

> to be critic-at-large of things as they are. I want to find out everything there is to know about the intimate structure of things. I want to reduce the whole system to absurdity. I want to laugh the powers-that-be out of existence in a great winnowing gale of laughter.

His one idea is to publish Marion's biography, in the belief that it will be a racy document, thereby "testing the caliber of our magazines, our press, our Senators, our morality." Like all Behrman's radicals he is without organizational or political ties, and a violent individualist.

Marion, on the other hand, is too tolerant, too easily amused by what is open to graver questioning, for us not to feel, as Kurt does, that she is not so much tolerant as undiscriminating. If she were less volatile and he less impelled by blind and unreasoning hate—if she were a better artist or a woman whose life had been less determinedly casual, and his social rebellion had had some basis of reasoned thought and action, their conflict and parting would have a quality of universal, instead of only personal anguish.

Richard Kurt offers an interesting sidelight on Behrman's development. Seen in perspective, as a sequel to Roderick Deane, he represents a distinct advance in thinking. Deane's emotional instability was supposed to

be symbolic of social insecurity, but his existence was as
remote from any evidence of that insecurity as his penthouse was from the level of the street. Kurt at least
knows that injustice exists: he has seen the living evidence of it, in the murder of his father. He hates cant
and hypocrisy. In the finest speech in the play he cries
out:

> I see now why the injustice and the cruelty go on
> year after year—century after century—without
> change—because—as they grow older—people be-
> come *tolerant*. Things amuse them. If the time
> ever comes when I'm amused by something I should
> hate I hope they'll shoot me.

Yet Kurt is unreal, a "literary" radical who has no connection with any actuality of social protest. There are
plenty of would-be radicals of Kurt's type in existence.
But Behrman was trying to portray, not a would-be
radical, but a man whose honesty of purpose, expressed
in terms of action, would be in complete contrast with
Marion Froude's temperament and standards. In this
attempt he has failed, just as he failed to make anything
more than a "voice crying in the wilderness" of Hugo
Willens in *Rain From Heaven* or caricatures of Will
Dexter and Dennis McCarthy in *End of Summer*.

In his next play, *Rain From Heaven*, Behrman stepped
squarely into the social arena. True, there is a long
digression—a secondary comedy plot in which the
moronic Phoebe pursues the unfortunate Hugo, and
which nearly wrecks matters by its irrelevance and
puerility. But the play unquestionably revolves around a
triangular conflict between four people who express, almost as simply and clearly as the proponents of an old

morality play stood for qualities of character, three opposing political points of view—Fascism, liberalism, and
liberalism emerging into positive action. The principal
character is Hugo Willens, a German music critic whose
trace of Jewish blood makes him the victim of Nazi
persecution. Willens finds refuge and understanding in
the home of a wealthy English woman, the epitome of
enlightenment. In juxtaposition to them, Behrman
places an American financier who is busily fostering
Fascism in England, and a boyish young explorer—Rand
—who is unmasked before the end of the play as excellent potential storm-trooper material. In the end, despite
the fact that he and Lady Wyngate have come to love
each other, Willens goes back to Germany to fight the
Nazis.

Dramatically, *Rain From Heaven* is weak: a series of
polite drawing-room discussions punctuated by one
dramatic incident, when Rand's burst of jealousy leads
him to call Willens "a dirty Jew." Phoebe's pursuit of
Willens is completely unrelated to the main theme of
the play (Behrman might have made her a revealing
study of empty-headed and parasitic womanhood instead
of an encumbering caricature), and the young people,
whose disagreement represents the conflict between the
artist and the ordinary mere mortal, are superficially
drawn. But Willens himself is an extraordinary creation.
Into this character have gone more genuine feeling on
the part of the author than into any other character he
has drawn. Behrman feels profoundly the tragedy of
Willens' life, the injustice and the horror of the persecution which hounded him, the menace which hangs over
the civilized world. When Willens speaks we are lifted

from the grace and immunity of an English drawing room, to a world of harsh and agonizing realities.

But with all his passionate partisanship for Hugo Willens as opposed to the two demagogic Rands, Behrman fails to bring *Rain From Heaven* to anything like a satisfactory conclusion intellectually, hence dramatically. At its close Willens goes back to almost certain death, but his purpose—what he hopes to achieve, what he actually proposes to do—is dissipated in vague phrases. He never tells us anything more explicit than that he wants—

> to find certitude, if necessary to die for it—to investigate reality, to destroy the inhuman and rediscover humanity.

Later he says:

> I see now that goodness is not enough, that liberalism is not enough. I'm sick of evasions. They've done us in. Civilization, charity, tolerance, progress—all catchwords. We'll have to redefine our terms.

What precisely, in terms of action, in terms of reality, do these words mean? What are these phrases, used at a time when play should be resolved in terms of clear, cogent analysis and action, but catchwords with which Behrman is blurring his climax? We never know whom Willens proposes to fight, yet obviously he cannot expect to engage the Hitler regime singlehanded. We never know what he feels caused the Nazi cataclysm. There is no reference to any of the other crimes for which it stands liable, only the destruction of culture and the persecution of the Jews. We have here an excellent example of righteous indignation and honest thinking which proceed just so far and no further, which stop short of real analysis and hence beg the main issue.

In the playwright's introduction to the printed version of *Rain From Heaven*, there is a passage which throws a great deal of light on the author's thinking. In it he tells how the play had its origin in an incident he read of in a newspaper. A distinguished German critic, persecuted by the Nazis, turned for aid and sympathy to the grand old man of German literature, Gerhart Hauptmann, whom he himself had helped to raise to his present eminence. Hauptmann rebuffed him; the dark forces unleashed in Germany today had destroyed all mutual sympathy between the two men. This is the tragedy that impelled Behrman to write *Rain From Heaven*, for all his hopes for civilization are centered, so he tells us, in these two men and what they represent.

"From these two men," he writes, "two essences of what the race might hope to be," one might hope for "the emergence of a spirit and an understanding transcending the clamors and ferocities of the marching lustful mobs.——From where else? The mob is the same in nearly all countries, whether it engages in a pogrom in Russia, an Armenian massacre, a book-fire in Germany, a lynching bee in America. One does not expect anything from it but massacres or senseless villification or the 'stinking breath' which nauseated Shakespeare. Isolated fragments of the mob are equally predictable in their conduct, and therefore, for the playwright, quite uninteresting."

What strikes one here is the dramatist's total disregard for any factors of social or economic causation. Although his own craft demands the most scrupulous motivation for every act on the stage, he disregards the fact that social acts must have social or economic causes. Yet to overlook such causation and to deal in generalities is to fall into the trap of using catchwords which he himself decries so vigorously through the mouth of Willens. And the cast of mind which talks so contemptuously of mobs, in other words of the broad masses of humanity, and puts its faith instead in the individual—an "essence of what the race might hope to be"—is dangerously similar to the Fascist point of view, which sees the apex of social development, the only possible source of leadership, in single individuals, be they Führers or Duces.

The prejudice which makes Behrman talk in such broad and supercilious terms of "the mob" is what prevents his giving *Rain From Heaven* an effective conclusion. The only possible source of opposition to the Nazi oligarchy is popular and widespread opposition of the broadest kind. A Hugo Willens will never be able to re-establish culture and tolerance in Germany without the support of the population as a whole—workingmen, middle-class wage earners, and professional groups. To dismiss all but the individuals who represent the highest pitch of culture and self-consciousness and sophistication as "the mob" is to talk about a struggle against Fascism on a plane of sheer fantasy. *Rain From Heaven* shows, with devastating clearness, Behrman's own need to "redefine his terms," to "*investigate reality.*"

In *End of Summer* Behrman at first sight takes another step forward; not only do riches no longer bring immunity; they bring responsibilities. There are interlopers in the world of privilege and security—young men and old—jobless, resentful, outspoken. Behrman's thesis here is the illegitimacy of inherited and accumulated wealth. The two protagonists are Leonie Frothingham, representative of all the graces of affluence, and her daughter Paula, who rebels against the inequalities of a fortune which smiles on her and denies her friends the essentials of existence. In the end Paula throws in her lot with her friends and the penniless young radical she loves; what is more, she does so at her mother's behest, for Leonie has arrived at the conclusion that her life has brought her little real happiness because it has been aimless, and she does not want her daughter to repeat her tragedy.

Behrman has peopled *End of Summer* with a galaxy of brilliantly articulate characters who represent a wide range of conflicting ideas. Structurally, the play is diffuse and chaotic. In trying to gain range he has sacrificed dramatic compactness and tension. Many of the characters have no apparent place in what little plot exists. There is practically no connection between Paula's pursuit of Will Dexter, who is afraid to marry her because of what her money will do to his radical principles, and Leonie's wooing of the astute psychiatrist, Kenneth Rice. (The fact that *End of Summer* was originally written with Paula Frothingham as the central character, and was revised with Leonie in the position of principal interest because the Theatre Guild needed a vehicle for Ina Claire, goes far to explain the peculiarly desultory quality of the play's dramatic structure, and provides a good illustration of the craftsmanship fostered by our commercial theatre.)

The subject matter of *End of Summer*, which is immediate, vital, and dramatic, its whole rich stirring background of present-day life, are in striking contrast to the pallidness and artificiality of the characters. This is particularly true of the two "rebels"—Will and Dennis. If the boys are meant to be representative of the best in the movement that is stirring on American college campuses today against intolerance, militarism, and the restriction of civil liberties, then they are caricatures. Whatever Behrman may have intended, the play resolves itself into a comparison of the very flower of the "old order" (Leonie) with the least prepossessing elements of the new (Will and Dennis). The latter is described as "gawky, slovenly, and infinitely brash—an officer of the National Student Federation" (a progressive organization of college students); actually he is abominably rude and opinionated. Will talks a great deal about his radical principles and activities, but both melt away before the charm of Paula's mother (the same is true of Dennis), and he is hagridden by the fear of being tainted by Paula's money. Inevitably the audience is left with the impression that Leonie is a darling, even if she is a brainless parasite, and that the young people are unbalanced kids with no manners, whose radicalism is only skin-deep and quite negligible.

All too frequently the dialogue, which at times is brilliant, lapses to the level of cheap wisecracking:

> Why can't radicals be chic? I saw a picture of Karl Marx the other day and he looks like one of those ads before you take something.

Frequently the context of a line is such as to negate its meaning.

LEONIE

(*To Dennis*) Whatever you say, it's an exciting time to be alive.

DENNIS

That's because your abnormal situation renders you free from its major excitement.

LEONIE

And what's that?

DENNIS

The race with malnutrition.

Yet Dennis' role in the play, his whole relationship to Leonie (which is one of the most cordial friendship and admiration), is such as to contradict any impression such a speech might give of his opinion of Leonie; it becomes a flippancy.

Either the author, therefore, has created an impression the opposite of what he intended, or he is so much of two minds about the problems that perplex him that, like Stephen Leacock's young man on horseback, he is riding rapidly in all directions. To eat your cake and try to have it too, to deny and affirm simultaneously, is neither tolerance, nor within the bounds of dramatic plausibility. It gets Mr. Behrman into trouble in *End of Summer*, and it gets him into a terrible mess in *Wine of Choice*.

Here once again (and very much like Sidney Howard in *The Ghost of Yankee Doodle* during the same season), Behrman shows himself alert to the inconsistencies and inequities of the world, and yet recoils in horror and distress of mind from any change, or from what he conceives to be the only alternative. *Wine of Choice* deals with the emotional instabilities of Wilda Doran, a would-be film actress who wants a career, and is beset by four men who all love her. She unfortunately elects to love, and throw herself at, the radical who doesn't really want her. Chris is a young man of few words. He tries to mind his own business, to discourage Wilda's attentions, tu point out that they are unsuited to one another. He is seduced by her very much against his will, and he gives her no false hopes. Yet while thus ostensibly playing fair with Chris, Behrman manages to make him appear as cold-blooded and unprincipled a villain as ever wronged fair maiden. In fact, he draws the character in cold hatred. Eschewing all political labels (aside from a few cracks about executions and liquidation), he nevertheless conveys the idea that Chris' brand of "revolution," which is obviously supposed to be socialism (though Behrman never permits him to discuss it), is the sole danger confronting the world today. This is a position Mr. Behrman would undoubtedly deny, just as in the introduction to the published play he carefully denies that Chris is "the factual portrait of an individual Communist." The meaning to audiences however is clearly that the menace to civilized mankind today lies, not in the Fascist ideology which menaced Hugo Willens and all he stood for in *Rain From Heaven*, but on the left. There is not a single reference to the danger of Fascism or reaction of any kind throughout the play. Once again we have a political argument—for what else are Ryder Gerrard's tirades against Chris?—in a vacuum, and a radical who, while giving lip service to humanity, is a caricature that embodies the author's personal antagonisms and has about as much relation to actuality as a Charlie McCarthy.

In all probability, Behrman is still as sincerely antifascist as when he wrote *Rain From Heaven*. But *Wine of Choice* is not an antifascist play. It is, in effect, an anticommunist play in which the cards are stacked to facilitate Red-baiting, and as such it does Mr. Behrman's unquestioned talent and intelligence less than justice. Such a stand on his part is due to his failure to come to grips with the problems which preoccupy him, to a tendency to write from hearsay rather than experience and to assume the point of view of the people about whom he is writing.

No one wants Mr. Behrman to begin writing proletarian drama. His talent—and it is not inconsiderable—is clearly to write, in not too serious a vein, of a certain class of people whom he knows intimately. But he must widen and deepen his experience beyond that class in order to see it in perspective, in its proper relation to society as a whole. He will then not only acquire a healthier point of view towards the people he writes about, but a wider knowledge of the world outside his particular milieu may enable him to solve some of his problems as a dramatist: thinness of action, lack of concrete incident, superficiality of characterization, and the recurrence of one pattern of action—the parting and frustration of a man and woman who cannot understand each other or surmount their differences of opinion. This last is only one projection (the eternal radical is another) of Behrman's own conflict—of his failure to integrate his instincts and his thinking. The answer lies outside his present limited field of inquiry.

IV Maxwell Anderson

None of our leading playwrights, with the exception of Eugene O'Neill, have written as consistently without compromise as Maxwell Anderson, who has shaped public taste rather than conformed to it, and has followed the dictates of his own interests and artistic standards rather than those of the box office. Anderson believes that "our theatre is the one really living American art," that the theatre, "more than any other art, has the power to weld and determine what the race dreams into what the race will become"; [1] out of this noble conception has come his allegiance to blank verse as the highest form of a great art. He has never deliberately set himself to write a "hit," although a large number of his plays have fallen into that class. Audiences have been attracted to his work by its craftsmanship and its dramatic effectiveness, not by any expectation of cheap sensationalism or empty laughter. An Anderson play, they know, is the

[1] Introduction, *Winterset*.

expression of its author's ideas, uttered with candor and integrity; it represents the best he is capable of.

His own life has shown no lack of the same qualities. He taught school, and lost his job for talking pacifism to his pupils. He worked on a newspaper, and lost his job for his outspokenness. And when he felt that the standard he wished to achieve in the theatre was incommensurate with writing for Hollywood, he abandoned the latter.

His work is of great interest, not only because of its variety, or because his proportion of successes has been so high. Nor is it due solely to his excellence as a craftsman, or to his extraordinary feat of winning the public to a form of theatre which, at first sight, would seem to be the last to appeal to our audiences nowadays—the poetic drama. It is for all these things, but also because he has used the theatre as an exalted tribune from which he has expounded a personal philosophy. It is therefore only giving him his due if we concern ourselves at some length with what he has to say as well as how he says it, the more so because there is an increasingly striking correlation between the quality of his writing and the validity of his thinking.

In contrast with his later preoccupation with the historical past and his use of blank verse, Anderson's first half-dozen plays (with the exception of *White Desert*) were in prose, and the majority of them were contemporary and highly realistic in tone. Nevertheless the seeds of his latter-day confusion and pessimism are already present in them. From the beginning he has shown himself unable to grapple with the basic causes of the problems he dealt with, to extract the full human or social implications from his subject matter. For all their expertness, *What Price Glory?*, *Saturday's Children*, and *Gypsy* show a lack of penetration which presently made it possible for Anderson to immerse himself in poetic idealism and believe that therein lay the salvation of the modern world and the modern theatre alike.

1

What Price Glory?, by Anderson and Laurence Stallings, is not an antiwar play, but a highly realistic play about war as fought by professional soldiers. Such propaganda value as it may possess, owing to its depiction of some of the less savory aspects of modern trench warfare, is pretty well canceled by the glorification of the daredevil, "he-man" qualities of Captain Flagg and Sergeant Quirt.

Compared to the moving picture *All Quiet on the Western Front*, directed by Lewis Milestone, *What Price Glory?* is a tabloid. *All Quiet* is concerned with what happens, bodily and spiritually, to men whom war snatches ruthlessly out of the pattern of their normal lives. *What Price Glory?* has no such philosophical perspective. It never questions the wholesale slaughter of men to gain political or economic ends, as an institution; it scarcely deprecates it. Occasionally Captain Flagg rebels, not at the necessity of leading his men to death, but only at the circumstances under which it must be done—the necessity of fighting when they are tired, or attacking at *too* murderous a cost. If he is cynical over the purpose of the Great War ("that world-safe-for-democracy slush"), he nevertheless pursues the profession of soldiering for eight dollars' a day soldier's pay.

There's something about this profession of arms, some kind of damned religion connected with it you can't shake. When they tell you to die you have to do it, even if you're a better man than they are.

Who are "they"? This is the crux of the matter, but it is never pursued. "What a lot of God-damned fools it takes to make a war," sighs Quirt at the last as he wearily prepares to go back into action, but his closing line is only "Hey, Flagg, wait for baby!" Today such a consciously "hard-boiled" attitude appears as much romanticism as the aura of gallantry which still hung over the war (as far as the theatre was concerned) in 1924, and which Anderson and Stallings were trying, with their brand of realism, to dispel. By identifying the forces of evil in the play with nothing more fundamental than vainglory, bureaucracy, and the traditional ineptitude of G.H.Q., *What Price Glory?* is, by the standards of 1938, precisely the evasion of reality which the authors wished to avoid.

On the plane of theatrical effectiveness there is no fault to find with *What Price Glory?* It is a tautly constructed, well-written, and fast-moving play. The picaresque rivalry between Captain Flagg and Sergeant Quirt, pursued in many lands and by many seas, of which we here glimpse only one episode (the struggle over Charmaine) has wide appeal. The seesawing rise and fall of the fortunes of first one and then the other of the two antagonists combines tension and humor, and the salty dialogue is still as full of life as when it first shattered theatrical conventions fifteen years ago.

After two more collaborations with Stallings, neither of them successful, Anderson wrote *Outside Looking In,* still not an independent piece of work since he dipped into Jim Tully's *Beggars of Life* for his material. Despite its great dramatic possibilities, *Outside Looking In* is a desultory and aimless play because it lacks a clear-cut conflict. The conflict is there ready to hand—it is even implicit in the title of the play: there is no struggle more bitter than the one which rages between the human beings who have been cast out from society, and the society which, having barred them from its shelter, is put on the defensive against their depredations. This conflict Anderson practically ignores, except for some long speeches. The action centers, not around Red and Edna's flight from the police or even the antagonism between the hobos and the law, but around the hobos' rivalry for supremacy among themselves or for the possession of Edna. Consequently there is no development, no climax, no point, only a succession of racily written episodes each entertaining in itself, but lacking any cumulative force or direction.

2

Saturday's Children was Anderson's first independently written play. It is an amusing and touching comedy about the problems of young married life on a shoestring, and if the treatment in general is light and humorous the serious overtones are unmistakable. Bobby Halevy, terrified at the prospect of a lifetime as a stenographer or a family dependent, "catches" young Rims O'Neil, just as her sister Florrie "caught" her husband before her. Once married, however, she finds that she has been tricked into something which society had taught her was the be-all and end-all of a girl's existence but which amounts to nothing more than servitude. She revolts, and swings to the opposite extreme. As she tells Rims:

What we wanted was a love-affair—just to be together and let the rest go hang—and what we got was a house and bills and general hell——I want my love affair back. I want hurried kisses and clandestine meetings and a secret lover. I don't want a house. I don't want a husband. I want a lover.

She gets one; the curtain goes down on Rims' visit to the little boardinghouse room where Bobby has set up housekeeping, not as her husband, but as a forbidden afterhours' visitor.

The trouble is that Bobby mistakes freedom from an impossible burden for irresponsibility. Life cannot be lived on the principle of just "being together and letting the rest go hang." By her negation of marriage in favor of an affair she is escaping into romanticism, and so is the playwright, since his proposed "solution" overlooks the fundamental need for stability in an emotional relationship. And when Anderson leaves Bobby and Rims pretending that they are lovers in order to preserve their independence and avoid the responsibility of a common home, he is not only storing up future heartaches for them; he is evading the fundamental cause of the trouble, which is an inadequate standard of living. Plenty of marriages go on the rocks for other than economic reasons; but in this case Anderson makes it quite clear that the nagging, scrimping, and worrying incident to living on two tiny salaries is at the bottom of their quarreling. Yet neither Rims nor Bobby ever questions the society which places them in such an impasse, and neither, apparently, does the playwright.

Ellen Hastings in Gypsy is Bobby a a few years later;

it is as if Anderson had realized the falsity of his conclusion to *Saturday's Children* and had decided to face the consequences inherent in Bobby's flight from responsibility in quest of "freedom." Ellen's emotional life lacks both honesty and stability, and leads to tragedy. Yet despite the logic of such an outcome, *Gypsy* illustrates to perfection John Howard Lawson's thesis that one of the weaknesses of present day playwrights is their negation of the individual will. Their characters are helpless, ridden by all kinds of "fate"; fortuitous, religious, cosmic, psychological, hereditary. Ellen cries out against her nature, but she cannot help herself; she is will-less. Blame is put on her mother, a nymphomaniac, who likewise "cannot help" being what she is. Yet there is nothing obscure about Ellen's plight; it overtook a good many members of her generation, and had less to do with what kind of women their mothers were, and more with a profound sociological change which was taking place in morals and mores during the nineteen-twenties. Ellen is what prohibition, postwar disillusionment, and flight from reality, the recession of religious belief the cult of feminine emancipation, the rising tide of Hollywood movies and tabloid journalism, and the perfecting and wider knowledge of contraceptives all made of a weak character who lacked the capacity to assimilate these novelties. The pages of Judge Ben Lindsey's writings are full of her. But according to Maxwell Anderson she is only an unfortunate young woman plagued with bad heredity and a worse upbringing, loose in a society where young people habitually settle down to smoothly married domesticity.

3

Gods of the Lightning, the joint work of Anderson and Harold Hickerson, is based on the Sacco-Vanzetti case. There are of course certain changes: only one of the two men, railroaded to the electric chair for a murder neither committed, is a foreigner and an Anarchist; the other is an I.W.W.; both are labor organizers, working actively in a trade union. The play revolves, moreover, around a dual theme. One is the martyrdom of Macready and Capraro at the hands of a justice whose class complexion makes it a travesty of the word. The other is the futility of the work and death of these men, expressed in the character of Suvorin, an extraordinary figure compounded of hatred, cynicism, and demoniac power. Suvorin hates oppression yet mocks those who fight against it, believes in nothing, and in the end escapes unscathed from the fate of Macready and Capraro. *Gods of the Lightning* is the first clear example of a pattern of thought and its dramatic embodiment, which Anderson was to use with little fundamental alteration for the next ten years.

It is certainly a curious mixture. There is no doubting the intensity of conviction of the two men who wrote the play. With unsparing outspokenness and savage skill they show up the institution of "class justice" for what it is worth. The scenes in which the State's Attorney shepherds his uneasy witnesses back into line under the threat of blackmail, and the eloquent court-room scene, are among the most bitter and forthright indictments of injustice in the service of vested interest that have ever been penned for the stage.

What then is the reason for the introduction of the

sinister figure of Suvorin? It seems hardly likely that the authors felt the need for additional dramatic material to bolster up the plot. Suvorin serves only a mechanical role in forwarding the action; his discovery of the stool pigeon, his confession of the murder for which the two men are being railroaded, his escape from the death house, are none of them dramatically indispensable. In fact, they are the least credible incidents of the play and as such weaken its impact, which depends on complete plausibility. Suvorin also weakens it insofar as his philosophy completely negates everything for which Mac and Capraro lived and died. There would be little reason to include him, therefore, if he did not express to some extent the point of view of the authors, and this probability is born out by the tenor of much of Anderson's subsequent work. Suvorin regards all struggle as fruitless. He is contemptuous of the workers for whom the two martyrs are sacrificed. He believes only in hatred. Listen to him when he uncovers a supposedly trusted union man as a spy:

> How many years have I sat listening to fools' talk? Five years—ten years. And what have I learned from you?——that you know nothing—that you learn nothing! Uplifters you are, dreamers, reformers, thinking to make over the earth. I know you all and you are fools——The earth is old. You will not make it over. Man is old. You will not make him over. You are anarchists, maybe, some of you socialists, some of you wobblies, all of you believers in pap. The world is old and it is owned by men who are hard. Do you think that you can win against them by a strike? Let us change the gov-

ernment, you say. Bah! They own this government, they will buy any government you have. I tell you there is no government—only brigands in power who fight always for more power! It has always been so. It will always be so. Till you die! Till we all die! Till there is no earth!

Here is negation, futility, made absolute. The last act, as Philip Stevenson has pointed out,[2] belongs almost entirely to Suvorin and Rosalie—the one embodying futility, the other personal grief and bitter resentment of the cause for which the men have died. It is true that Rosalie's last speech, which brings down the curtain, is a plea for justice:

> Don't whisper it! Don't whisper it!——That's what they'll want you to do—whisper it—keep quiet about it—say it never happened—it couldn't happen—two innocent men killed—keep it dark—keep it quiet—no! No! Shout it!——Shout it! Cry out! Run and cry! Only—it won't do any good—now.

Yet her anguish is personal, infused more with a sense of her own loss than an understanding of the issues involved. And there is no escaping that despairing last admission: "It won't do any good—now."

There is no one to affirm the value of continued struggle, to see the whole episode in proper perspective, as one link in a long heroic saga. The tragedy of the two men is isolated, to a great degree, from what they stand for. This is because the authors, despite all their

[2] "Maxwell Anderson, Thursday's Child," *New Theatre*, September, 1936.

resentment of "class justice," are nevertheless primarily interested in the suffering of two *individuals*, rather than in the class which is the collective victim of an attitude of which we here see only one example. It was perfectly legitimate for Hickerson and Anderson to write a play focused primarily on the two principal victims. The importance of such a point of view lies in its relation to Anderson's whole development. He has never been closer to any mass movement than he was in *Gods of the Lightning*, or once again, years later, in *Valley Forge*. Primarily his interest is in individuals, in isolated rebellion far removed from contact or root in the great masses of people. These two tendencies, hopeless pessimism and individualism, first clearly discerned in *Gods of the Lightning*, develop in time into the fatal confusion and inconclusiveness of *Winterset* and the sterility of *The Masque of Kings*.

4

Once established, the pattern is followed with extraordinary consistency. It is not as long a step as it might seem from the Sacco-Vanzetti case to the court of Queen Elizabeth, if one looks beneath the outward trivia of time and personages to the mood and ideas expressed in both *Gods of the Lightning* and *Elizabeth the Queen*. When Elizabeth cries, "The rats inherit the earth," it might be Suvorin speaking. Having examined the results of class oppression, Anderson turns to a consideration of the effects and attributes of power on those in high place, to discover that the strong and unjust are themselves not immune from suffering and injustice.

In certain respects *Elizabeth the Queen* marks a new phase of his growth. With it Anderson's writing gains

additional scope, almost a new dimension. In an introduction to the published version of *Winterset* he has set
forth what he holds to be the aims and the significance
of poetic drama. "Prose is the language of information
and poetry the language of emotion. . . . Under the
strain of an emotion the ordinary prose of our stage
breaks down into inarticulateness, just as it does in life.
Hence the cult of understatement, hence the realistic
drama in which the climax is reached in an eloquent
gesture or a moment of meaningful silence."

Anderson sees the theatre today, because of its domination by prose as journalistic, "dominated by those
who wish to offer something immediate about our political, economic or social life." He himself wishes, and
believes that audiences desire, that it should take up
again "the consideration of man's place and destiny in
prophetic rather than prosaic terms." This can be done
only by returning to the poetic, emotional tradition of
the theatre, "the poet to be prophet, dreamer and in-
terpreter of the racial dream."

It is true that the present-day theatre offers few
examples of the self-expressive articulateness which
Anderson's poetic characters boast of. In going back to
verse, Anderson has likewise gone back to the tradition
of unreal dialogue—the long speech, "unpacking the
heart with words." This has been done in prose, witness
the writing of O'Neill, Lawson, Odets. There is no
"meaningful silence" in *The Children's Hour* when the
two schoolteachers kneel in front of the fire, or in *Biography* or *Ned McCobb's Daughter*, or even in *Street
Scene*; there is, however, by contrast with Anderson's
technique, brevity, compactness, an absence of rhap-
sodizing. The danger is, that in eschewing the realism of

"journalistic social comment" for poetic prophecy, the writer will lose his grip on the reality which must necessarily be the basis of dreaming if it is not to be idle vaporing and self-delusion. A dream can be, not only the setting of a goal, the embodiment of a hope, but an escape from the difficult and the necessary. Anderson himself confesses to having "only a faith that men will have a faith" even after "they have lost the certainty of salvation through laboratory work" which is their faith today. The test of his thesis of the importance of poetic drama must be the stature, the significance of the aspirations and dreams and hopes which the use of poetry in the theatre liberates in the dramatist.

On the first count he seems justified. Nowhere in the theatre today do we have such a series of highly developed, visionary, articulate characters as Anderson has created, with the single exception of Eugene O'Neill. Elizabeth is the first of those extraordinary characters—introspective, self-conscious, articulate, highly intellectualized—who live simultaneously on two closely interrelated planes of thought and action, in the world about them and in the "room of the mind": Pablo Montoya, Washington, Mio Romagna, Rudolph of Habsburg. But what do these characters envisage for themselves and for the race? Let us examine in detail a number of his poetic dramas.

Elizabeth the Queen, although simple in main plot outline—the vicissitudes of Elizabeth's stormy affair with the Earl of Essex, is nevertheless complex, since the two principal characters have continually changing aspects, and in addition to their own kaleidoscopic selves hold in their minds continually shifting images of each other. Essex is sincere, if a man with two strong con-

flicting aims of which first one and then the other dominates, may be called sincere. He loves the Queen, but he
will not subordinate his love to his overweening egotism
and desire for a position above even Elizabeth's. Elizabeth, on her part, is alternately woman and ruler, at one
moment keenly aware of the dangers of Essex's hot-
headedness and vanity, at another the helpless prey of
her feelings. As queen she outwits the earl at the
moment when he is master of her palace by trickery; as
woman she stops him when he turns to go to his execution, crying "Lord Essex! Take my kingdom. It is
yours."

The main temper of the play is unquestionably one of
consistent, bitter disillusionment and cynicism. The
other characters, the statesmen who surround the Queen
—Cecil, Raleigh, Bacon—are one and all schemers and
intriguers, their actions governed only by lust for power.
To hold power is inevitably to traffic in it and be corrupted by it, Anderson would seem to say; the councilors
of Elizabeth's court are kin to the Continental Congressmen of *Valley Forge* and the corrupt legislators of *Both
Your Houses*. (On the other hand, what we are told of
the people is little better: "beef-witted bastards" and
"drunken children," Elizabeth calls them on different
occasions.) When Cecil and his colleagues present the
Queen with evidence of Essex's treachery, she lashes out
at them:

It's your day, Cecil.
I daresay you know that. The snake-in-the-grass
Endures, and those who are noble, free of soul,
Valiant and admirable—they go down in their prime,
Always go down.———

——*The snake-mind is best—*
One by one you outlast them. To the end
Of time it will be so—the rats inherit the earth.

To Essex, in the hour when even her faith in his love is shattered, she cries:

I trusted you,
And learned from you that no man can be trusted.
I'll remember that.——
——*This is the end.*
It comes late. I've been a long while learning.
But I've learned it now. Life is bitter. Nobody
Dies happy, queen or no.

In her loneliness, her concentrated, intensely personal anguish in which she is imprisoned, her sense of being pitted against a baleful fate, she resembles many of Anderson's characters. "Always I've known too late that I was alone," says Pablo Montoya; "we are alone, always alone," cries Mary Stuart; Oparre recognizes that "I've never known you, and I'm alone"; and Mio Romagna is "outcast of the world, snake in the streets." Each one echoes Elizabeth's haunting sense of tragedy and loss, of the evanescence of happiness, of the human soul beset by forces which change it, despite itself, into an alien thing:

The years are long, and full of sharp wearing days
That wear out what we are and what we have been
And change us into people we do not know,
Living among strangers.

It makes little difference whether Anderson's men and women live and suffer in the sixteenth century or the nineteenth or the twentieth, whether they are Roman

Catholics or Jews or hard-boiled agnostics—one and all they cry out for help to the same vague ruling spirits; they are weighted down by a sense of predestined fate it is beyond their power to avoid. Trapped as they are, individual will is of no avail. Anderson's whole conception of history, judged from *Elizabeth the Queen*, *Mary of Scotland*, *Night Over Taos*, and *The Masque of Kings*, is of a mystical process without rhyme or reason, completely divorced from any relation of cause and effect.

This is particularly apparent in *Mary of Scotland*, where the conflict between Elizabeth and Mary, historically a vast complex of motives and forces, is narrowed down to the opposition of the two ethical principles of good and evil. Mary is tolerant, generous, and gentle. Elizabeth is a sinister and baleful figure, spinning a huge web of intrigue in which to catch her apparently innocent victim. Because no real cause is shown for her hatred of Mary, her persecution of the Scottish queen appears mere rancor and intolerance. Now as a matter of fact there were good solid reasons why Elizabeth, and England with her, dreaded Mary's presence in Scotland and the Spanish influence her religion made inevitable; the Catholic reaction under Mary Tudor, and her marriage to Philip II of Spain, had given the newly emerged English middle class an unpleasant taste of what it might expect of a Catholic neighbor and pretender to the throne. But in making the bigoted John Knox sole representative of Protestantism, and Mary's magnanimity synonomous with Catholicism, Anderson opposes pure sweetness and light on one hand to pitch-black on the other. He completely ignores the cruel and fanatic manifestations of Catholicism, as well as the many economic and social justifications for the Reformist movement: the ecclesiastical decay of the Catholic Church, its temporal power and corruption, and the dead weight of its teachings on the awakening curiosity and enterprise of a new era.

Without making his play an historical treatise, Anderson might have taken some account of these fears and motives; to omit them completely amounts to distortion. Every writer of historical plays and novels has practiced such distortion, from Shakespeare on down the list. The question here is: where does it lead Anderson, what use does he make of his license? In *Mary of Scotland* it leads him once again into futility and negation, since Elizabeth's triumph over Mary, because of the values with which he has invested the characters, amounts to the victory of evil over good. Mary's heroic insistence at the close, "And still I win—" is only the playwright's apologia, similar to, and of no more value than, Esdras' final affirmation at the tragic conclusion of *Winterset*:

> yet is my mind my own,
> yet is my heart a cry towards something dim
> in distance, which is higher than I am
> and makes me emperor of the endless dark
> even in seeking—

In such passages as these the poet is voicing an emotional faith which is in direct contradiction with the logic of his reasoned thinking. What emerges from Anderson's plays, one after another, is belief in a useless gallantry which almost invariably goes down to defeat, which avails nothing, but which is yet, in some mystical heart-warming way, worth-while and noble for its own sake. This philosophy has earned him the reputation of idealist, since its outstanding expressions—the characters of Mary Stuárt, Mio Romagna, Van Van Dorn, Oparre, and Rudolph of Habsburg—are all animated by motives and standards of conduct above any material considerations. It would be more accurate to call it romanticism, since such a philosophy amounts to an acceptance of failure and disillusionment as the only possible outcome of effort by the best of humanity.

In *Mary of Scotland* the nemesis of inconclusiveness and sterility which lurks in such thinking for the playwright is not yet apparent. For one thing, the pattern has not yet worn thin with repetition; it is vigorously and effectively executed in dramatic terms. *Mary of Scotland* is first-rate theatre; it moves with tragic power to its inevitable conclusion. By interweaving the course of Mary's fortunes in Scotland with the scenes in Elizabeth's council chamber the tension of the successive stages of Mary's ruin are heightened; the calculating frozen immobility of the Whitehall room where Elizabeth spins her web are in masterly contrast to the vigor and color of the Holyrood scenes. Mary is the more pitiful in that she is a completely unconscious victim. But the audience knows, having heard Elizabeth's schemes:

It is not easy to thrust a queen from her throne, but suppose a queen were led to destroy herself, led carefully from one step to another in a long descent until at last she stood condemned among her own subjects, stripped of force, and the people of Scotland were to deal with her for us?

By dint of whispers and rumors Mary's name is blackened; by the device of urging Mary to do one thing

Elizabeth drives her to do another, simply to defy the mandates of the English queen. In many ways Mary is akin to Elizabeth in the earlier *Elizabeth the Queen*: in her feeling of helplessness before a stronger power:

> the gods set us tasks, my Lord,
> that we must do.

In her anguished sense of solitude and loneliness:

> God help all women
> Here in this world, and all men. Fair fall all chances
> The heart can long for—and let all women and men
> Drink deep while they can of their happiness. It goes
>   fast
> And never comes again. Mine goes with you,
> Youth, and the fund of dreams, and to lie a while
> Trusted, in arms you trust. We're alone, alone,
> Alone—even while we lie there we're alone,
> For it's false. It will end. Each one dies alone.

Elizabeth, on the other hand, has now become completely the queen whom we saw earlier still struggling with the woman who wished only to follow her own heart.

>   I'm old by now
> In shuffling tricks and the huckstering of souls
> For lands and pensions. I learned to play it young,
> Must learn it or die. It's thus if you would rule;
> Give up good faith, the word that goes with the heart,
> The heart that clings where it loves. Give these up and
>   love
> Where your interest lies, and should your interest change
> Let your love follow it quickly. This is a queen's por-
>   ridge

And however little stomach she has for it
A queen must eat it.

If *Mary of Scotland* is technically a fine piece of work, considerably less can be said of its literary quality. In the earlier *Elizabeth the Queen* and *Night Over Taos*, Anderson's blank verse had a bareness and simplicity which led to the charge that he was stiff and uncomfortable in the medium. In *Mary of Scotland*, on the other hand, he has been acclaimed for bringing back to the theatre "the full flooding beauty of the English language." Yet he lapses repeatedly into triteness, poverty of imagery, and sentimentality. Here he first displays his obsession with the visual images of fire and flame, which echo throughout his verse in *Winterset, The Masque of Kings, The Wingless Victory*, and *High Tor*, and give a cloying quality to the lyric speeches of Mary and Bothwell.

There is aching
Fire between us, fire that could take deep hold
And burn down all the marches of the West
And make us great or slay us.

Other images reappear constantly, in this and in his later plays: the wind, night, the passing of time. It is a curious fact that Anderson's metaphors, his use of words, his rhythms, are most fresh and arresting, not in his lyric passages, but when he is voicing hatred or contempt or bitterness, as in the speeches of Trock, Mio, Rudolph of Habsburg, and Washington, or in more measured passages of intellectual contemplation: Judge Gaunt, Franz Joseph. The simpler characters who speak from their hearts—the Empress Elizabeth, Miriamne, Mary Tudor,

Lise—never attain the same incisiveness or significance of utterance.

Both *Night Over Taos* and *Valley Forge*, Anderson's next two verse plays, are inferior to his Elizabethan plays as theatre, for two different reasons. In *Night Over Taos* the historical thinking is so confused as to weaken the dramatic structure of the play. Pablo Montoya, feudal lord of the principality of Taos in New Mexico in the year 1847, finds his rule menaced from within by popular dissatisfaction with his despotism and the restlessness of his sons and from without by invasion by the growing young American republic. To allow Montoya to submit voluntarily, as he does, to destroy himself in order to clear the way for the forces against which he has, up to now, fought so uncompromisingly is, as Philip Stevenson points out, completely false: "The Montoyas of decaying social orders do not abdicate voluntarily." [3] They never have and they never will. What is, in this case, historical distortion, is also dramatically an unpardonable inconsistency; it closes the play, as is so often the case with Anderson, in an aura of sentimentality. The proud and ruthless Montoya has taken poison; Felipe, his son, and Diana, potagonists of the new order, who owe their lives to his death, kneel beside his chair.

FELIPE
If I could help you—
DIANA
Or I.
Curtain.

Valley Forge is badly constructed, and static; there is too much talk and too little action, and the entire Mary

[3] *Ibid.*

Phillips episode—an arbitrarily introduced romantic interlude—is irrelevant, not the least of its weaknesses
being the question: how does the lady acquire the vital
information concerning the consummation of the
French alliance, which she gives Washington in his
hour of need? [4] But *Valley Forge* possesses the inestimable advantage of making a great affirmation, and of
telling a great story: the epic of the Continental army,
pitted not only against the British regulars but against
the inefficiency, selfishness, and double-dealing of the
Continental Congress. Characteristically, the affirmation does not come until Anderson has made this conflict the basis for an attack against all governments as
such in the best anarchist tradition.

They're all alike, and have one business, governments,
and it's to plunder. This new one we set up
seems to be less efficient than the old style
in its methods of plundering folk, but give them time;
they'll learn to sink their teeth in what you've got
and take it from you!

Bitter disillusion even leads one of the generals, Stirling,
to contend that monarchy is the best form of government because a king is more easily put out of the way
than the machinery of a democracy.

Do you know what I think of governments, by and large,
I mean in general? They're run by pimps
who get kicked out of hot-houses for picking
the customers' pockets. This one we've got—we made it,
set it up, picked the best men we could find

[4] The audience only knows that Howe specifically decided *not* to
tell her that particular piece of news.

and put them in—and their brains began to rot
before the year was out. It rots a man's brains
to be in power, and he turns pimp and picks pockets;
the scavengers! At least, when you have a king
you can chop his head off.

Washington himself is not untouched by the general
despondency and confusion of mind; he is apparently
fighting for an ideal of whose realization he has only
the faintest hope.

What I fight for now is a dream, a mirage, perhaps,
something that's never been on this earth since men
first worked it with their hands, something that's never
existed and never will exist unless we make it and put
it here—the right of freeborn men to govern themselves in their own way.—Now men are mostly fools,
as you're well aware. They'll govern themselves like
fools. There are probably more fools to the square
inch in the Continental Congress than in the Continental
Army, and the percentage runs high in both. But we've
set our teeth and trained our guns against the hereditary
right of arbitrary kings and if we win it's curfew for
all the kings of the world.——It may not be worth
doing. When you deal with a king you deal with one
knave, fool, madman or whatever he may be. When you
deal with a Congress you are dealing with a conglomerate
of fools, knaves, madmen and honest legislators, all
pulling different directions and shouting each other
down. So far the knaves and fools seem to have it.
——So far our government's as rotten as the sow-
belly it sends us. I hope and pray it will get better.
But whether it gets better or worse it's your own, by

God, and you can do what you please with it—and what
I fight for is your right to do as you please and
wish without benefit of kings.——If you've lost
interest in this cause of yours—we've lost our war,
lost it completely, and the men we've left lying on
our battlefields died for nothing whatever—for a
dream that came too early—and may never come true.

This speech is unjust to Washington's state of mind
at Valley Forge. There is no evidence whatever to show
that he doubted the ultimate validity of the ideal he
was fighting for. Therefore it affords us one more clue
to Anderson's cast of mind. But this time the last word
is not with the powers of darkness. At the close of
Valley Forge there is a passage unique in his writing.
In a moment of complete disillusionment when Washington has discovered that Congress is negotiating with
the British behind his back, he puts the question,
whether to fight on or not, to his men. They reject any
submission or compromise. For once in Anderson's
plays the individual, the leader, the lonely intellectual
and thinker, draws new faith from the strength and
will of the many. Behind the corruption and cynicism of
power lies the great reservoir of the masses of common
people—the rank and file. In them Washington finds
strength to rededicate himself to the common cause:

>   *the forge was cold*
> *that smelted these fellows into steel—but steel*
> *they are.——*
>   *If this war*
> *were made for trade advantages it would end tonight.*
> *It was made over subsidies or some such matter,*
> *but it's been taken over. Let the merchants submit*

*if that's any good to you,[5] then come out and find
my hunters—and backwoodsmen, and beat us down,
into the land we fight for. When you've done that,
the king,may call us subjects. For myself, I'd have
died within if I'd surrendered. The spirit of earth
moves over earth like flame and finds fresh home
where the old's burned out. It stands over this my
country in this dark year, and stands like a pillar
of fire to show us an uncouth clan, unread, harsh-
spoken, but followers of dreams, a dream that men
shall bear no burdens save of their own choosing,
shall walk upright, masterless, doff hat to none,
and choose their gods! It's destined to win, this
dream, weak though we are. Even if we should fail
it's destined to win!*

Throughout the length and breadth of Anderson's
work there is no other affirmation such as this. With
Valley Forge it seemed as if he had taken the first step
in freeing himself from his burden of mysticism and
futility. Any such expectation, however, was dashed by
Winterset and his subsequent three verse dramas.

4

The story of *Winterset* is that of a seventeen-year-old
boy, Mio Romagna, whose father was electrocuted for a
paymaster robbery and murder which he denied having
committed up to the day of his death. The elder Romagna was an Anarchist, and Mio believes that he was
framed because of his political beliefs. A college professor has discovered that an important witness in the case
—Garth Esdras—was never called. Mio reads the professor's pamphlet and comes to find Garth and discover

[5] He is addressing Howe.

whether he knows anything that did not come out at
the trial. In the opening scenes of the play, two other
figures converge on the miserable Esdras tenement
dwelling under the shadow of a great bridge: Trock, a
notorious gangster, guilty of the crime for which Romagna died, and Judge Gaunt, who presided at Romagna's trial. Gaunt has lost his reason from worrying
over his thirteen-year-old verdict against Romagna.
The professor's pamphlet sends him wandering, a victim of amnesia obsessed by the desire to find Garth and
establish the fact that the latter has no further evidence
which might cast any further light on the Romagna
case, and thereby justify his verdict. Trock is determined to make Garth keep his mouth shut.

At a moment when Trock is unnerved by the re-
appearance of a man whom he thought he had killed,
Mio wrests from him an avowal of his guilt. Thereafter
Trock turns the tables on the boy by trapping him in
the dead-end street where the Esdras family live, and
shoots him down when he tries to escape. Meanwhile
Miriamne, Garth's young sister, and Mio have come
to love each other at sight. But torn between her love
and her devotion to her brother, whose life she also
knows to be in danger, Miriamne shields Garth at Mio's
expense and in so doing is instrumental in trapping
him for Trock. She too dies, over Mio's body, because
the gangster realizes that she too heard his confession
and is a menace to his safety.

In *Winterset* Anderson unquestionably set himself
his most difficult task to date. He treats in blank verse,
not of historical material or royal lovers, but of a modern
theme and of the contemporary New York underworld,
of subject matter and characters which have been

stripped of all glamour for his audience by the newspapers and the moving pictures. Whatever one's opinion of the play—and it aroused widespread controversy—it ranks as a courageous effort and an undoubted contribution towards enriching the domain of the theatre.

Winterset is discussed here at such length because it offers an unusual opportunity of examining the processes of the playwright's mind, and of the effect of his thinking on the manipulation of his craft. It is melodrama, on a high plane, but melodrama notwithstanding; it is a lyric love story; and it is an intellectual examination of the nature of truth and justice. It is also—and herein lies the difficulty for the critic striving for detachment in order to assess the play purely in terms of theatre—the fictitious story of the son of Sacco and Vanzetti, united into one character, Bartolomeo Romagna; as such it is a kind of sequel to the Anderson-Hickerson *Gods of the Lightning*. Before discussing it from this latter point of view it is imperative that it be analyzed without reference to any such external considerations, solely from the point of view of the dynamics of the play itself.

Technically, Winterset combines the deftest craftsmanship with serious flaws. The murder of Shadow, which indirectly furnishes Mio with his opportunity to wrest the truth from Trock, is expertly foreshadowed from the very beginning of the play. The exposition of the extraordinarily intricate conflicting motives which animate Trock, Mio, Judge Gaunt, and the Esdras family is brilliantly accomplished in a masterly first act which also sets forth Anderson's familiar thesis of the corruption incident to the holding of power, and the class nature

of justice, which he first attacked in Gods of the Lightning.

I don't think of anything you can't buy, including life,
honor, virtue, glory, public office, conjugal affection
and all kinds of justice, from the traffic court to the
immortal nine. Go out and make yourself a pot of
   money
and you can buy all the justice you want. Convictions
obtained, convictions averted. Lowest rates in years.

There is humor as well as grim irony in the episode of
the policeman and the hurdy-gurdy grinder, seen against
the dark background of the Romagna case and with the
moral driven home by the dead man's son: "That's in
the best police tradition. Incite a riot yourself and then
accuse the crowd." The love scenes are infinitely touching, and the character of Mio, compounded of humor,
courage, vindictive hatred, and lyricism, with the flavor
of a pungent personality, is a magnificent acting role,
of which Burgess Meredith made the most in Guthrie
McClintic's Broadway production of the play. The
scene in which Mio wrings an avowal from Trock while
a freak thunderstorm rages outside the squalid basement
tenement is one of the most electric in our theatre.

   Unfortunately, with Mio's cry of release and triumph
at this point, the play reaches its high point; thereafter the author's grasp weakens. Crushed (at the very
moment of triumph) because Miriamne's loyalty to her
brother takes precedence over her love for him, Mio
literally relinquishes his victory. He has Trock in the
palm of his hand, for he knows his guilt; the corpse of
the murdered Shadow in the next room will send him
to the chair, and the police are on hand. But either for

Miriamne's sake or from anguish at her betrayal—it is
not made clear which—he does not press his advantage.
When the policemen fail to find the body and accuse
him of kidding them, and Miriamne asks, "You have
dreamed something, isn't it true?" he says, "Yes—I was
dreaming," and thereby writes his own epitaph. The
policemen go, Trock goes, and only when it is too late
does Mio follow, to tell the world of his discovery of
Trock's guilt, and to find himself trapped, instead, by
the gangster and his henchmen. Miriamne, full of remorse, comes out to join his dark vigil in the shadow of
the great bridge piers. Then hope rises again. Carr, another young vagrant, comes in, passing by the gunmen
who do not know he is Mio's friend. Mio has the chance
of sending Carr for help, and of telling him of his discovery—of escaping himself or at least seeing that the
truth survives him and clears his father's name. But because the truth implicates Miriamne's brother he does
not do so. For this there is some reason, though, as we
shall see later, it weakens the major premise of the play.
But not at least to send Carr for help is dramatically
inexcusable.

In other words, for an act and a half Anderson is writing a play about a boy whose sole purpose in life is to
clear his father's name, if not to avenge him. Suddenly,
however, he allows him to abandon the purpose which
is the root action of the play, and, violating every principle of character which he has so carefully established in
the first part, brings about a catastrophic denouement
which he invests with a completely false aura of tragic
inevitability, since dramatically there is nothing inevitable about it. Why doesn't Mio jump into the East
River, always full of passing boats, and swim for safety?

Why, if the playing of a hurdy-gurdy brings an enraged policeman to the spot a few hours earlier, does not the sound of Trock's shooting, first of Shadow and then of Mio, bring the police on the scene? Why doesn't Mio fire his gun as a signal for help? And why, as we have already asked, does he not at least tell Carr that he is ambushed by thugs and send him for help—for Carr passes by the ambushed gangsters a second time without trouble.

Melodrama cannot afford such flaws. On the intellectual level there are others no less serious. Take the whole question of Judge Gaunt's role in the play and the playwright's attitude towards him. It was largely due to Gaunt that Mio's father was sent to the chair on extremely flimsy evidence; the judge's charge to the jury was so biased as to be deliberately prejudicial. Yet during the greater part of his presence on the stage his gentleness, his conscience-ridden anguish, his pitiable condition cannot fail to arouse compassion, or at the most condemnation touched with compassion, in the minds of the audience. To Mio he may be a "venomous slug," a "cobra"; but *dramatically* he is invested with considerable nobility, a quality which was strengthened in Richard Bennett's performance of the role.

Indeed, the case of Judge Gaunt offers an outstanding example of how the playwright's treatment and *emphasis* can so color a character or an idea as to completely change its value from what might have been the author's intention, or at first glance appear to be the case. In the long scene between Mio and Gaunt, the latter again and again asserts his good faith in the matter of the Romagna trial, declaring that he weighed the evidence scrupulously, that he searched his soul for traces of prejudice;

Mio's bitter accusations are in themselves proof of nothing but the boy's own fiery conviction of his father's innocence. At the close of the scene the judge has won the advantage, since he has succeeded in making Mio doubt his own sanity and the validity of the conviction which has literally enabled him to live; perhaps, Gaunt insinuates, Romagna was guilty, and Mio's own obsession is proof of the father's irresponsibility and guilt. The ground seems to be crumbling under Mio's feet.

Then suddenly the situation is changed. Mio wrings the truth from Trock. His father was innocent. He turns on Gaunt.

> You lied! You lied!
> You knew this too!
>> GAUNT
>
> (low)
> Let me go. Let me go!
>> MIO
> Then why
> did you let my father die?

Gaunt's answer is a damning self-indictment of his role as a weapon in the hands of the ruling class:

> Suppose it known——justice once rendered
> in a clear burst of anger, righteously,
> upon a very common laborer,
> confessed an anarchist, the ruling found
> and the precise machinery of the law
> invoked to know him guilty—think what furor
> would rock the state if the court flatly said:
> all this is lies—must be reversed? It's better
> as any judge can tell you, in such cases,

holding the common good to be worth more
than small injustice, to let the record stand,
let one man die. For justice, in the main,
is governed by opinion. Communities
will have what they will have, and it's quite as well,
after all, to be rid of anarchists. Our rights
as citizens can be maintained as rights
only while we are held to be the peers
of those who live about us. A vendor of fish
is not protected as a man might be
who kept a market. I own I've sometimes wished
this was not so, but it is.

This is the most crucial speech in the play, for it is the only statement of why Bartolomeo Romagna really died, of the reason for the situation that is the center of the play and that made Mio what he is. It is important to emphasize that it *is* the only statement—that it is never commented upon, amplified, substantiated. It occupies only a fraction of the time which Gaunt has spent, up to now, in self-justification. Placed as it is in the action, in an arbitrarily created pause in which Mio is filled to bursting with the knowledge he has gained, with Trock collecting his wits again, and the tension between the two at a terrific pitch, the speech assumes the value of an irrelevancy.[6] Moreover, Gaunt's self-indictment is concluded in these terms:

> *the man you defend*
> *was unfortunate—and his misfortune bore*
> *almost as heavily on me. I'm broken—*

[6] This was obvious in the production when the actor playing Mio had a difficult time "sustaining" the pause during whch Gaunt spoke.

*broken across. You're much too young to know
how bitter it is when a worn connection chars
and you can't remember—can't remember.*

These are very nearly Gaunt's last words, and they
create an unmistakable aura of pathos in which he
makes his final exit, leaving behind him the impression,
not of hypocrisy or guilt, but of what a difficult and
thankless task it is to be a judge, and of what a fine old
man he really is!

If Anderson wanted to reveal and excoriate the class
basis of justice in *Winterset*, which appeared his purpose
at the outset, he signally failed to do so, and the reason
for his failure lies in his sentimentalization of Judge
Gaunt. The judge's tragedy grows on him, to the exclusion of that of Mio or Romagna or the countless
Romagnas of the working class. There is certainly excellent dramatic material in the case of a man who is the
victim of a conflict between his feelings as a decent
human being and the prejudices which, as a judicial
pawn, he must express. But then he is either guilty of
weakness or hypocrisy, or he is trapped by circumstances,
which he either surmounts, or submits to in self interest.
In *Winterset* the logic of the play leads incontrovertibly
to the conclusion that Judge Gaunt was guilty of prejudice and hatred born of class interest, but the author
nevertheless portrays him as a helpless old man who
meant well and in return suffered for it by losing his
mind. It is a confused and distorted conclusion which
throws the play completely off balance. Nor does it
right itself after Gaunt's exit, since, as we have already
seen, the final act abandons the theme upon which the
play started out in favor of a Romeo and Juliet finale.

No less significant is the character of Esdras and the
position he occupies, particularly at the close of the play.
With his useless wisdom, his purposelessness, his hopelessness, Esdras is the incarnation of futility, of a philosophical idealism completely dissociated from reality.
Yet Anderson so constructs his play as to make Esdras
the survivor who pronounces over the bodies of Mio and
Miriamne, the two young people who stood for hope
and strength, a valedictory which is unequaled for its
empty idealism, whose phrases are devoid of any significance in terms of actuality. Now either the architecture of the play fails utterly to convey the dramatist's real
meaning—which in the case of a craftsman such as
Anderson is hardly likely—or it expresses his intention
justly and we are driven to analyze it. The message of
Winterset, as conveyed in this denouement is that effort
and strength are of no avail. A vague emotional concept
is the be-all and end-all of existence. Best of all is to
die young.

> *To die*
> *when you are young and untouched, that's beggary*
> *to a miser of years, but the devils locked in synod*
> *shake and are daunted when men set their lives*
> *at hazard for the heart's love, and lose.*

The important issue of the play is, therefore, not the fate
of Bartolomeo Romagna, not justice, not even the
tortured conscience of the judge, but the love of two
children.

> *And these*
> *who were yet children, will weigh more than all*
> *a city's elders when the experiment*
> *is reckoned up in the end. Oh, Miriamne,*

and Mio—Mio, my son—know this where you lie,
this is the glory of earth-born men and women,
not to cringe, never to yield, but standing
take defeat implacable and defiant,
die unsubmitting.

These are fine words. But they cannot hide the fact that
to submit is exactly what Mio did when he abandoned
the defense of his father's good name for the love of a
girl he had known only a few hours. At this point, in-
terestingly enough, the curtain fell during Guthrie
McClintic's production of the play; the rest of Esdras'
speech, as written (and published), proved anticlimactic
and too long-drawn-out in the playing. But it is vitally
important, nevertheless, as a statement of the playwright's credo.

>   I wish that I'd died so,
> long ago; before you're old you'll wish
> that you had died as they have. On this star,
> in this hard star-adventure, knowing not
> what the fires mean to the right or left, nor whether
> a meaning was intended or presumed,
> man can stand up, and look out blind, and say:
> in all these turning lights I find no clue,
> only a masterless night, and in my blood
> no certain answer, yet is my mind my own,
> yet is my heart a cry towards something dim
> in distance, which is higher than I am
> and makes me emperor of the endless dark
> even in seeking! what odd and ends of life
> men may live otherwise, let them live, and then
> go out, as I shall go, and you. Our part
> is only to bury them.

This, then, is the outcome of "the consideration of man's place and destiny in prophetic rather than prosaic terms." This is the "racial dream." [7] Here is the culmination of the idealistic romanticism whose progress we have been watching. And it is at this point, when Anderson has dismissed everything except the contemplation of man's ultimate idealistic goal as "odds and ends of life men may live otherwise," that we must recognize the fact that *Winterset* is intellectually a sequel to *Gods of the Lightning* and that Mio Romagna is the son of Sacco-Vanzetti.

Ten years previously the Sacco-Vanzetti case stirred Anderson to a scorching indictment not without weaknesses in its logic but nevertheless uncompromising in its anger and condemnation. In *Winterset* he compromises all along the line. The judge has become an object of curiosity and pity, and the son of his victim turns on his heritage with bitter despair:

deliver me from the body of this hate
I've dragged behind me all these years——

Miriamne, if you love me
teach me a treason to what I am and have been
till I learn to live like a man!

These words strike one like a blow. They smack of the weakling and the renegade. It is perfectly possible that a boy who had suffered as Mio had might be seized with horror of the agony which had constituted his entire life. But Anderson has been at pains to show us that Mio is no ordinary boy. He is of heroic stuff, he is hard-boiled, he is a fanatic with a single obsession. Anderson has put

[7] See p. 89.

Mio's love and admiration for his father into some of the finest lines of the play.

When I was four years old
we climbed through an iron gate, my mother and I
to see my father in prison. He stood in the death-cell
and put his hand through the bars and said, My Mio,
I have only this to leave you, that I love you,
and will love you after I die. Love me then, Mio,
when this hard thing comes on you, that you must live
a man despised for your father. That night the guards
walking in flood-lights brighter than high noon,
led him between them with his trousers slit
and a shaven head for the cathodes. This sleet and
rain that I feel cold here on my face and hands
will find him under thirteen years of clay in
prison ground. Lie still and rest, my father,
for I have not forgotten. When I forget
may I lie blind as you.

To his friend Carr, who tries to reason with him of the hopelessness of his purpose, he cries out:

This thing didn't happen to you.
They've left you your name
and whatever place you can take. For my heritage
they've left me one thing only, and that's to be
my father's voice crying up out of the earth
and quicklime where they stuck him. Electrocution
doesn't kill, you know. They eviscerate them
with a turn of the knife in the dissecting-room.
The blood spurts out. The man was alive. Then into
the lime pit, leaving no trace. Make it short shrift
and chemical dissolution. That's what they thought

of the man that was my father. Then my mother—
I tell you these county burials are swift
and cheap and run for profit——

The moment when he suddenly turns against all these
things is only a few minutes after his discovery that his
lifelong dedication is vindicated; he has heard Trock's
confession and Judge Gaunt's admission of his con-
nivance. But because justice against Trock would involve Miriamne's brother, because he is tired and at
Trock's mercy, he suddenly abandons everything his life
has stood for up to that moment; and not only abandons
it but turns on it with hatred.

      I've groped long enough
through this everglades of old revenges—here
the road ends.——

      I think I'm waking
from a long trauma of hate and fear and death
that's hemmed me from my birth—and glimpse a
life to be lived in hope.

In his anguish he cries out to Miriamne, "Teach me how
to live and forget to hate," and she answers, "He'd have
forgiven." "Who?" asks Mio, and she tells him, "Your
father."

Anderson has come a long way since *Gods of the
Lightning*. One remembers the final courtroom speeches
of Capraro and Macready. And one cannot refrain from
following the example of Philip Stevenson in quoting
the last letters of Sacco and Vanzetti in this connection.
"Forgiven?" asks Stevenson. For Vanzetti wrote, "I
don't forgive my murderers. It would be to betray my
loved ones, my ideas, my comrades, the best of mankind,

all the future generations and myself." [8] He wrote, not from an animus of personal hatred, but from a profound conviction that justice, and the righting of wrong, were the most important things in life. It was a point of view which the author was inclined to share when he wrote *Gods of the Lightning*, but which he had nearly lost when he came to write *Winterset*. Enough of it survived to furnish the initial impulse of the play and to kindle a fine blaze in the first act. But in the end, love becomes more important, and to die young appears the greatest desideratum of all.

The result, purely from the standpoint of theatrical effectiveness, is poor construction and an unsatisfactory conclusion. As far as the playwright himself is concerned, *Winterset* shows a deteriorating sense of values, growing sentimentality, the increasing impediment, dramatically, of his futility and pessimism, and inability to resolve a situation which has all the elements of positive struggle and affirmation in any terms but those of vague verbiage and defeat. The same pattern will be repeated, with only superficial variations, with the suicide of Rudolph Habsburg in *The Masque of Kings*, and of Oparre in *The Wingless Victory*, and the capitulation and flight westward of Van van Dorn in *High Tor*.

5

The Wingless Victory, a story of miscegenation in the year 1800, is a tragedy of intolerance. Anderson is lashing out at the hypocrisy and smugness of false Christianity when he excoriates the Puritan persecution of the Malay princess whom Nathaniel McQueston brings back

[8] Stevenson, Philip, "Maxwell Anderson, Thursday's Child," *New Theatre*, September, 1936.

from his seven years' adventuring in the South Seas as his wife. Having gained great wealth in his enterprises, McQueston, who genuinely loves his wife, tries to buy the good will of the town. He not only fails, but himself becomes poisoned by the hatred which surrounds him and Oparre and which drives them into complete isolation, and acquiesces to the elders' demand that he send Oparre away. Knowing that she faces death if she returns to her barbaric people, since she has become a convert to Christianity and married a white man, and brokenhearted by Nathaniel's desertion, Oparre kills herself and her two dark-skinned children.

Anderson's theatrical instinct has left him in the lurch in *The Wingless Victory*. The character of Nathaniel is badly fumbled; his sudden hatred of his wife is unprepared for, in precisely the same way that Mio's *volte-face* in *Winterset* is dramatically unbelievable. Moreover, in *The Wingless Victory* Anderson the poet is at his worst. The writing is for the most part undistinguished, and some of it is incredibly bad:

In a sea of agony, where one surge follows
after another, to beat us down before
there's a chance to rise, in a sea of fire, where waves
of fire wash over me, I must know that, must still
know we were happy once, and he gave that
as he gives us torment now! Oh, stubby fingers,
dearer than my own eyes that see them, dearer
because they are like this, he wants us no more
and we must go! Oh, web of beauty, woven
of his delight, woven in mystery, worn
so proudly, he puts you off, discards you now,
still warm with him. Now to retrace our steps

while the oceaned agony follows, washing down
the sands in fire! Now to go on alone—
Now to go on alone!

It is apt here to recall Anderson's justification for verse drama: "Under the strain of an emotion the ordinary prose of our stage breaks down into inarticulateness, just as it does in life. Hence the cult of understatement, hence the realistic drama in which the climax is reached in an eloquent gesture or a moment of meaningful silence.[9] But could anything savor more of "understatement" than Nathaniel's explanation to his brother Ruel when the latter bursts into the cabin to find him kneeling by Oparre's body?

NATHANIEL

Come in. Oparre's dead—
and the children.

                RUEL

God! I knew it.

And could anything be more ludicrous than Nathaniel's protest when the dying Oparre tells him she has poisoned her two young daughters?

Damn you! What right
had you to kill the children?

The principal rock on which *The Wingless Victory* founders is failure to relate the individual tragedy of Oparre concretely to a larger issue. Anderson does extend his observations to intolerance and hypocrisy *in general*: the brutality of the Puritans towards Oparre becomes an indictment of false Christianity, and Oparre

[9] Introduction, *Winterset*.

in several passages excoriates the race's assumption of superiority; she tells her husband:

> I hold you free of blame.
> You're but one of a colorless tribe, a tribe that's said:
> Those who are black are slaves, to be driven, slept with,
> beaten, sent on, never loved. Beyond law we are,
> reptilian, to be trodden.——
> We are less than you.
> You part the earth among you, burdening us
> with your labor and your lust. Among yourselves
> you think to breed and rule, breed up in men
> a race of kings to climb the centuries
> on us who bear you.

But is it not extraordinary that an American writer should attempt such a theme without a single reference to our own particular problem of race prejudice and exploitation—the problem of slavery and of postslavery oppression and discrimination as they have existed, and continue to exist, in the Southern states? In 1800, when Anderson sets the date of his play, slavery was already a violent issue. North and South were in continual collision over the principle of human bondage, the Northern states having abolished it by statute, the South upholding it. Why, therefore, did Anderson choose as the scene of his conflict a New England town, and make the Puritans his examples of racial prejudice? Was it in his mind to show that human beings might be progressive as far as legislation went—willing to bar an institution which was of no importance to them economically —and yet be bigoted and cruel when it came to any personal relationship with colored peoples? There is no evidence that such was his intention. Why did he make the victim of his tragedy a Malay princess? To show that race prejudice acknowledges no distinctions of breeding, class, and intellect? If so, then he is palpably in error, since oppression and prejudice increase as we go down the social scale.

Anderson has only skimmed the surface of as profound and dramatic a social problem as exists today. At every point in *The Wingless Victory* the emphasis is wrongly placed. Inevitably, therefore, the tragedy appears forced and artificial, completely lacking in the universality which lay within the playwright's reach. *The Masque of Kings* shows a similar disregard for the values implicit in his material. Dramatically it is one vast fallacy. According to Anderson, Rudolph of Habsburg is dragged, quite against his reasoned judgment, into a conspiracy to overthrow his father's tyranny. Having condemned the scheme as harebrained, he joins it nevertheless because it offers a means of rescuing his mistress from the clutches of the emperor. At the moment of success he stops short and relinquishes his victory, not only because he realizes that he cannot maintain himself in power without the same harsh methods for which he abhors his father's regime, but because he has discovered that Mary Vetsera's love for him is tainted, since she first came to him as a spy in the pay of Franz Joseph. The fact that she abandoned her unsavory task the moment she fell in love with him makes no difference to Rudolph; her "treachery" is the last straw which destroys his faith in humanity and reform. He surrenders to the emperor, retires to Mayerling, and drives his sweetheart to suicide by his cynicism. Then, rediscovering in her death the loyalty he had lost all belief in, he refuses to compromise with his father, and kills himself.

It seems to be the playwright's intention to show the tragedy of a man who lacked the courage and strength to accept certain evils which are the inevitable accompaniment of change and progress, of the liberal who refuses to resort to the violence he abhors. But the play itself does not prove his case. At the very beginning Rudolph states the point of view which, at its close, is supposedly the outcome of what has taken place in the meantime. In the second scene of Act I he sees that

A government will end as it begins,
and if it builds on slaughter it will stand
on slaughter till it falls.

He will have to follow his father's example of autocracy and oppression if he overthrows the latter by violence. When, therefore, he abandons the unexpectedly successful rebellion, saying,

I am the thing I hate—
when I entered this room and knew I owned it,
and knew I'd touched Franz Joseph's power, then
virtue went out of me to him; I was not the same
and any man who sits here in his place will
be as he was, as I am—

he has actually not changed in any respect from what he was or believed at the opening of the play; there has been no real development.

Again, in Act I, he forswears the winning of his ends by force, saying that he has "caught a vision of what a man might do if he were king." In the end he bitterly denies the possibility.

the faith I had
was baseless as a palace of the winds

anchored in clouds, a faith that I had found
a use for kings, a faith that with skill and wisdom
and infinite tolerance, infinite patience, I,
the heir of all the Habsburgs, might strike out
a new coinage of freedom, cut new dies for the mind
and lift men by their bootstraps till they walked
the upper air. This is the faith of fools,
but I had it, and I lost it.

Why? Regardless of its merits, what has happened in the play to make him lose belief in the possibility of *peaceful* change? He has not tried it. He has merely engaged in a palace cabal, come face to face with the necessity for using force against those who are willing to use force against him, and quit. Why the complete denial and renegation of *other* methods? Obviously only because Anderson needs to have his hero stripped of all faith, all illusions, for his final tragic climax. But he has failed to provide adequate motivation for the change.

Two things strike us in *The Masque of Kings*. One is Anderson's fondness for introducing love into his plots as a crucially decisive factor. With incurable romanticism, love—disillusioned or betrayed or triumphant—tips the scales in *Night Over Taos*, in *Valley Forge*, in *Winterset*, and in *The Masque of Kings*. That is to say, it alters what would otherwise be the normal development of the plot. It is as if Anderson were driven to use it as a device in order to avoid pursuing certain implications to their logical conclusion or thinking a problem through to its fundamental premises. Secondly, we are aware that this is historical drama for its own sake, devoid of all contemporary implications. *The Masque of Kings* carries no real meaning for modern audiences; it is pure pageantry. As in *The Wingless Victory*, we are reminded of the *particularity* of Anderson's thinking, his concern with the individual, rather than seeing the individual as representative, or a part of, anything greater than himself. The arraignment of Austro-Hungarian absolutism and the dissolute Viennese imperial court is too special. Because history is more and more clearly revealed as the dynamic working-out of certain basic principles, the historical dramatist, or novelist, or epic poet, cannot confine himself to recounting a court cabal, and not have his work suffer in importance and interest. To "tell sad stories of the death of kings" is no longer enough. Above all, what is needed is a grasp of the forces at work in history, an understanding which is not apparent in Anderson's work.

Rudolph of Habsburg's final speech shows up with great clarity both the truth and the falsehood of Anderson's historical outlook. The Habsburgs are vestigial remains of a dying order:

We are all ghosts, we three,
walking the halls of Europe in a dream
that's ended, a long masquerade of kings
that crossed the stage and stumbled into dark
before we came. We are the shadows cast
by medieval conquerors, a rout
of devil-faces, thrown up long ago
by the powers beneath erupting, but long dead
and gone to slag.

So far so good. But what of the future?

Now the earth boils up again
and the new men and nations rise in fire

to fall in rock, and there shall be new kings,
not you or I, for we're all past and buried,
but a new batch of devil-faces, ikons
made of men's hope of liberty, all worshipped
as bringers of the light, but conquerors,
like those we follow. I leave the world to them,
and they'll possess it like so many skulls
grinning on piles of bones. To the young men
of Europe I leave the eternal sweet delight
of heaping up their bones in the same piles
over which their rulers grin. To the old and
dying I leave their dying kingdoms to be ploughed
by the new sowers of death—fools like myself
who rush themselves to power to set men free
and hold themselves in power by killing men,
as time was, as time will be, time out of mind,
unto this last, forever.

Now this is Anderson speaking, not Rudolph, because
there is no necessity, either of character or in history, for
the prince to utter such sentiments. He might, with perfect truth and consistency, have lamented that he was
before his time, that he was helpless because the forces
working from below among the people were not yet
strong enough to throw off the yoke of tyranny and that
without them he could do nothing; that the world must
inevitably pass through a holocaust in the process of
evolution, but that evolve it must and could, slowly and
haltingly, as history had already proved in America, in
the curbing of the divine right of kings in England, in
the overthrow of absolutism and feudalism in France.

The reason Rudolph ignores these things and speaks
as he does is because, in the last analysis, Anderson him-

self does not care about them; he believes in the essentially ignoble nature of man, in the submersion of the occasionally noble exception by the vast mass of mediocrity and unworthiness; he is not interested in man's circumstances and his bettering and mastering of them. By an extraordinary mental short circuit he sees that the nature of those who hold power unjustly is rotted by the evil they do, that in such cases man's nature flows *from* his circumstances, and thus in turn creates greater evil. But, with the single exception of *Valley Forge*, he is unable to reverse his line of reasoning and believe that man can progress upwards as well as down, can do good and thereby further improve himself.

Why do so many of Anderson's plays end in death, self-inflicted or otherwise? Although such conclusions occur in most of the Greek and Shakespearian tragedies the motivation is different. With the Greeks the convention arose from a religious idea of fate and guilt; in Shakespeare the hero expiates, by his death, for some major tragic fault: witness Macbeth, Lear, Hamlet, Coriolanus, Othello, Antony.[10] With Anderson the fatal outcome is also the result of a philosophic concept: the inevitable end of all that is worthwhile and noble, in death and failure:

> those who are noble, free of soul,
> Valiant and admirable—they go down in their prime,
> Always go down.——The rats inherit the earth.

6

What is true of Anderson's somber verse dramas applies equally to his lapses into lighter vein, in prose. For

[10] A. C. Bradley, *Shakespearean Tragedy.*

all its racy wisecracking and the irrepressible ribaldry of Congressmen Sol Fitzgerald, *Both Your Houses* attempts an indictment of corrupt government and fails, because the corruption is never traced to its source. It is treated as an inevitable appendage to democracy, and the young Galahad who tilts a lance against the professional politicians can offer no alternative except the eventual wrath of the voters.

In *High Tor* Anderson once again vents his ire against the money-changers, in a genuinely comic sequence in which two real-estate crooks are trapped in mid-air in a steam shovel, and hang there throughout a thunderstorm. However the alternative to chicanery and commonplace is flight—flight to the top of a mountain on the shores of the Hudson River, flight into a nostalgic dream of ghosts from a dead past, flight to the West, a West which to the playwright still seems to offer the comfort of an open frontier. The dying Indian tells young Van van Dorn—

> Nothing is made by man
> but makes, in the end, good ruins.

To which Van rejoins, "I can hardly wait."

Most recently, in *The Star Wagon*, in which Anderson has let his taste for whimsy run unchecked, a scientific genius, goaded past endurance by his wife's dissatisfaction with his weekly pittance while the company makes millions out of his inventions, constructs a time machine and travels back twoscore years to see whether life would have been preferable if he had taken another turning, gone in for enterprise instead of invention, and married differently. His discovery is that he was right all along, a conclusion which loses nothing by the fact that his boss sees the light and promises to exploit him somewhat less. Even his invention of the time machine proves nothing sensational:

Nothing changes the world. Every new thing we find just makes it more mysterious. And maybe more terrible.——I'm not different. I'm just a little man, like the rest, only more stupid about most things.

Thus the commonplace becomes glorified; man's everyday routine existence is tinged with gallantry, a subtle device for perpetuating it. There is an unmistakable similarity of tone in Anderson's last play and the most recent works of Eugene O'Neill and George Kaufman—*Ah! Wilderness*, and *You Can't Take It With You*. Wistfully our playwrights are turning to the humdrum and the familiar, endowing them with the glamour of a sentimental nostalgia, after the familiar manner of women's magazines. The pattern of flight, of escape, is unmistakable.

Criticism is functionless if it does not attempt to pierce beneath the excitement and plausibility with which the life and immediacy of performance, quite properly, invest a play, and assess its less superficial values, its point of view and the consistency with which it is expressed. It is of enormous importance to point out where the thinking of our leading dramatists is, consciously or not, leading them. It is not trivial that they appear to say one thing when in reality they mean quite another; it is not irrelevant to point out what values they emphasize as worthwhile, what they exalt or ridicule. No play is better than the system of ideas it expresses. Molière, Ibsen, Pinero, Chekhov, Tolstoi, Hauptmann,

Schnitzler, Strindberg, Galsworthy, Shaw, have achieved enduring literary quality in direct proportion to the soundness, honesty, and consistency with which they handled their material. *Ghosts, The Cherry Orchard,* and *The Weavers* are great plays because they follow the implications of their subject matter uncompromisingly to a logical conclusion. If Varya had married Lopahkin, if Oswald Alving had been spared the final horror, if the truant Liliom had escaped death and "gone straight" for the rest of his life in Molnar's poignant fantasy, these plays would have suffered from the same dislocation and falsity which are the ruin of *Winterset.*

The American theatre has produced enduring drama only when its playwrights have had the honesty and courage of their convictions, and have seen, thought, and spoken straight. No amount of theatrical talent or literary endowment can serve as substitute for these attributes: of this Maxwell Anderson, next to O'Neill the most talented writer of his generation, has been striking proof. Less talented or versatile writers than he have written better plays for that reason. Anderson is wrong in thinking that poetry alone can be the salvation of the theatre. It may help to dignify it, but it cannot cover up sentimentality or straighten out fallacious thinking.

Maxwell Anderson has been at his best, in recent years, when he was angry. But because his anger lacks any basis for hope, for a constructive point of view towards what disgusts him, it must in the end turn back upon itself, and render him peevish and despairing. Fine words and despair are not enough on which to nurture a dramatic talent; Anderson's latest plays show a marked decline. Yet his great gift is apparent whenever he permits himself to write immediately and simply about human beings. In *High Tor* and *The Star Wagon* there are flashes of the insight and humanity which were so evident in *Saturday's Children* and *Gods of the Lightning*. If their author can go back to the source of all drama—experience of people, of life as they live it—he may gain a new knowledge which can still redeem him from his present somber convictions.

V   Eugene O'Neill

Eugene O'Neill's pre-eminent position in the American theatre is a curious phenomenon. In view of the extraordinary promise of his early work, his career has been one long-drawn-out anticlimax. Some of his most ambitious undertakings have been resounding failures, and to award honor for intention rather than achievement would involve a substantial re-evaluation of our drama in which many names distinguished by their failures alone would come to the fore. As far as O'Neill's undoubted contributions to our theatre go, it is still true that not all the psychological profundity and architectural sweep of *Strange Interlude* and *Mourning Becomes Electra* can surpass the dramatic force and emotional reality, the imaginative richness, of those early plays of the sea and of simple people: the *S. S. Glencairn* one-act plays, *Anna Christie* and *The Emperor Jones*. They came straight from O'Neill's direct experience of life in the days when he shipped around the world on small tramp steamers, and for that reason they have a truer sense of human character, of real tragedy, than when he was exploring the psyche with the aid of Freud or searching for an ultimate meaning in modern life.

Our successful playwrights have mostly gone to college and then into journalism. O'Neill spent years seeing life at first hand in surroundings that were neither middle class nor intellectual. Before he began his first play at the age of twenty-four he had seen and done enough for the impulse thus derived to last him through a dozen years of playwrighting. The strain of introspection and analysis which crops up as early as *Diff'rent* (1920) and *The First Man* (1921) is still unable to subdue the passionate and dramatic utterance which welled up in the sea plays, and to a certain extent in *The Hairy Ape* and *All God's Chillun Got Wings*. Since then O'Neill has made undoubted contributions to our theatre but they are largely intellectual and technical in nature, and with the single exception of *Mourning Becomes Electra*, the later plays fall below the level of his earlier work. The audiences which first thrilled to the beat of the tom-tom through the East Indian jungle, and heard Chris Christopherson rail against "dat old davil sea," experienced the finest theatre O'Neill has evoked up to now.

Not only was it of a high order; it was something totally new. There is no underestimating O'Neill's contribution in bringing new subject matter and new life into the postwar theatre, infusing it with fresh imagination and vitality, greater honesty, and a poetic vision which sprang, not out of vapid fantasy but from a realism till then undreamt of. The fact that today no aspect of life is debarred on asthetic grounds from our theatre, its variety and vigor and outspokenness on many subjects, are due in great measure to the O'Neill of 1919–23. He has been acclaimed as largely responsible for the so-called renaissance of the American theatre during the nineteen-twenties. Certainly he contributed a mighty initial impulse to it, and he has been in the forefront of experiment and serious effort ever since. Like Maxwell Anderson, he is a creative artist devoted to a medium for which he has the most profound respect. His absorption in it has been such that he has never written a line for the motion pictures, in which undivided allegiance he stands practically alone among present-day playwrights.

Dramatic: that was the essential quality of the younger O'Neill, a quality sufficiently strong to compensate for any crudities or shortcomings. He built his plays around the conflict, dramatically expressed, of character with character, human beings with nature, instinct with circumstance. Later he too often became content with posing a situation, implicit with conflict, and then allowing it to degenerate into an argument devoid of theatrical action or development, with stating ideas baldly and statically in so many words (and a great many of them!), instead of embodying them in living characters.

In its most extreme form this tendency produced *Welded, The Great God Brown, Dynamo,* and *Days Without End*; even *Strange Interlude* is weakened by it. When a playgoer complains of an evening's theatregoing that "it wasn't a play," he is not necessarily being dogmatic about whether or not there were three acts, a hero, and a climax. He is asserting the axiom that the theatre is an emotional medium (Brecht, Pirandello, and others to the contrary notwithstanding) in which ideas are best conveyed from the brain of the author to that of the spectator by way of the emotions, as a painter must communicate his concept through the eye and the musician through the ear. It is a principle of which O'Neill has too often lost sight. The masks in *The Great God Brown*, the asides in *Strange Interlude* and *Dynamo*, the dual personality of John Loving in *Days Without End* are only mechanical means for externalizing a proneness to introspection and discursiveness already displayed by Curt and Martha Jayson in *The First Man*, Michael and Eleanor Cape in *Welded*, the Cabots in *Desire Under the Elms*, Yank in *The Hairy Ape*, and Ella Downey and Jim Harris in *All God's Chillun Got Wings*.

Gradually the psychologist has submerged the dramatist. The result has been that, in his capacity of dramatist-psychiatrist, O'Neill has concentrated his attention increasingly on the abnormal. He ceases to recognize such simple, commonplace instincts as friendship, ambition, emulation, pride, boredom, joy of living, as basic human motives; they disappear from his plays. Instead, normally sublimated instincts ride his characters like furies. Except in *Marco Millions* and *Ah! Wilderness*, there is not a play in which one or more of the principal characters do not succumb to madness or hysteria or both. Humanity acquires a psychopathic quality present in life but not considered as the norm. O'Neill treats it as if it were the norm. The artist, under the obligation of viewing life sanely and as a whole, yields to the psychiatrist, to whom a scale of values is irrelevant. This tendency has been accentuated by O'Neill's devotion to the Freudian view of the subconscious, with its emphasis on the sexual origin of our impulses.

If O'Neill the dramatist is continually embroiled with O'Neill the psychologist, he is also in perpetual conflict with O'Neill the philosopher. To the latter, life is not explicable in scientific terms alone. He must go beyond them and search for an ultimate meaning which will justify human suffering as well as explain it. This quest is his principal preoccupation as a playwright; he himself has said so.[1] That it should have brought him to a vague and mystical pantheism, and eventually—perhaps only temporarily—to an acceptance of Catholicism as the solution for the intellectual skeptic of modern times, is an amazing paradox, in view of the profoundly scientific turn of mind which his psychological preoccupation reveals. For ten years this strange dualism runs through his work: a need for faith no less than knowledge, emotional as well as intellectual appeasement, comfort as well as understanding.

In voicing this dualism O'Neill is typical of the rebellions, the frustrations and doubts, that beset the intellectuals of that highly complicated era, the nineteen-twenties. More than any other group they were caught in its contradictions. They could not dissipate their post-war disillusionment in unreasoning cynicism. Their intellectual equipment compelled them to reject alike religious orthodoxy, patriotism, the cruder forms of Bohemianism and the gospel of prosperity, yet their background and habits of thought still cut them off from belief in new goals and new forms of action. Individualism was moribund, collective effort hardly yet a dream. The prevailing literary patterns of the period were therefore, as Granville Hicks has pointed out, either escape or frustration.[2] Both were admirably suited to the Freudian treatment, and resulted in the neurosis, the

---

[1] See page 195.
[2] Granville Hicks, *The Great Tradition*, Chapter VII.

alternating longing and despair, so often found in
O'Neill.

In contrast to other writers of the period, however,
O'Neill has never outgrown this phase. While other
novelists and playwrights have gone on to deal with
those questions which have assumed greater importance
than the condition of an individual soul, O'Neill has
adhered with very little change to the problems and
solutions which he evolved as early as 1923. The similarity of his thinking since then has often been successfully concealed by the variety, in form and subject
matter, of his plays, but it exists nevertheless. He is
forever arriving at the same conclusion and embarking
anew on the same quest. Passages taken at random from
his writings over a period of ten years are practically indistinguishable, the one from the other.

Michael Cape, in *Welded* (1923):

You and I—year after year—together—forms of
our bodies merging into one form; rhythm of our
lives beating against each other, forming slowly the
one rhythm—the life of Us—created by Us!—beyond us, above us!

Nina Leeds, in *Strange Interlude* (1927):

There . . . again . . . his child! . . . my child
moving in my life . . . my life moving in my
child . . . the world is whole and perfect . . . all
things are each other's . . . life is . . . . and the is
is beyond reason . . . questions die in the silence
of this peace. . . . I am living a dream within the
great dream of the tide . . . . breathing in the tide
I dream and breathe back my dream into the tide

. . . suspended in the movement of the tide, I feel life move in me, suspended in me——

Rueben Fife in *Dynamo* (1928):

That's the right place for us to love—atop of that hill—close to the sky—driven to love by what makes the world go round—by what drives the stars through space!——Our blood plasm is the same right now as the sea was when life came out of it. We've got the sea in our blood still! It's what makes our hearts live. And it's the sea rising up in clouds, falling on the earth in rain, made that river that drives the turbines that drive Dynamo!

Lazarus, in *Lazarus Laughed* (1926):

There is only life! I heard the voice of Jesus laughing in my heart; "There is Eternal Life in No," it said, and there is the same Eternal Life in Yes! Death is the fear between!——Once as squirming specks we crept from the tides of the sea. Now we return to the sea! Once as quivering flecks of rhythm we beat down from the sun. Now we re-enter the sun! Cast aside is our pitiable pretense, our immortal ego-hood, the holy lantern behind which cringed our Fear of the Dark! Flung off is that impudent insult to life's nobility which gibbers: "I, this Jew, this Roman, this noble or this slave, must survive in my pettiness forever!" Away with such cowardice of spirit! We will to die! We will to change! Laughing, we lived with our gift, now with laughter give me back that gift to become again the Essence of the Giver! Dying we laugh with the Infinite! We are the Giver and the Gift!

Kublai Khan, in *Marco Millions* (1924):

In silence—for one concentrated moment—be proud of life! Know in your hearts that the living of life can be noble! Know that the dying of death can be noble! Be exalted by life! Be inspired by death! Be humbly proud! Be proudly grateful! Be immortal because life is immortal. Contain the harmony of the grave and the womb within you! Possess life as a lover—then sleep requited in the arms of death!

Juan Ponce de Leon, in *The Fountain* (1922):

Fountain Everlasting, time without end! Soaring flame of the spirit, transfiguring Death! All is within! All things dissolve, flow on eternally! O aspiring fire of life, sweep the dark soul of man! Let us burn in thy unity!——O God, Fountain of the Eternal Becoming which is Beauty!——One must accept, give back, become oneself a symbol! ——O Fountain of Eternity, take back this drop, my soul!

Cybel, in *The Great God Brown* (1925):

Always spring comes again bearing life! Always again! Always, always, forever again!—Spring again! —life again!—summer and fall and death and peace again!—But always, always, love and conception and birth and pain again—spring bearing the intolerable chalice of life again!—bearing the glorious, blazing crown of life again!

John Loving, in *Days Without End* (1933):

I know. Love lives forever! Ssh! Listen! Do you

hear?—Life laughs with god's love again! Life laughs with love!

These passages reveal something else beside repetitiousness: the undistinguished quality of much of O'Neill's writing. The same banal poetic images—references to the sea, to the tide, to rhythm, harmony, the dream that is life, the unity of the cosmic process—recur constantly. There is a complete absence of characterization, of individualization. Shuffle these speeches around, put Cybel's in the mouth of Kublai Khan or let Lazarus speak the words of Ponce de Leon, and no incongruity is apparent, no integrity of character has been violated. This, too, is evidence of imaginative poverty. Rhythmic recurrence of sounds and images is a basic poetic principle. It is O'Neill's misfortune that he has been unable to evoke sufficiently significant or beautiful phrases for their recurrence to be anything but a trial.

In the matter of style, as in other respects, O'Neill's work falls sharply into two parts. When he was employing the colloquial, unpolished language of racial or working-class types in *Anna Christie*, *The Emperor Jones*, the one-act plays, *The Hairy Ape*, and in the first three scenes of *All God's Chillun Got Wings*, he was able to create characters with a colorful individualized speech. His feeling for the language of our times in its crudest forms, for the argot of poverty and ignorance and brutality that boils out of the slums, out of the heart of living and action, is nothing short of magnificent; here his writing attains the level of the first rate and comes the nearest he ever achieves to poetry. The speeches of Yank and Burke and Jones and the Dreamy Kid have an authentic poetic quality conspicuously absent from the poetic vaporings of Lazarus and Dion Anthony and Reuben Fife. It is when he takes to the ordinary speech of refined, educated people, which co-incides with his abandonment of drama for philosophiz-ing, that O'Neill becomes trite, flavorless, and poetic in the very worst sense of the term. His ability to charac-terize through dialogue vanishes, and his characters all talk exactly alike.

1

The story of that summer of 1916 at Provincetown which launched O'Neill on his career and saw the birth of a theatre is an oft-told tale. It witnessed the first per-formance of *Bound East for Cardiff*, which was repeated when the Provincetown opened its doors in New York the following winter. The three following years saw the production of *The Long Voyage Home, Ile, The Rope, Where the Cross Is Made, The Moon of the Caribees,* and *The Dreamy Kid*—all one-act plays.

O'Neill's connection with the Provincetown is a strik-ing illustration of what association with a small experi-mental theatre can do for a young author. The tiny playhouse on Macdougal Street enabled O'Neill to see his early work on the stage and learn from it at a time when one-act plays were barred from the commercial theatre. It gave him the opportunity of actually working in a theatre, an experience not many playwrights have had, to their loss. Lastly it permitted him to find his audience slowly while he was finding himself, free from that crippling compulsion of the Broadway theatre to write a play that will be easily negotiable and earmarked for success, during his formative years. It was not until four years after the first appearance of *Bound East for*

Cardiff that O'Neill's first full-length play appeared on Broadway: *Beyond the Horizon*, presented in the winter of 1920. Six months before the Provincetown produced *The Emperor Jones*, often regarded as the beginning of his success, *Beyond the Horizon* had already won the Pulitzer Prize. During the next year three managements beside the Provincetown presented O'Neill plays, but the little theatre in Greenwich Village continued to play a vital role in his career. The experimental productions, scenically far superior to the Broadway level at that time, which it gave to *The Emperor Jones*, *The Hairy Ape*, and *All God's Chillun Got Wings*, contributed not a little to their renown; in return they made the Provincetown.

O'Neill's one-act plays, particularly those now grouped together under the name of *S. S. Glencairn*, are required reading for any student of the theatre. No more than vignettes of the sea and its people, they are written with a brevity and spareness that are in striking contrast to his later prolixity. In a few lines O'Neill achieves a degree of feeling, of compassion, unique in his writing; because of their very simplicity, the dying Yank, the nostalgic Olson, move us as do no other figures he has since put on the stage. These plays have a truth, an absence of contriving, that bespeak the ease and spontaneity of genuine artistic expression which, in the theatre of 1919–20, amounted to a revolution. In *Ile*, and *Where the Cross Is Made* [3] there is already a striving after effect, a quality of melodrama; but it is good melodrama, and the effects are justifiable. In *The Dreamy Kid* the two styles fuse; the conflict between the Dreamy's desperate predicament and the urgency of the dying woman's wish and her feverish delusions, create a

[3] Later developed into the three-act play *Gold*.

tension of atmosphere and action in the highest degree theatrical.

The Dreamy Kid is a young Negro gangster who, having killed a man in a brawl, comes to the bedside of his grandmother, who has sent for him because she is dying. Superstitious fear that he will suffer if he does not obey her wish triumphs over his fear of the police. While he is with her the tart Irene comes to warn him that the police are closing in on him; while he deliberates a plan of escape, the trap is closed. The curtain falls on the Dreamy barricading himself in one corner of the room, with the dying woman babbling on in delirious oblivion of what is taking place around her.

The Dreamy Kid illustrates O'Neill's innate talent for characterization, dialogue, pace, contrast, and mounting suspense. The characterization of the Dreamy—braggart, callous, brave, superstitious—as achieved within the limits of a single act, is nothing short of superb. Every circumstance, every line, contribute to the mounting tension: our knowledge of his predicament before he appears, his endless haggling quarrels with Ceely Ann and Irene, the contrast between the sick woman's dreams and her grandson's desperate plight, and his efforts to hide the truth from her. Theatrically O'Neill has never written anything more effective.

Until he wrote Strange Interlude, the play which contributed most to O'Neill's reputation was undoubtedly The Emperor Jones, already rated among the few classics of the modern theatre. By conventional standards it is hardly a play at all. Its text runs for only thirty-five pages; speech, excepting for the first and last scenes, is limited to Jones' monologue of rising terror, and much of its effectiveness lies in the stage pictures and pantomime.

There is no orderly structure of acts building to a climax; instead, its whole duration is one agonizingly drawn-out climax, like a tooth-ache, due in parge part to the use of the tom-tom, savage and unremitting symbol of a man's heartbeat steadily increasing in tempo and volume, until it filled the tiny Provincetown theatre with an ocean of clamorous sound and lifted the hearers out of their seats.

Using the incident of a Negro who made himself Emperor of Haiti for a brief period, O'Neill built up the story of a Pullman porter who had fled from the United States because he had committed a murder, and who sets himself up as the absolute ruler of a West Indian island. When his power wears thin and the natives desert to the hills, planning rebellion and revenge, Jones plunges into the jungle in an effort to escape to the coast. The man's extraordinary personality, compounded of cleverness, unscrupulousness, and great courage, has been delineated in an initial scene with a white trader, Smithers, who first reveals the incipient rebellion to him. Once in the jungle Jones is defeated, not by his rebellious subjects, but by his own past, racial as well as individual, which, under the weight of guilt and fear, breaks through his thin veneer of sophistication. His recently acquired sense of self-confidence and power are as nothing in comparison with the hundreds of years of ignorance and oppression that are his racial heritage. In successive scenes of nightmare delusion he relives the various stages through which his people have passed, a *via dolorosa* to civilization and a freedom not yet attained: his life as a Pullman porter; the southern chain gang; the slave trader's block; the slave ship; the paganism of a savage African tribe. Unnerved by his ghosts, Jones loses his sense of direction and finally emerges from the forest at the exact point where he entered it, only to fall a prey to the waiting natives who had foreseen just such an outcome.

Because of its subject *The Emperor Jones* must be considered on basis other than that of theatrical effectiveness; the same is true of *The Dreamy Kid*. The treatment of the Negro in the theatre clearly reflects the concepts and prejudices current among even the most intelligent elements in our society. While the stage has not, in general, sunk as low as the moving pictures in caricaturing the Negro race as happy-go-lucky and indolent, capable at best of idiotic cheerfulness and blind loyalty to its "masters," it has only in recent years, in such plays as *Stevedore* and *Marching Song*, grappled with the realities of the Negro problem. These plays showed racial prejudice as rooted in social thinking that has originally as a conscious purpose the perpetuation of race divisions and class relationships which dissolve at the recognition that the Negro race is equal in all respects to the white.

Prejudice is insidious. It seeps into our attitude, no matter how enlightened and unprejudiced we may fancy ourselves, unless we clearly understand its origins and struggle unceasingly against it. It forbids any casual treatment of the Negro in art or literature out of social context and without a complete understanding of the problem. The danger of the presentation of a Negro gangster, a Negro coward, a lazy Negro is that they will never be considered as individuals by an average white audience; always such a characterization will represent to them the race as a whole, thus bolstering their sense of racial superiority and reinforcing their prejudices, *however latent.*

What is true of the Negro is no less true of the Jew
and other racial groups, and of the militant working
man, the prostitute and the pacifist, to cite only a few
instances. All victims and opponents of established relationships, be they political, economic, or social, will
suffer from any presentation which does not take into
serious account the forces of which they are the victims,
and which anything but the most searching honesty
will reinforce.

Our playwrights, except for the few with a high degree of social consciousness, have ignored this fact. The
result has been such heedless grotesques of the Negro
race as those in *You Can't Take It With You* and *The
Petrified Forest*, or the less overt but no less dangerous
treatment of the Negro in O'Neill's plays. Strikingly
enough, O'Neill is the only one of our leading successful
dramatists to devote a play primarily to the American
Negro. But only in *All God's Chillun Got Wings* did
he consider him in a social framework; this play will be
discussed in detail later. In *The Dreamy Kid* and *The
Emperor Jones*, both of which depict a Negro as an un-
scrupulous adventurer, O'Neill is, despite his artistry,
guilty of the same irresponsibility which infects his colleagues; they are excellent instances of how "artistic detachment" and "artistic truth," so-called, lend themselves to reactionary prejudice and to the perpetuation
of injustice.

Anna Christie belongs to the group of early plays at
one end of his career, and *Mourning Becomes Electra*
at the other, which prove that O'Neill is at his best
when his creative instinct is emotional rather than intellectual in origin. None of these plays deal primarily

in *ideas*; they are about living people in tragic circumstances, and such ideas as they may contain are implicit
in the characters and the action itself. The characters
in *Anna Christie*, a tragedy of the New York water front,
are among the most finely executed in our theatre. As
in *The Dreamy Kid*, the playwright's ability to communicate keeps abreast of his psychological insight; every
line is telling and authentic. Using only the conventional methods of dramatic narrative and exposition,
O'Neill conveys as much of the workings of the human
mind, the conflicting passions and instincts of Anna and
Chris and Burke, as he ever succeeded in doing with
more complex and less theatrical methods in *The Great
God Brown* and *Strange Interlude*.

The tragedy in *Anna Christie* results from Chris Christopherson's desire to save his daughter from the sea
which he knows only as an implacable enemy. Anna's
life inland is as cruel as anything the sea could hold in
store for her, and it is from the sea, after illness and
despair have driven her back to her father, that she does
finally wring some small measure of happiness. But her
past life comes between her and the Irish sailor Burke
and before she has convinced him that it was not of her
own choosing and that he is the first man she has really
loved, he and her father, in drunken misery, have signed
to sail on the same ship for a long voyage. From the
first the brooding premonition that the sea will, in the
end, claim its full toll of lives, has hung over the play,
and Chris voices it at the close:

It's funny. It's queer, yes—you and me shipping
on the same boat dat vay. Ay don't know—it's dat
funny old davil sea do her vorst tricks, yes. It's so.

BURKE

(*Nodding his head in gloomy acquiescence—with a great sigh*)
I'm fearing maybe you have the right of it for once, divil take you.

Anna Christie is thus a fatalistic tragedy. Anna tells her father, "You ain't to blame. You're yust—what you are—like me." Men and women are blind puppets. It is a conception that O'Neill abandoned almost as soon as he had formulated it for the more modern thesis that a cause exists for all things, good and evil. That it is possible to write of tragedy which arises from known human causes with undiminished poignancy and increased validity is nowhere proved more effectively than in that other play of the sea, Herman Heijerman's *The Good Hope*, where the blame for the high toll of life exacted in the trade of merchant shipping is put, not on an "old davil sea" but on the unprincipled owners who send their crews to sea in rotten-bottomed boats to avoid repair costs or in order to collect insurance. The sailor has been made a rolling stone and a drunkard by the conditions under which he must work in order to live. This degree of "realism" O'Neill has never reached, least of all in *Anna Christie*.

2

O'Neill has used the theatre increasingly as a forum from which to consider man's relation to the universe, itself tragic because it is so patently unsatisfactory. Most of his plays are cast in the form of a question, a search: how can man find fulfillment in sexual love, in the pursuit of wealth, in the face of racial barriers or the indifference of our society to art? To what God can he turn? How can he find peace and faith in the face of insoluble contradictions in his own nature? *Beyond the Horizon*, written in 1918, is the first link in a chain of thought which stretches with hardly a break down to *Days Without End* in 1933.

Robert and Andrew Mayo in *Beyond the Horizon* represent two fundamental conflicting tendencies in human nature—the dreamer, who seeks to escape from the drudgery and responsibility of life, and the practical man who extracts a meaning and a dignity from routine drudgery. Both men are in love with Ruth. The tragedy is precipitated by Robert and Ruth's fatal error: Ruth mistakes her passing infatuation with Robert's romanticism for real love, while Robert allows his love for her to tie him down to a life for which he has neither the physical strength nor the taste. Thus a temporary attraction ruins three people's lives, for Andrew tries to overcome his love for Ruth by going to sea in his brother's ship, and finally dissipates his fine feeling for the earth and the dignity of labor in grain speculations; Robert succumbs to failure and illness, and loses Ruth's love; and Ruth, after transferring her dreams to Andrew, who in the meantime has forgotten her, relapses into hopelessness. Andrew comes home too late to save Robert's life, and presumably too late to redeem Ruth from apathy or to recover his own sense of values.

The play ends on a note of confused idealism which leaves us completely in the dark as to what it is supposed to prove. Robert dies, seeing in death the freedom he has so long desired, that horizon beyond the hills which has beckoned to him all his life, and warning his brother that happiness can be won only through suffering and

that he must marry Ruth. Are we supposed to be witness-
ing the same kind of arbitrary dislocation of human lives
as occurs in *Anna Christie?* Robert's verdict is nearly as
fatalistic as Anna's:

> Why did this have to happen to us? It's damnable!
> ——I'm a failure and Ruth's another, but we can
> both justly lay some of the blame for our stumbling
> on God.

Is God as casual and cruel a nemesis as "dat old davil
sea"? It would seem so, since even in the exercise of their
wills the characters in *Beyond the Horizon* are trapped
by forces within themselves they cannot control. Yet
there is a fundamental difference between *Beyond the
Horizon* and *Anna Christie*. Here the protagonist is unmistakably man in the general, man in conflict with himself, the human spirit asking questions of life, breaking
itself in helpless aspiration and frustration. The characters and the problems are universal, not particular; generalization, with its extraordinary effect, in the case of
O'Neill, of dramatic disintegration, has already begun.
Beyond the Horizon is its first toll, despite the realistic
treatment of farm life, which gives it a significant place
in our dramatic development, and its idealistic aspiration, which also struck a new note.

The theme of man's search for a niche in the universe,
for power to understand and express himself, re-emerged
three years after *Beyond the Horizon*, in *The Hairy Ape*.
It was a striking occasion in more ways than one, since
it marked O'Neill's return, after a lengthy excursion into
realism, to the expressionistic technique. The poetic
and dreamy Robert Mayo becomes the turbulent, in-
articulate Yank, the Hairy Ape. But if Robert Mayo was

a generalization of man, Yank is only the symbol of a force: the power, the strength which are the eventual source of all activity, all achievement—and which is found in one class—the working class. This symbolism is in itself sound; O'Neill nevertheless falls into the error of regarding what is essentially a social as a philosophical problem.

O'Neill envisions the working class trapped between two "worlds"; barred from the jungle, home of man in his completely unthinking state of brute force, by the consciousness of its power, and from the world of make-believe for which it provides the foundation by its integrity and reality. At the start of the play Yank "belongs," because he makes a real, irreplaceable contribution, to society, and therefore believes in himself. At that time Carl Sandburg was already hymning the magnificence of industrial America and the glory of the men whose sweat and blood had built her. There are passages in The Hairy Ape which are almost pure Sandburg:

Hell in de stokehole? Sure! It takes a man to work in hell! Hell, sure, dat's my favorite climate. I eat it up! I git fat on it! It's me makes it hot! It's me makes it roar! It's me makes it move! Sure, o'ny for me everything stops. It all goes dead, get me? De noise and smoke and all de engines movin' de woild, dey stop. Dere ain't nothin' no more! Dat's what I'm sayin'. Everything else dat makes de woild move, somep'n makes it move. It can't move witout somep'n else, see? Den yuh get down to me. I'm at de bottom, get me? Dere ain't nothin' foither. I'm de end! I'm de start! I start somep'n and de woild moves! It—dat's me!—de new dat's moiderin' de old! I'm de ting in coal dat makes it boin; I'm steam and oil for de engines; I'm de ting in noise dat makes yuh hear it; I'm smoke and express trains and steamers and factory whistles; I'm de ting in gold dat makes it money! And I'm what makes iron into steel! Steel, dat stands for de whole ting! And I'm steel—steel—steel! I'm de muscles in steel, de punch behind it!

But the destruction of the Hairy Ape's self-confidence, of his feeling that he "belongs," has neither rhyme nor reason. It is brought about by Mildred, symbol of the effete, worn-out privileged class which subsists on Yank's strength. Her horror and loathing when she is brought into the stokehole face to face with "unknown, abysmal brutality, naked and shameless," hurts Yank's feelings, and he wants revenge—the unspoken insult of her presence and her look of contempt have robbed him of his self-assurance. He loses his grip, throws up his job, tries to join the I. W. W. in the hope of direct and violent action against the powers Mildred represents. But he is too naïve and outspoken and the Wobblies reject him. Finally he wanders crazily into the zoo and, hailing a giant ape as his brother, lets the animal out of his cage and dies in his ferocious embrace. The concluding line in the stage directions reads: "And, perhaps, the Hairy Ape at last belongs."

Just what does all this mean? Symbolism, even fantasy, must have some sort of logic. What is the significance of Yank's spiritual collapse because of a petty insult? Why do the I. W. W. reject him? Why the insane episode in the zoo? From the moment of Mildred's entrance into the stokehole Yank ceases to

be a valid symbol and becomes merely a deranged individual incapable of adjustment within the social mech-
anism. But even as an individual he has no reality because the factor that produced his maladjustment—
Mildred's "insult"—has no meaning. What really drives
the Yanks of this world into morbid depression and
madness? The loss of their jobs through overproduction
and mechanization, industrial accidents, long hours, and
low wages. Not one of these things is even mentioned
in O'Neill's play. What might easily account for his
confusion and mental collapse—the terrible conditions
of work in the stokehole—bad ventilation, the speed-up,
the long hours of back-breaking toil—are to Yank a
source of pride.[4] Yank's frenzied beating against his
prison bars, in itself a legitimate symbol of class frustration, should lead to some more significant denouement
than a lunatic's death in the monkey house. The Hairy
Ape is a long way from being "revolutionary propaganda," as Joseph Wood Krutch has termed it.[5]

What was unquestionably effective in the play, and
assumed tremendous proportions at the time of the original production because of its novelty, was O'Neill's
uncompromising use of the stark and brutal in life for
stage purposes. He employed realistic material in settings, language, and characters, in an unrealistic, highly
imaginative manner; and the hurly-burly, the dirt and
noise and terrific heat of the stokehole, the fantastic
violence of the stage picture with its steel bastions and
flaming open furnaces, and its sense of frantic, agonizing
toil, opened new vistas in the theatre.

[4] Scenes I, III.
[5] Introduction, Nine Plays, Eugene O'Neill, Nobel Prize edition,
Random House.

In *All God's Chillun Got Wings* O'Neill tackled a social question more straightforwardly than he was ever to do again. It is a dual problem, of miscegenation on the one hand and of the sensitive color-conscious Negro trying to improve his position in the world on the other. While Jim Harris is still at school, and during his later attempts to qualify for the Bar, he is constantly paralyzed by race-consciousness:

> I swear I know more'n any member of my class. I ought to. I study harder. I work like the devil. It's all in my head—all fine and correct to a T. Then I'm called on—I stand up—all the white faces looking at me—and I can feel their eyes—I hear my own voice sounding funny, trembling—and all of a sudden it's gone in my head—there's nothing remembered—and I hear myself stuttering—and give up—and sit down——They don't laugh—hardly ever. They're kind. They're good people. (*In a frenzy*) They're considerate, damn them! And I feel branded!

This profound self-consciousness affects his feeling for the white girl, Ella. He cannot love her sanely, straightforwardly; his love has a quality of abasement which precludes any possibility of a healthy relationship between them. From the moment they come to Harlem to live as man and wife they are surrounded by prejudice. Marriage to a white woman cuts Jim off from his own people and increases his sensitivity, while marriage to a Negro brings to the surface in Ella all the prejudice which is the imposed heritage of her race. She becomes desperately afraid that Jim may prove himself her intellectual superior. The strain drives Ella insane and

Jim neurotic. She causes him to fail in his Bar examinations, threatening him with murder if he should succeed; then, her end accomplished, her madness takes the form of a double regression, to her childhood when she and Jim played together without any race consciousness whatever, and historically, to slavery and the toleration of Jim by a benevolent and superior mistress. Jim, crushed by his adversities, is filled with religious beatitude and accepts his suffering as a martyrdom!

Obviously, *All God's Chillun Got Wings* contains a strong admixture of truth and distortion. After a strong first act in which he clearly indicates the social roots of prejudice, O'Neill allows the conflict to degenerate into a psychic antagonism between two individuals, an antagonism whose social causes are allowed to lapse in the background. It is significant that after the first act O'Neill takes the two antagonists out of the world which has so profoundly conditioned their relationship, and completely isolates their neurotic conflict. Moreover he passes from the scene of their wedding straight to the Harlem apartment to which they return from France, already well along the road to emotional disaster. He gives us the beginning and end of the tragedy, and entirely omits its development.

Small wonder therefore that he goes so far afield, at one point even shifting blame for the catastrophe from society to a long-suffering Deity, when he has Jim tell Ella

> Maybe God can forgive what you've done to me and maybe He can forgive what I've done to you; but I don't see how He's going to forgive Himself.

And despite his condemnation, undoubtedly sincere, of

prejudice, O'Neill gives unmistakable evidence himself of latent prejudice, as in Jim's plea to Ella to marry him, with its vicious emphasis on color and its use of the "slave-master" pattern of thought, or more generally in his portrayal of Jim as weak, ineffectual and unbalanced. It is necessary to stress once again the importance of keeping the social basis for character, and for the prejudice with which O'Neill is here concerned, clearly in the foreground, unless the treatment is not to degenerate, as it does in *All God's Chillun Got Wings*, into false emphasis of the issues really involved, and a portrayal of the Negro race which is the opposite of what the author may have intended.

Lastly, his failure to penetrate to the basic roots of race prejudice leads O'Neill to accept its inevitability, as tragedy without rational cause must always be accepted. The Negro's struggle for equality and recognition, as exemplified in Jim Harris, is a fruitless one. "Dere's one road where de white goes on alone; dere's anudder where de black goes on alone," says Mrs. Harris, and Jim's sister Hattie adds, "Yes, if they'd leave us alone." Thus only by racial segregation, itself an implicit admission of inferiority, can the Negro hope to attain any satisfaction, a philosophy as false as it is pernicious.

O'Neill and his admirers have repeatedly answered the charge of undue pessimism that has been leveled at him by pointing to the triumphant mysticism of plays like *Lazarus Laughed, Beyond the Horizon* and *Days Without End.* Yet whenever his plays have a basis in social reality, as in *The Hairy Ape, All God's Chillun Got Wings,* and *Dynamo,* and repeatedly when the conflict is purely individual, they follow a pattern of frustration and physical or spiritual death. Greed, sexual disharmony, social maladjustment, the sensitivity of the creative artist out of harmony with our material scale of values—O'Neill has analyzed them all. Yet he has shown himself unable to draw an iota of assurance or positivism out of anything but an emotional conviction. Where in his plays is there a Trofimov or a Vershinin to point to a healthier future, to put a name to the sickness which afflicts the characters who populate his plays and the society which their very existence indicts? You will not find one, because, unlike Chekhov, O'Neill himself is touched with the death he delights in depicting.

3

O'Neill has been called the Freudian dramatist. The sexual impulse, thwarted and awry, is to him a first cause for many evils. Curiously enough, he has only once succeeded in building a really good play on it, in *Mourning Becomes Electra*. Elsewhere it is a subject which sees him at his most discursive and argumentative; always he regards it, despite poetic paeans, with profound morbidity. One can look far and wide in his plays without finding a happily married or sexually harmonious couple. Dramatically such figures do not appear to interest him.

One of the earliest and most extreme of his plays on the subject is *Welded*, which introduces to us, in the person of Michael Cape, the tortured idealist straining desperately to achieve realization, self-expression, understanding, and harmony, who is to reappear as Eben Cabot in *Desire Under the Elms*, Ponce de Leon in *The Fountain*, Dion Anthony in *The Great God Brown*, Reuben Light in *Dynamo*, Orin Mannon in *Mourning Becomes Electra*, and John Loving in *Days Without*

End. This resemblance is no superficial coincidence; one and all they seek an answer to the same question, which is the very essence of O'Neill himself: man's need for peace and certainty, in his emotional life, in his religion, in his scheme of life. Take the description of Michael Cape.

> His unusual face is a harrowed battle-field of super-sensitiveness, the features at war with one an-other—the forehead of a thinker, the eyes of a dreamer, the nose and mouth of a sensualist.

Here O'Neill is not describing an individual face, but one which embodies all the characteristics of a type, and has very nearly the abstraction of a symbol. The use of the term "masklike" is indicative; it recurs frequently in his later plays, and leads naturally to the use of masks themselves, with their emphasis on the abstraction and stylization of qualities instead of the direct human presentation of those qualities.

The title *Desire Under the Elms* states quite explicitly that the play deals with human appetites; those involved are sexual desire and passion for the land. The peculiar character that these assume in the play, their distortion and intensification, are the outcome of generations of inbreeding, Puritan repressions, back-breaking labor tilling the rocky New England soil, and a loveless religion, hard and stern as the land.

Ephraim Cabot is a lonely old man, whose extraordinary vitality has been warped by his religion and the ferocity of his struggle with the land into something grasping and sterile.

> When ye kin make the corn spout out of stones
> God's livin' in yew.——Stones. I picked 'em up and

piled 'em into walls. Ye kin read the years o' my
life in them walls, every day a hefted stone, climbin'
over hills and down, fencin' in the fields that was
mine, whar I'd made thin's grow out o' nothin'—like
the will o' God, like the servant o' His hand. It
wa'n't easy. It war hard, an' He made me hard fur it.

No one has ever understood his feeling for the land and
for his God, a "hard an' lonesome" God. His wife was
a gentle weak woman whom he worked to death, and he
hates her son Eben for resembling his mother, to the
point where he wants yet another son for his heir. So
he marries Abbie, an orphan who has spent most of her
hard life working for others, who wants her own "hum',"
and who possesses enormous animal vitality and senu-
ality. That vitality, finding little satisfaction in Ephraim,
turns naturally to Eben. When she bears a son, it is
Eben's, not Ephraim's. But the latter, ignorant of the
truth, taunts Eben with losing the farm to his baby
stepbrother, and Eben, enraged, accuses Abbie of using
him to bear a child who, as Ephraim's son, will take the
farm away from him. To prove her love for him, Abbie
kills the child. Eben is horrified by her crime, and calls
the sheriff. Then, a prey to love and remorse, he gives
himself up with her as an accessory. Ephraim Cabot is
left without an heir to tend his farm, "hard an' lonesome"
as his God.

Desire Under the Elms marks O'Neill's complete acceptance of the Freudian theory of the libido. The
mother-incest theme is clearly stated in the initial stage
directions.

(Two enormous elms are on each side of the house.
They bend their trailing branches down over the roof.

*They appear to protect and at the same time to subdue.
There is a sinister maternity in their aspect, a crushing
jealous absorption. They have developed from their in-
timate contact with the man in the house an appalling
humanness. They brood oppressively over the house.
They are like exhausted women resting their sagging
breasts and hands and hair on its roof, and when it rains
their tears trickle down monotonously and rot on the
shingles.)*

Following the pattern thus stated, Eben Cabot is impelled at every step by the image of his dead mother.
He desires the farm because he believes his father cheated
her of it. He goes to the village whore because she has
been his father's before him, and he feels that he is aveng-
ing his mother by taking her away from him. The same
motive originally lies behind his affair with Abbie, which
deepens into love when he identifies her directly with
his mother. The climax of the tragedy, Abbie's murder
of her son for Eben's sake, goes back to the woman who
tried to find compensation for an exhausting and loveless existence in her love for her son.

Parallel to the incest motive runs the influence of a
religion which has lost its spiritual content. It is his
stern and grasping religion which makes Ephraim
identify his sexual and possessive impulses to the point
where he tells Abbie

> Sometimes ye air the farm an' sometimes the farm
> be yew. That's why I clove t' ye in my lonesomeness.
> Me an' my farm has got t' beget a son.

But even his possessiveness is sterile and destructive. "I
hain't a-givin' it to no one," he tells Abbie of the farm

at one point, and she answers, "You can't take it with ye!"

CABOT

(*Thinks a minute—then reluctantly*) No, I calc'late not. (*After a pause—with a strange passion*) But if I could, I would, by the Etarnal! 'R if I could, in my dyin' hour, I'd set afire an' watch it burn—this house an' every ear o' corn an' every tree down t' last blade o' hay! I'd sit an' know it was all a-dyin' with me an' no one else'd ever own what was mine, what I'd made out o' nothin' with my own sweat an' blood.

Despite Eben's selfish sensuality and hardness, he has a strength and stature which are eloquent testimony to virility of his stock, and to the ravages which religion has wreaked on it. Thus the background of the Cabots' tragedy is not purely psychological and individualistic; but, as usual with O'Neill, social factors are pushed into the background, or ignored. The impact of the play is thereby weakened, and greater significance is permitted its more repulsive elements than is necessary or even justifiable. *Desire Under the Elms* lacks humanity because it becomes a study in perversion. It falls short of tragedy because O'Neill fails to grasp the real basis from which the tragedy of the Cabots derives.

He continued his investigation of the libido in *The Great God Brown*, one of the most baffling plays he, or anyone else for that matter, ever wrote. Elaborately symbolic, it is also scientific in approach, an extraordinary mixture of psychoanalysis and mysticism. It combines a study in dual personality with a contrast between two diametrically opposed human beings—a maladjusted artist and a successful businessman—and throws in for good measure, a dramatic summation of the history of the human soul for the past two thousand years, and an indictment of American Babbittry. The obscurity arose from superimposing different patterns of thought upon one another, patterns which at times flowed the one into the other and at other times showed no relation and connection whatever, and O'Neill was obliged to write at some length in explanation of the "mystical pattern which manifests itself as an overtone to *The Great God Brown*, dimly behind and beyond the words and actions of the characters."

> It was far from my idea in writing *Brown* that this pattern of conflicting tides in the soul of Man should overshadow and thus throw out of proportion the living drama of the recognizable human beings—Dion, Brown, Margaret and Cybel. I meant it always to be mystically within and behind them, giving them a significance beyond themselves, forcing itself through them to expression in mysterious words, symbols, actions they do not themselves comprehend. *And that is as clearly as I wish an audience to comprehend it.* It is Mystery—the mystery any one man or woman can feel but not understand as the meaning of any event—or accident—in any life on earth. And it is this mystery I want to realize in the theatre. [Italics mine.]

Rarely has an explanation itself been more unintelligible, and an initial reading of *The Great God Brown* goes far to explain why. What we take in is little more than this: Dion Anthony, a sensitive, introverted boy, is pushed into the profession of architecture by his parents, merely because Anthony's employer, Mr. Brown, is educating *his* son William, a friend of Dion's, to be an architect. Dion and William Brown both love Margaret; she chooses Dion, but she never knows his real self, which he conceals behind a mask in her presence. Torn by inner conflicts, Dion drinks heavily. At Margaret's plea, Brown, now a rising architect, gives Dion a job; Dion supplies the creative, imaginative elements in Brown's work. Dion begins visiting a prostitute, Cybel, with whom he has a purely platonic relationship, because she alone understands him. He dies, willing his mask to Brown, who buries his body in the garden and uses the mask to take Dion's place with Margaret without her discovering the substitution. But Brown inherits Dion's inner conflicts along with his mask, and succumbs to them just as Dion did. The police discover Brown's own discarded mask, and believe that Brown has been murdered. They kill Brown in the belief that he was an unknown accomplice of Dion's in murdering Brown.

Upon further examination we separate the different influences which have determined Dion's lack of inner harmony. We trace his abnormal sensitivity to the fact that once as a child he was drawing a picture in the sand and another boy in whose goodness he had always believed (William Brown) rubbed the picture out because he could not draw anything so good, destroying Dion's faith in the good in Man and God alike. The other profoundly formative influence in his life was his relationship with his mother, whose absorption in him and the dependence on security and comfort in a hostile world thus engendered, drive Dion to see all women in the mother image.

The enormous complexity of Dion's character and the significance of the many allusive interjections that at first appear meaningless only become apparent in O'Neill's own explanation. Dion Anthony, we discover, is not only an individual, he is the symbol of a profound contradiction in the human spirit dating from the superimposition of a new ethical and religious system on the old creed of paganism. Even the name is symbolic:

> Dion Anthony—Dionysius and St. Anthony—the creative pagan acceptance of life, fighting eternal war with the masochistic, life-denying spirit of Christianity as represented by St. Anthony—the whole struggle resulting in this modern day in mutual exhaustion—creative joy in life for life's sake frustrated, rendered abortive, distorted by morality from Pan into Satan, into a Mephistopheles mocking himself in order to feel alive; Christianity, once heroic in martyrs for its intense faith now pleading weakly for intense belief in anything, even Godhead itself.

Dion's soul is thus in mortal conflict with itself, as contrasted with the unimaginative placidity of Brown, who does not feel disharmony because he is empty of any force which might turn disruptively upon itself. Dion is tortured by his spiritual wealth; Brown is spared any such suffering because of his mediocrity.

One must quote at length from O'Neill's own explanation of the Dion-Brown conflict in order to plumb the full complexity of his scheme of thought:

> Brown has always envied the creative force in Dion which he himself lacks. When he steals Dion's mask of Mephistopheles he thinks he is gaining the

power to live creatively while in reality he is only
stealing that creative power made self-destructive by
complete frustration. This devil of mocking doubt
makes short work of him. It enters him, rending
him apart, torturing him and transfiguring him until he is even forced to wear a mask of his Success,
William A. Brown, before the world, as well as
Dion's mask toward wife and children. Thus Billy
Brown becomes not himself to anyone. And thus
he partakes of Dion's anguish—more poignantly,
for Dion had the Mother, Cybel—and in the end
out of this anguish his soul is born, a tortured Christian soul such as the dying Dion's, begging for relief, and at last finding it on the lips of Cybel.——
Dion's mask of Pan which he puts on as a boy is
not only a defense against the world for the super-
sensitive painter-poet underneath it but also an integral part of his character as the artist. The world
is not only blind to the man beneath it but also
sneers at and condemns the Pan-mask it sees. After
that Dion's inner self retrogresses along the line of
Christian resignation until it partakes of the nature
of the Saint, while at the same time the outer Pan
is slowly transformed by his struggle with reality
into Mephistopheles. It is as Mephistopheles that
he falls stricken at Brown's feet after having condemned Brown to destruction by willing him his
mask, it is the Saint who kisses Brown's feet in ab-
ject contrition and pleads as a little boy to a big
brother to tell him a prayer.

Here is confusion worse confounded. We may legiti-
mately wonder whether such a complex and primarily

intellectual conception belongs in the theatre at all. In *The Great God Brown* the conflicts which are so endlessly described are never dramatized; we do not see characters in action. We never see evidence that Brown is "an uncreative creature—inwardly empty and resourceless"—we are only told that such is the case. We do not see the incidents which make Dion what he is, nor do we see anything of the creative spirit which we are repeatedly told tortures him; we see only its ravages.

Repeatedly man and symbol get in each other's way. When Dion takes to drink we do not know whether he does so in the role of the frustrated artist or as the victim of an Oedipus complex or because a false religious and ethical pattern of behavior has been imposed on the pagan spirit of mankind. The transference of Dion's creative power to Brown is abysmally obscure; how can Brown receive a force which must cease to exist at a man's death? What is the meaning of the destruction of Brown's own personality? (Brown's exploitation of Dion's talent to his own profit during the latter's lifetime might corrupt and destroy Brown, but this possibility O'Neill appears to overlook.) There is additional confusion in the fact that Dion *wills* his mask to Brown, while O'Neill himself states in his explanation that Brown *steals* it. Why the two conflicts, completely different in themselves, between one aspect of Dion and Brown on the one hand, and between the two aspects of Dion on the other? If O'Neill wanted to dramatize the problem of dual personality, of conflicting instincts and qualities, in a human being, individual or typical, why did he not make use of one character who appeared in different guises in accordance with the personality which predominated at the moment, after the fashion of Dr.

Jekyll and Mr. Hyde? And lastly, on what plane are we to consider all these things—on that of fantasy, or symbolism, or reality?

A certain image of that complex and tragic figure, modern man, cursed with an irreconcilable heritage in which religious, emotional, and philosophical concepts are hopelessly at war, undoubtedly emerges from *The Great God Brown*. Its very confusion is eloquent, and we sense in it more than a trace of self-portraiture, for the conflicts of Dion Anthony are to be a certain degree those of O'Neill himself. The mere attempt, however inchoate the results, to probe the human soul in such depths, to perceive and state its contradictions, is not without dignity. But the author's choice of form is fundamentally false. The subject matter of *The Great God Brown* does not belong in a play. The fact that symbol and generality yield only occasionally to individual human and emotional appeal is not the point; the impersonality of *Everyman* has a theatricality of its own different from that of *Romeo and Juliet*. The issue is one of clarity, or the lack of it, and the difference between *relation* and *action*.

How O'Neill came to submerge the instincts and technique of the dramatist so completely is apparent from reading a passage in a letter he wrote to Arthur Hobson Quinn in April, 1925.

I'm always, always trying to interpret Life in terms of lives, never just in terms of characters. I'm always acutely conscious of the Force behind—(Fate, God, our biological past creating our present, whatever one calls it—Mystery certainly)—and of the one eternal tragedy of Man in his glorious self-destructive struggle to make the Force express him instead of being, as an animal is, an infinitesimal incident in its expression. And my profound conviction is that this is the only subject worth writing about and that it is possible—or can be—to develop a tragic expression in terms of transfigured modern values and symbols in the theatre which may to some degree bring home to members of a modern audience their ennobling identity with the tragic figures on the stage. Of course, this is very much of a dream, but where the theatre is concerned, one must have a dream, and the Greek dream in tragedy is the noblest ever! [6]

What O'Neill is proposing here is the very negation of theatre. It is all very well for a philosopher or a poet or essayist to try to "interpret Life in terms of lives, never just in terms of character," to be "acutely conscious of the Force behind" and the "one eternal tragedy of Man in his glorious self-destructive struggle to make the Force express him instead of being——an infinitesimal incident in its expression," etc., etc. But such preoccupations spell disaster for both the novelist and the playwright, who must, by the very nature of their medium, communicate with their audiences in terms of "characters" and "lives," excepting in the case of explicit fantasy or allegory, whose intention must then be unmistakable. Conflict, character, action—these categories distinguish the theatre from other forms, they are its essence. What will best bring home to an audience its "ennobling identity with the tragic figures on the stage" will be the universality of individual characters, by virtue of their

[6] Arthur Hobson Quinn, *History of the American Drama*, revised edition, F. S. Crofts & Co., 1936, Part II, p. 199.

reality (as distinguished from realism of presentation). And that reality will grow out of the dramatist's understanding of their circumstances, their predicaments, their human traits. No modern audience has experienced more complete and poignant identification with the figures in a play than in the case of characters conceived three hundred and fifty years ago, because Shakespeare thought in terms of living human beings and their tragic or comic circumstances, and not in terms of their philosophical relation to Life or Man or a "Force," and because he expressed his awe and exaltation at the mystery of life in poetry whose images came out of homely life: death is "an undiscovered country"; life is a "brief candle," "the world is a stage," and mortal men and women are "golden lads and girls." If a man thinks clearly and with imagination and sets about writing plays his philosophy will be apparent, directly or indirectly, in his writing. But if he makes his thinking the be-all and end-all of his work he will stifle his creative instinct at its source, with words.

In the closing scene of *The Great God Brown* there is a speech by the dying Billy Brown, which is a kind of prelude to *Lazarus Laughed*.

> I know! I have found Him! I hear Him speak! "Blessed are they that weep for they shall laugh!" Only he that has wept can laugh! The laughter of Heaven sows earth with a rain of tears, and out of Earth's transfigured birth-pain the laughter of Man returns to bless and play again in innumerable dancing flames upon the knees of God.

Not only is the theme heralded, but the passage itself indicates the quasi-poetry in which O'Neill's next opus

is couched. It is a chronicle of the life and teachings of
Lazarus whom Jesus raised from the grave. He comes
back from death to teach men that it does not exist:
death is only man's fear of what a cessation of living may
bring. Lazarus' previous existence was a Joblike series of
misfortunes. But when he died—

> In the dark peace of the grave the man called Laza-
> rus rested. He was still weak, as one who recovers
> from a long illness—for, living, he had believed his
> life a sad one! He lay dreaming in the croon of
> silence, feeling as the flow of blood in his own veins
> the past re-enter the heart of God to be renewed by
> faith into the future. He thought, "Men call this
> death"—for he had been dead only a little while
> and he still remembered. Then, of a sudden, a
> strange gay laughter trembled from his heart as
> though his life, so long repressed in him by fear, had
> found at last its voice and a song for singing. "Men
> call this death," it sang. "Men· call life death and
> fear it. They hide from it in horror. Their lives are
> spent in hiding. Their fear becomes their living.
> They worship life as death!"

In successive scenes Lazarus' gospel is shown at work
among the hostile Jews and the followers of Christ, the
crowds in which stir dreams of a resurgent Greece liberated from the Roman yoke, even in the Emperor Tiberius and his unsavory heir Caligula. Tiberius begins to
fear that Lazarus' creed, which denies the existence of
death, may undermine his rule, which rests on men's fear
of death. He summons Lazarus to Rome, where the
latter miraculously wins over the degenerate court, Caligula, the Emperor's wife Pompeia, momentarily even

Tiberius himself. He uncovers the source of their cruelty in their despair and fear. But he is forced to admit that, like Christ, he has come before his time: "Men forget. It is still too soon." Those he has won turn against him, again from fear. He is burned to death and Caligula, who owes him most gratitude, pierces his heart with a spear on the funeral pyre. Yet even his death is a triumph, his last words an affirmation: "There is no death."

There is little pretense of dramatic structure in *Lazarus Laughed*; each episode is detached, except for the unifying thread of the prophet martyr's gospel, and the progression towards tragedy (or triumph). Packed with symbolism, with long undramatic speeches, with characters only rarely individualized, as in the case of Miriam and Caligula, it is more of an allegorical pageant or poem than a play.

Although the conception is not lacking in stature, its grandeur is only that of a façade. Behind it is nothing more than a vague, undifferentiating, endless reiteration: "There is no death—death is dead—laugh, laugh." When Lazarus is already on the funeral pyre, Tiberius and the crowd beg for some hint of illumination: "Why are we born? To what end must we die?" Lazarus' answer is:

> Yes! (*His voice a triumphant assertion of the victory of life over pain and death*)—O men, fear not life! You die, but there is no death for Man!

Surely we may ask for something a little more explicit, even in an abstract poetic work? There must be some basis even for rapture excepting in the briefest and simplest lyric, such as *Pippa Passes*. Stretched out over four acts the belief that death is nonexistent and life a magnificent cosmic privilege, dwindles to mere vaporing. Faith in life, divorced from any belief of *how* it should be lived, of the importance of freedom, comfort, decency, dignity, and endeavor, not as abstract concepts but translated into actual standards of living and behavior, and of how they may be practiced and maintained, is vacuous. With Granville Hicks we feel that "we cannot affirm life in the abstract; we can only affirm the value of those forces in life that work for ideal ends. His inability to discover those forces, and show them to us, robs O'Neill of all vitality. Indiscriminate hope is as pointless as indiscriminate despair, as his manner of turning from one to the other shows." [7]

The fear of solitude, of the isolation of self which overtakes us even in the midst of crowds of friends, has haunted O'Neill as it haunts every artist. In *The Great God Brown* he traces it back to a psychological causation: the young boy, his trust overthrown and his sensitivity bruised, puts on a mask, an armor, of self-protection. But in *Lazarus Laughed* O'Neill abandons such scientific conclusions and proclaims that man needs only courage and buoyancy to overcome any sense of solitude:

> Man's loneliness is but his fear of life! Lonely no more! Millions of laughing stars there are around me! And laughing dust, born once of woman on this earth, now free to dance! New stars are born of dust eternally! The old, grown mellow with God, burst into flaming seed! The fields of infinite space are sown—and grass for sheep springs up on the

[7] Hicks, *The Great Tradition*, p. 254.

hills of earth! But there is no death, no fear, nor loneliness! There is only God's Eternal Laughter! His Laughter flows into the Lonely Heart!

Of the real basis of this feeling of loneliness, man's inability, as yet, to think and aspire and act in any way but individually, when changing conditions in a mechanized world demand a new collective ideal, collective activity, O'Neill has not a glimmer.

The poetry and writing in *Lazarus Laughed* reflect the puerility of its underlying idea, as the passages quoted indicate. One looks back from them to the spare, authentic speech of *Anna Christie* and *The Long Voyage Home* with incredulity. In line with the writing is the preciosity of the monstrously involved system of masks which O'Neill has evolved to express an elaborate symbolism. The crowds, or chorus, are masked in accordance with the following scheme:

There are seven periods of life shown: Boyhood (or Girlhood), Youth, Young Manhood (or Womanhood), Manhood (or Womanhood), Middle Age, Maturity and Old Age; and each of these periods is represented by seven different masks of general types of character as follows: The Simple, Ignorant; the Happy, Eager; the Self-Tortured, Introspective; the Proud, Self-Reliant; the Servile, Hypocritical; the Revengeful, Cruel; the Sorrowful, Resigned. Thus in each crowd (this includes among the men the Seven Guests who are composed of one male of each period-type as period one—type one, period two—type two, and so on up to the period seven— type seven) there are forty-nine different combinations of period and type. Each type has a distinct predominant color for its costumes which varies in kind according to its period.

In addition there are variations according to racial types: Greek, Roman, Jewish. Since facial pantomime except of the most exaggerated kind or nearness in make-up cannot project beyond a certain number of rows in the theatre unless the audience is equipped with opera glasses, only a small proportion of an audience could take in such subtle variations in contour and physiognomy as O'Neill has here prescribed, let alone figure out, from these variations, the particular aggregation of qualities they are intended to symbolize! And even if they could, what purpose, beyond giving an impression of the manifold variations human personality is capable of, can all this folderol serve?

4

The theatre has heretofore distinguished between action and observation or reflection, appropriating the first-named as its particular province, in explicit contrast to the latter. The conception of psychological cause and effect as action in itself, and therefore directly within the realm of theatre, first makes its appearance in O'Neill's *Strange Interlude*. The aside, in which characters speak their conscious as well as sub-conscious thoughts out loud in a stylized monotone while other characters on the stage remain immobile, has its origin in his desire to convey more of the obscurely mixed workings of our minds on the stage than have ever been displayed there before. O'Neill tries to show, dramatically, that we do good, not only from a desire to do good, but often from a desire to do evil, and vice versa, and in so doing he enters a field which has ordinarily belonged to the novel.

By "strange interlude" O'Neill seems to mean that period in a woman's life during which she is sexually reproductive. Nina at forty-five, according to the stage directions, is an old woman. (Because of her biological function, O'Neill conceives of woman as being at the very heart of the cosmic process. God the Father is to him a meaningless concept, a contradition of the role of woman in furthering life and making it possible.)

Before the play begins Nina Leeds had loved Gordon Shaw, who was killed flying in the Great War. Because they never lived together Nina has come to idealize him and to feel that she is guilty of having failed him. As the play opens she is trying to assuage her feeling of guilt by promiscuity among the wounded and crippled soldiers. At the suggestion of Ned Darrell, a young doctor interested in her psychosis, she marries Sam Evans, in the hope of having children by him, and perhaps eventually coming to love him. When she is already pregnant his mother reveals to her that there is insanity in Sam's family. She is forced to submit to an abortion; but out of a sense of loyalty, she does not divorce him, nor does she tell him why they have no children.

Sam, conscious that she does not love him, blames himself for the fact that they have no child; his work suffers, he begins to go to pieces. Nina asks Ned Darrell to enable her to have a child. Darrell, moved by his sense of fairness, and also by Nina's physical attraction for him, consents. He and Nina fall in love; Nina wants to divorce Sam and marry Darrell. But the latter, afraid of Nina's disrupting his scientific career, and also unwilling to hurt Sam, who is his friend, leaves the country, after

having told Sam that Nina is carrying his—Sam's—child.
Nina resigns herself.

A year passes. Nina is happy in her child and husband,
Sam in his wife and son. Man and woman alike are fulfilled, because they are continuing the race; O'Neill's insistence on this point is significant. Then Darrell comes
back; he has gone to pieces and abandoned his work and
is determined that Nina shall divorce Sam and marry
him, and that he shall have his rightful child. But now
Nina is obdurate. She still loves him, but she will not
give up what she has for his sake. For complete satisfaction and happiness she must remain Sam's wife at
the same time that she is Ned's mistress. She needs husband, lover, son, and the old family friend, Charlie
Marsden, who has assumed the image of her father to
her.

This point, at the end of the sixth act, marks the high
point of success in the "experiment" made by Nina and
Darrell. Thereafter matters go awry again. Nina's son,
named after Gordon Shaw, hates Darrell, because he
feels instinctively that there is more than friendship between him and his mother; he turns from Nina to his
supposed father, Sam. Later, however, Nina discovers in
him the reincarnation of her early hero and love, Gordon
Shaw, from whose ghost she has never been freed.
When young Gordon falls in love and becomes engaged
to Madeline Arnold she cannot bear to give him up to
another woman, and tries to break up the engagement.
She begs Darrell to tell Madeline that there is insanity
in Sam's family; but Darrell, free from the bondage of
his love for Nina, refuses "to meddle in human lives
again."

Meanwhile Nina is forty-five and, according to

O'Neill, an old woman. Evans has a stroke; before he dies she becomes reconciled to him and her neurotic hatred of Madeline and the desire to absorb young Gordon, disappear, symbolic of the approaching close of the sexual span of her life. Darrell goes back to his scientific work, and in a highly symbolical conclusion Nina turns at long last to Marsden, who has loved her all along; but she turns to him as to her father, and their love has become the peaceful affection of old age. The intervening years since she left her real father, her association with "the Gordons" and its accompanying relationships, are seen merely as an interlude to final peace. And in a concluding scene O'Neill pronounces the farewell to that "strange interlude" between childhood and age; life itself is only "a strange dark interlude in the electrical display of God the Father."

Within the strict delimitations he has set himself, O'Neill has been amazingly comprehensive. He has shown Nina with every type of man: the scholar, the businessman, the writer, the scientist, the athlete, young and old, and in every possible relationship she can bear to a man—father and daughter, mistress and lover, husband and wife, son and mother, friend and friend. The other women who appear are important only in their relation to the men with whom Nina's life is bound up; briefly we see Mrs. Evans as Sam's mother and Madeline as young Gordon's sweetheart. Thus O'Neill confines himself solely to the different phases of the sexual relationship.

As seen from this outline the play is structurally a tightly knit psychoanalytical case history. Thanks to the use of the aside which enables O'Neill to dramatize an incident on several planes simultaneously, there are scenes of truly extraordinary significance and power, such as that in which Nina persuades Darrell to give her a child. Listen to Darrell's thoughts as he hears Nina's proposal:

> Let me see . . . I am in the laboratory and they are guinea pigs . . . in fact, in the interest of science, I can be for the purpose of this experiment, a healthy guinea pig myself and still remain an observer . . . I observe my pulse is high, for example, and that's obviously because I am stricken with the recurrence of an old desire . . . desire is a natural male reaction to the beauty of the female . . . her husband is my friend . . . I have always tried to help him. . . .

Sensing that his detachment is threatened, he tries to rationalize his emotions:

> Am I right to advise this? . . . yes, it is clearly the rational thing to do . . . but this advice betrays my friend! . . . no, it saves him! . . . it saves his wife . . . and if a third party should know a little happiness . . . is he any the poorer, am I any the less his friend because I saved him? . . . no, my duty to him is plain . . . and my duty as an experimental searcher after truth . . . to observe these three guinea pigs, of which I am one. . . .

In scenes such as this O'Neill achieves his purpose of unraveling the intricacies of human motivation. Unfortunately they occur all too rarely. There are long stretches of *Strange Interlude* which are annotations for a play rather than a finished dramatic piece of work, full of self-inventories, mere catalogues of emotion. Too often the aside becomes a convenient way of conveying information to the audience, after the manner of screen captions in the days of silent moving pictures. Too often again, asides and dialogue alike are written in long, cumbersome sentences, which are repetitious, and difficult to understand, and a trial to actor and spectator alike. Compared to *Mourning Becomes Electra*, *Strange Interlude* is an uneven, slovenly piece of work.

The apparent profundity of the play is likewise deceptive. Attention has already been called to its narrow compass. It is confined to one problem, that of sex, which is thoroughly explored. But what kind of perspective is it that ignores every other phase of life? Moreover, the sexual force is shown as profoundly destructive unless it is harnessed to the reproductive function. Only in their child do Nina and Sam attain fulfillment and self-confidence. There is no recognition of the enrichening of life through sexual experience which does not result directly in procreation. Nina has only two moments of complete fulfillment and contentment. One comes when she feels her child moving in her womb:

There . . . again . . . his child! . . . my child moving in my life . . . my life moving in my child . . . the world is whole and perfect. . . .

The second occurs when she voices her possession of the three men—Darrell, Sam, and Marsden—husband, lover, and father-friend—and of the child upstairs.

My three men! . . . I feel their desires converge in me! . . . to form one complete beautiful male desire which I absorb . . . and am whole . . . they dissolve in me, their life is my life . . . I am preg-

nant with the three! . . . husband! . . . lover! . . .
father! . . . and the fourth man! . . . little man!
. . . little Gordon! . . . he is mine too! . . . that
makes it perfect! . . .

The unbroken continuity of life transmitted from one
individual to another, passing from the energy of the
sun into the stream of human life and eventually back
into a force of which our life is but one expression,
furnishes O'Neill with exultant satisfaction. What actually happens is that he comes to mistake the process for
an end in itself, seeing in it the very meaning of the
universe. Thus, as already shown in *Lazarus Laughed*,
he glories in something which he never really evaluates
and whose direction he does not examine. And it is for
this reason that, despite O'Neill's own poetic exaltation,
the characters in *Strange Interlude* are themselves beset
by confusion and despair, excepting in rare moments of
individual fulfillment. Nina longs continually to attain
again the simplicity and innocence of the days before
"all this tangled mess of love and hate and pain and
birth" began. To Darrell life is repeatedly a "madness"
or a "bloody mess." This is inevitable, since like the
great crowd of spectators of Lazarus' martyrdom in the
Roman amphitheatre they can only ask helplessly
"Why? To what end?" There is no answer excepting
the empty one vouchsafed Nina at the close:

Forget the whole distressing episode, regard it as an
interlude, of trial and preparation, say, in which our
souls have been scraped clean of impure flesh and
made worthy to bleach in peace.——Our lives are
merely strange dark interludes in the electrical display of God the Father!——It will be a comfort to

get home—to be old and to be home again at last—
to be in love with peace together—to love each
other's peace—to sleep with peace together!—I'm
so contentedly weary with life!

The definition of life as "a strange dark interlude in the
electrical display of God the Father" may be oddly at
variance with O'Neill's many references to life as a positive force, since he here identifies life with the lapse
between the expressions of that force—in other words,
with nothingness. But in general the conception of our
individual existences as mere purgatories before that
greatest desideratum of all, the peace of a comfortable
death, is unmistakably clear. It is a strange nirvana for
an adventurous spirit.

This then is what the acclaimed profundity of Strange
Interlude amounts to. In the words of Charmion von
Wiegand, "Of what use to visit the fantastic world of
the unconscious when the secrets brought back are no
more valuable than this dried sea-weed of desire and
these broken shells of lost hope? O'Neill has found no
buried treasure in this Saragossa sea of the soul. This is
cheap dross like the treasure sought for so many years
by the hero of Gold, who knew all the time that what
he was seeking was brass." [8]

If The Great God Brown suffered from obscurity,
Dynamo, which followed close on Strange Interlude, is
practically opaque. Here the tendencies towards dramatic and intellectual confusion culminate in complete
theatrical disintegration, from every point of view. Dramatic values give way to argument, character to intellectual concepts thinly disguised as people. The ending

[8] Charmion von Wiegand, "Eugene O'Neill," New Theatre, September, 1935.

leaves us completely in the dark as to the author's intention, as does much of the obscure symbolism throughout the play. All we can be certain of is that O'Neill intended Reuben Light's quest to exemplify the plight of the "surviving religious instinct today," loosed from the old moorings and in search of new holdfasts, torn between the positive and the negative elements in life. The former are represented by the Fife family, in which the father believes in science, in the power of electricity, while the mother and daughter symbolize the sexual life force, the ability to reproduce. Reuben Light's parents, on the other hand, stand for all that is sterile and dying —the strangling possessive love of the mother for her son raised to the height of perversion and the religious orthodoxy and intransigence of the father.

Through a profound emotional and intellectual upheaval Reuben Light tries to free himself from the domination of his parents—from his abnormal love of his mother and terror of his father. But when at last he finds in electricity the God he has been seeking he invests it with the qualities of his previous fixations. The two great creative forces become one. Dynamo, creator of electricity, is "like a woman—like Ada's mother—or mine—a great dark mother." It is also a merciless Moloch. Reuben's new faith leads him to madness and self-destruction. Along with his crazed love for Dynamo, which has assumed the complete mother image, his passion for Ada has continued, but he believes that in the eyes of Dynamo sex is sinful, that her "jealousy" demands that he kill Ada. He does so, then, terrified, turns to Dynamo, "pleading like a little boy" and crying—

I don't want any miracle, Mother! I don't want to

know the truth! I only want you to like me, Mother!
Never let me go from you again! Please, Mother!

Whereupon he falls to his death. There is no clue as
to whether he has deliberately sought suicide or been
carried away by his unbalanced brain in an attempt to
embrace Dynamo. The curtain falls on Mrs. Fife pound-
ing the body of the generator in "a childish fit of anger"
and crying,

> What are you singing for? I should think you'd be
> ashamed! And I thought you were nice and loved
> us!—You hateful old thing, you!

What does all this mean? Why does the new god—or
goddess—"Whose song is the hymn of eternal generation, the song of eternal life," actually bring only death—
to Ada, to Reuben? Why the conflict between the two
life principles, which forces Reuben to sacrifice Ada to
Dynamo's "jealousy"? What does O'Neill want us to
think? That faith and skepticism, sex and science, orthodox religion and atheism, alike lead to madness and destruction? That the search for knowledge and faith can
lead only in a circle, from the shelter of mother love
through experience and wisdom, through disillusionment and cynicism and despair back to the primordial
desire for mother comfort? What we grasp most clearly
of all is the degree of O'Neill's Freudian obsession, since
he is content to reduce Dynamo, highest expression of
the machine age, to a religious and sexual symbol, when
clearly the problem today is the practical one of mastering the machine before it destroys us, of constructing a
rational society which will benefit instead of suffering
from the advances of science!

5

In *Mourning Becomes Electra* O'Neill made deliberate and avowed use of an old pattern, one of the greatest in the Greek tragedies, reinterpreting it in the light of modern knowledge and substituting for the classic fates and furies the psychological laws of cause and effect. Its theme, like that of its Greek original, is retribution, payment by the children for the sins of the fathers, to the last farthing. The concept of retribution as an ethical necessity was an inheritance from tribal society in which blood was the basis of a collective responsibility and which decreed that the members of a family or a tribe were each and all responsible for the wrongdoing of one of their number. Having discarded the ethical concept, modern society has encountered the idea of retribution in another form, in which blood is once more the bond. For scientific heredity decrees that the sins of the guilty shall be visited on those who may be ethically innocent; this is the theme of *Ghosts*, and, less clearly, of *Mourning Becomes Electra*. In the latter, the wages of wrongdoing are paid, not through the blood and tissues, but by minds and emotions twisted awry, psychologically determined by heredity and environment alike. Because of this fundamental line of reasoning *Mourning Becomes Electra* is as tightly wrought as any play ever written. The first of the three plays, *The Homecoming*, consists of four acts; *The Hunted* has five acts, and *The Haunted* is in four. There is no break from play to play, no change in scene or characters—each act leads with shattering inevitability into the next. Nor is there a loose thread or weak link in motivation and development throughout the five hours of the trilogy. *Mourning Becomes Electra* is O'Neill's masterpiece in dramatic craftsmanship.

The background before the opening of the action itself is vitally important, since it contains the point of origin of the entire tragedy—the happenings for which everything we witness serves as expiation: Abe Mannon's jealousy and brutal treatment of his brother Dave and the latter's mistress, the nurserymaid Marie Brantome. Back of the episode itself, however, lie a whole complex of motives strongly resembling the background of *Desire Under the Elms*. The two strongest characteristics of the Mannons are their religion and their family feeling. Their puritanism is stark and loveless, a composite of inflexible moral rectitude, callous self-interest, the stern inhibition of emotion and a religious instinct which has hardened into a fear of life and a brooding over the thought of death. Ezra Mannon's thoughts turned to life for the first time during the war, when death became so common as to lose all meaning:

> That's always been the Mannons' way of thinking. They went to the white meeting-house on the Sabbath and meditated on death. Life was a dying. Being born was starting to die. Death was being born. How in hell people ever got such notions! That white meeting-house. It stuck in my mind, clean-scrubbed and white-washed, a temple of death!

Similarly stern and inflexible is the hold of the Mannon dead over their descendants. Again and again the characters in the play look up to the portraits on the wall and cry out against the tyranny of dead men, who, like unto themselves, yet rule them as judges and executioners.

Abe Mannon, father of Ezra Mannon and grand-

father of Lavinia and Orin Mannon, was also in love
with Marie Brantôme. When he discovered that she was
having relations with his brother David he threw them
both out of the house, despite the fact that Marie was
pregnant, and forced David to sell him his share of the
family business at one-tenth of its value. Then he pulled
down the house in which his brother had disgraced the
family (and gotten the better of him), and built the
present Mannon home in which the action of the play
takes place—a veritable "temple for his hatred," as Christine Mannon calls it. Subsequently, still before the opening of the play, after David had committed suicide and
her young son Adam run away to sea, Marie Brantome,
starving and ill, wrote to David's nephew, Ezra Mannon,
begging for help. But Ezra, a true son of his father, never
answered her letter, and she died in the arms of her son
who came home just in time to find her on her death-
bed.

The Mannon men were all attracted by women who
were their temperamental opposites. Both Abe and Dave
loved the foreigner Marie Brantome; Ezra married Christine—foreign, exotic, warm-blooded. Before their marriage she had loved Ezra—"so handsome in his lieuten-
ant's uniform—silent and mysterious and romantic."
But her love did not survive the cold brutality of her
wedding night, the puritan horror and repression of passion and sensuality. Lavinia, her first child, was conceived in hatred, of which Lavinia herself was always instinctively aware, and as a result of which she transferred
her love to her father. Orin was born after Christine had
become reconciled to her marriage, "in order to live," and
during her pregnancy Ezra was away with the army of
Mexico, so that it seemed as if Orin were wholely her

child while Lavinia was Ezra's. The girl grew up to resemble her father and to love him with an unhealthy intensity; the same relationship developed between the boy and his mother. Lavinia was hard and silent and mannish, Orin a soft and affectionate weakling.

It was Lavinia and Ezra who forced Orin to join the army at the outset of the Civil War. Deprived of the one human being she cared for, Christine fell in love with Adam Brant, Marie Brantome's son and now a sea captain. He reminds her of Orin, because of his general resemblance to all the Mannons but in temperament he resembles Christine, due to his foreign mother. Like her, he is all that the Puritans are not—healthy-minded, sensuous, almost pagan. His feeling for the South Sea islands is a symbol of his whole nature. (These islands recur like a theme throughout the trilogy, always in contrast to the puritanism of the Mannons.) Brant's love for Christine, although deep and sincere, has its subconscious origin in a desire for revenge on the whole family. He and Christine become lovers. Lavinia is also attracted to Adam, and he flirts with her as a screen for his affair with Christine. When Lavinia discovers the relationship between her mother and Adam she becomes not only jealous on her own account but furious at the wrong Christine is doing her father.

The action which begins at this point skillfully discloses this complex background during the course of the first play. Ezra Mannon comes back from the war resolved to break down the barriers that have grown up between him and his wife. But it is too late. Because Lavinia has threatened to tell her father of her mother's infidelity unless she gives up her lover, Christine, with Adam's aid poisons Ezra. And so Ezra pays the forfeit for his treatment of Marie Brantome, and his father's cruelty before him.

But the end is not yet. At Ezra's death Lavinia is already suspicious of her mother. The second play shows Christine's expiation for the murder and Adam's for his complicity. The figure of Lavinia, already growing in significance and stature througout *The Homecoming*, assumes in *The Hunted* the proportions of a goddess of vengeance, with Orin as her tool. The scourge that Lavinia uses to bend Orin to her will is his love for his mother. By fanning his jealousy of Brant to the point of frenzy Lavinia goads him into murdering the sea captain. The crime drives him over the verge of sanity. Looking down on the dead man he sees the family resemblance:

> This is like my dream. I've killed him before—over and over.——Do you remember how the faces of the men I killed (in the war) came back and changed to father's face and finally became my own? He looks like me, too! Maybe I've committed suicide!——If I had been he I would have done what he did! I would have loved her as he loved her—and killed father too—for her sake!

Brant's death and her fear of Lavinia drive Christine to take her own life. Remorse at having helped drive her to her death completes Orin's mental derangement. The close of the second play is prophetic of the horrors to come: Lavinia attempts in all good faith, to soothe him with the words "You have me, haven't you? I love you. I'll help you forget."

In *The Haunted* it is the turn of Lavinia and Orin, who pay the forfeit for the death of their mother and Brant. Their torture is subtle and long-drawn-out, and before the end is reached their identification with the personalities of the dead father and mother is complete, with all the complexity of behavior patterns such a change implies. Lavinia, under the influence of a visit to the South Seas, has become the image of her mother. She falls prey to the same fits of anger her mother had, uses her very words. She longs to forget the past in a healthy normal life and only her fear of leaving Orin, now completely unbalanced, and of his revealing their secret, prevent her from marrying Peter Niles. Meanwhile Orin has become jealous of her. The mother-son pattern of feeling, superimposed upon that of brother and sister, has led to that of husband and wife. The past is closing in on them, imprisoning them. Orin clearly foresees their destiny; malignantly he hints at the relationship fate has in store for them. Revolted by the prospect Lavinia goads him to suicide as she once goaded him to murder; she sees no other way of freeing herself from the past. But after his death she realizes how impossible the accumulation of death and guilt and horror have rendered her marriage to Peter. She would inevitably ruin Peter's life. Happiness is not for her. She sends him away with a trumped-up story of her immoral behavior in the South Sea islands, and enters the Mannon house to live out her life shut away with her ghosts.

Orin had said in taunting bitterness to the Mannon portraits on the walls, "You'll find Lavinia Mannon harder to break than me! You'll have to haunt and hound her for a lifetime!" Puritan to the last, this is the fate she metes out to herself:

I'm not going the way Orin and Mother went. That's escaping punishment. And there's no way

left to punish me. I'm the last Mannon. I've got
to punish myself. Living alone here with the dead
is a worse act of justice than death or prison! I'll
never go out or see anyone! I'll have the shutters
nailed close so no sunlight can ever get in. I'll live
alone with the dead, and keep their secrets, and let
them hound me, until the curse is paid out and the
last Mannon is let die! I know they will see to it
that I live a long time! It takes the Mannons to
punish themselves for being born!

And as the hired man begins closing the shutters, she
marches into the house, closing the door behind her.
Played by Alice Brady, it was one of the great moments
in modern theatre.

Why? Does the emotion with which we have been
wrung for five hours have its origin in terror and compassion, in our identification with the tragic figures on the
stage, or only in a consummate technical skill of the
grand guignol variety which has played on our nerves?
The degree of that skill is unquestionable. O'Neill has
employed every known theatrical device to build suspense
and an atmosphere of brooding tragedy. Repeatedly
he allows the characters themselves to express their instinctive forebodings. Recall how, before Christine ad-
ministers the poison, Ezra Mannon wrestles with the
foreboding that something is wrong in his house.

Something uneasy is troubling my mind—as if something in me was listening, watching, waiting, for
something to happen.——This house is not my
house. This is not my room or my bed. They are
empty——waiting for someone to move in! And
you are not my wife! You are waiting for something!

Downstairs, we know, Lavinia is "pacing up and down before the house like a sentinel." The tension is felt, not only by the audience, raising them to the highest pitch of nervous anticipation, but by Christine as well. It unnerves her so that once she has administered the poison she faints and drops the telltale box, which Lavinia promptly finds.

Again, there is the role of the chanteyman in the opening of the scene which builds to Brant's violent death and the first traces of Orin's madness. The singer serves not only to build up an eerie atmospheric background but to dramatize the fact that Brant is alone, that there is no watchman about, and that Brant himself is nervous and apprehensive. These are melodramatic devices, but they are good melodrama. Moreover O'Neill succeeds perfectly in maintaining a sense of inevitable tragedy without sacrificing the suspense as to what form the tragedy will take. From the beginning *Mourning Becomes Electra* is pitched to a tragic conclusion. Herein lies much of its harrowing effectiveness, and also its greatest weakness.

For there is no real reason why *Mourning Becomes Electra* should follow the tragic course it does. If we are able to maintain some degree of intellectual detachment in the face of the dramatist's skill, we are aware that certain alternatives are open to the Mannons. The motivation is psychologically flawless in that nothing takes place that could not have happened. But it does not follow that what occurred *needed* to have happened. In the words of Charmion von Wiegand, "More normal alternatives of action were open to all the characters than the one they chose of murder and blood, or which their author chose for them, *in mechanical imitation of the Attic pattern.*" [Italics mine.]

For the Agamemnon-Clytemnestra-Electra story is one whose origin and meaning were largely social in significance. To quote Miss von Wiegand again, "Attic tragedy based on this legendary history contains implications lost to modern audiences. For the Athenian spectator, the plays of Euripides and Sophocles had a meaning far beyond any single family tragedy of blood; they were ritual dramas whose choruses recounted the social history of the Greek race——In Attic tragedy, murder was not conditioned by mere personal pique or revenge, but by far wider social issues.——Here passion is inseparable from politics. O'Neill has built his version of the tragedy on purely personal motives without any profound social significance." [9]

This last is the crux of the matter. O'Neill's attempt in his own words, to "borrow the theme pattern of Aeschylus (and the old legends) and to re-interpret it in modern psychological terms with Fate and the Furies working from within the individual soul" is inadmissible because, wrenched from its context, the story becomes pure melodrama. Without the justification afforded by early Greek religion and morality in which the blood feud was a collective responsibility which took the place of objective law, the actions of his characters become arbitrary and unreal. In New England in the year 1865 legal recourse for murder existed. That Lavinia Mannon took justice in her own hands becomes a *violation* of the existing code rather than, as in the case of the Electra myth, conformity to it.

That she did so, O'Neill attempts to explain on psycho-

[9] Charmion von Wiegand, *ibid.*

logical grounds. But the substitution of psychological derangement for social compulsion does not remedy the fault. Like the diseased insanity of Oswald in *Ghosts*, Lavinia's actions are the fruit of distorted emotions and of her parents' antagonism. Like Oswald she is a victim. But Oswald's illness comes as a climax; it does not serve as the origin for a long series of crimes, for that would completely mar the social significance of the tragedy. In *Mourning Becomes Electra* on the other hand the entire action unrolls from Lavinia's twisted loves and hates. The causes·of her tragedy are lost in the welter of horror that ensues. Those causes, no less than in the case of Oswald Alving, are not arbitrary perversity, spontaneously engendered. They are social, as our initial analysis of the background of the plot clearly showed. The Mannon stock has deteriorated as the result of false ideals of family honor, an outworn, empty religion, a corrupted society, as the choral interjections of Ezra Mannon's fellow townsmen amply prove. The sexual perversion of the younger Mannons is a symptom. But O'Neill has hardly touched on the essential causes of the tragedy, and has allowed the symptom to obliterate the disease.

There is yet another flaw in *Mourning Becomes Electra*. With steady and almost maddening persistence throughout thirteen acts O'Neill relates every occurrence, every trait, back to the sexual impulse, or its distortion and frustration, just as he did in *Strange Interlude*. One cannot acknowledge as a great dramatist a playwright who persistently ignores any causation except that induced by sex. Some human beings, after all, are sexually normal! They grow up with happily married parents, and in their turn bear children who do not murder them. Other things happen to them. They lose their jobs. They go to war. They aspire to wealth or position out of native ambition or emulation or because they love their families and children. They encounter success and failure and sadness and joy; innumerable things happen to them for any number of reasons. But you will not find these things in the plays of Eugene O'Neill.

It is also noteworthy that for all his preoccupation with sexual problems O'Neill never admits any reason for sexual maladjustment excepting *previous* sexual maladjustment, save in the case of *All God's Chillun Got Wings*. Yet social workers and psychiatrists alike have testified that marriages are frequently wrecked and homes broken up because social frustration induces emotional disturbances. A man who has been out of work for a period of years suffers humiliation or nervous tension, whose emotional repercussions can corrode a marital relationship and set up further maladjustments among his children. But in this kind of causation, seemingly, O'Neill is not interested either.

6

Not the least extraordinary thing about O'Neill has always been the ability of his talent to vary, not only in subject matter (though his basic preoccupation was usually the same), but from very good to very bad. *Mourning Becomes Electra* came at a time when he seemed to have abandoned the limitations of the "well-made play" for good. And hard upon its mechanical perfection and intensity followed *Days Without End*, a reversion to all the faults of *Dynamo*, and that idyllic

daguerreotype, *Ah! Wilderness*. In the latter, the kindly
figure of Nat Miller, family man and solid small-town
citizen, is evidence that O'Neill can, after all, render the
commonplace motives and qualities of mind of a normal
human being. However dissimilar in theme and treatment with *Mourning Becomes Electra* and *Days Without End, Ah! Wilderness* has this in common with both:
it represents an intellectual and emotional return to the
past, an attempt to turn away from present-day problems
or to solve them by an unrealistic answer which dates
from the past. In *Mourning Becomes Electra* antiquity
furnished O'Neill with the skeleton of his plot and his
theme, while we have seen his attempt to invest it in
modern terminology, was nevertheless the ancient idea
of family revenge. In *Ah! Wilderness* the more recent
past is presented in a sentimental halo, as a time of
simple virtues and nostalgic charm. In *Days Without
End* the hero abandons the scientific for the orthodox
religious viewpoint; John Loving, still another projection of modern man, makes yet another halt on his
endless Calvary, this time at the shrine of Catholicism,
with which he assuages all his doubts and fears. Thus,
if straws show which way the wind is blowing, O'Neill's
last three plays offer unmistakable evidence that, at
least during a period of four years—from 1929 to 1933,
he was retrogressing intellectually.

In *Days Without End* O'Neill went back to the
clumsy and undramatic technique of the aside; this time,
however, the split personality of the hero, part skeptic,
part wistful believer, is played by two actors: "John's"
thoughts are uttered by his cynical, destructive half,
"Loving." The play is nothing more than a debate in
which different characters present opposing points of

view. They speak a dull and colorless prose, and even *The Great God Brown* cannot exceed some of the passages for turgid obscurity. The most significant of these, from the point of view of O'Neill's development, is one which contains as explicit a statement of a pro-Fascist philosophy as has appeared in the work of any of our major writers. Like so many of O'Neill's utterances it is far from lucid, but its implications are unmistakable. John, talking to the Catholic priest who is his mentor, is decrying the cowardice and futility of contemporary life, the deterioration of the idea of freedom. His evil self, Loving, interrupts him:

> Freedom was merely our romantic delusion. We know better now. We know we are all the slaves of meaningless chance—electricity, or something, which whirls us—on to Hercules!

> JOHN
>
> Very well, on to Hercules! Let us face that! Once we have accepted it without evasion, we can begin to create new goals for ourselves, new ends for our days! A new discipline for life will spring into being, a new will and power to live, a new ideal to measure the value of our days by!——We need a new leader who will teach us that ideal, who by his life will exemplify it and make it a living truth for us—a man who will prove that man's fleeting life in time and space can be noble. We need above all to learn again to believe in the possibility of nobility of spirit in ourselves! A new saviour must be born who will reveal to us how we can be saved from ourselves, so that we can be free of the past and inherit the future and not perish by it!

As an elucidation of the *Führerprinzip*, this can hardly be bettered. It is, in a somewhat different form, the same tendency which S. N. Behrman has voiced in his preface to *Rain From Heaven*. True, it is a philosophy which John presumably (not explicitly), abandons when he returns to the fold of the Church. But the idea is unquestionably present in O'Neill's mind. It is an idea to which the sensitive bewildered individual is inevitably driven by the chaos of irrationality which our society presents today, *unless* he finds the third alternative— not chaos, not salvation by a "leader," but the strength and promise which the ideal of collective effort for a common good holds out to him. It is an ideal to which only reality of experience can lead the writer today, and it is inevitably denied the writer who turns his back on life. Yet this, insofar as we can judge from his writings to date (O'Neill has given us nothing since 1933) is precisely what he has done. Joseph Wood Krutch quotes a remark once made to him by O'Neill: "Most modern plays are concerned with the relation between man and man, but that does not interest me at all. I am interested only in the relation between man and God." O'Neill has further stated, in a letter to George Jean Nathan: [10]

The playwright today must dig at the roots of the sickness of today as he feels it—the death of the old God and the failure of science and materialism to give any satisfying new one for the surviving primitive religious instinct to find a meaning for life in, and to comfort its fear of death with. It seems to me that anyone trying to do big work nowadays must have this big subject behind all the little sub-

[10] Quoted by Joseph Wood Krutch in his introduction to the Nobel Prize edition of O'Neill's plays, Random House.

jects of his plays or novels, or he is simply trying to scribble around the surface of things——

These two statements are closely related. In distinguishing so sharply between the religious and the material aspects of life, O'Neill is overlooking the fact that religion is inevitably a reflection of existing social relationships, and mirrors, not only men's aspirations and fears but the society which fostered both. The rise or decline of religious belief is therefore a social as well as a spiritual phenomenon. Failure to see the connection between "the death of the old God, etc., etc." and "the relation between man and man," and arbitrary exclusion of the latter from his consideration, relegates O'Neill to the position (to borrow his own words) of "simply trying to scribble around the surface of things."

If it is true that men and women are continually driven to ask "What is the point of life? Why are we alive?" what drives them to ask the question? Is it metaphysical perplexity, or is it because their most fundamental human instincts are frustrated by life as it is organized today? They want to work, steadily and securely; they want to marry and have children, in health and security; they desire a rounded, creative, abundant existence. They want, above all, to be able to feel that assurance that comes from knowing that the society of which they are a part is rational and sound, that it has for its purpose a common good that transcends the welfare of any small group of individuals. It is the impossibility of satisfying these desires which drives so many human beings today into skepticism, into neuroses of all kinds, into lawlessness and despair.

Yet when has O'Neill taken into consideration these

fundamental needs whose frustration lies at the roots of the doubt and distortion with which he does concern himself? In *Desire Under the Elms* he deals with Abbie's longing for a home and Ephraim Cabot's passion for the land, but both motives become confused with, and in the end submerged by other instincts—in the first case sexual passion and in the second religious obsession. In *The Great God Brown* Dion Anthony is an artist in conflict with a society whose standards of achievement are wholly material; but once again the problem is subordinated to sexual and religious complications. Always O'Neill puts the cart before the horse—he deals with man's search for a faith instead of first determining what undermined his faith, or portrays the horrors into which his twisted emotions plunge him without reference to the forces which must first have warped those emotions, a consideration which would inevitably bring him up against the factor that he dismisses—"man's relation to man." By denying, in that he persists in ignoring, the importance of this enormous field of human experience, O'Neill has invited the mystical confusion and pessimism which have kept his great dramatic gift musclebound.

VI Comedy

1 GEORGE S. KAUFMAN

Two arguments are frequently advanced against the
serious consideration of George Kaufman as a dramatist:
first, that his work is so much a matter of collaboration
that it is impossible to isolate Kaufman's contribution
to the plays jointly written by him and Marc Connelly,
Edna Ferber, Moss Hart, and others; second, that Kaufman himself makes no pretensions to being a serious
dramatist, since he is first and last a *showman*, intent on
turning out entertainment, whether it be in the form of
legitimate drama, musical comedy, or moving picture.
An expert in theatrical craftsmanship of all kinds, he
will contribute to the production of a "show" in any
capacity—direct, write the book of a musical, collaborate,
revise someone else's work, or hasten to wherever a play
may be in the doldrums of a catastrophic "tryout" and
by his deft carpentry in one week turn it into a hit of
stupendous proportions!

It is true that Kaufman has only one play to his sole

credit—*The Butter and Egg Man*—and that he is interested in every phase of theatrical activity whether it involves work that is primarily creative or not. But he —and his collaborators—have twice won the Pulitzer Prize (for what it is worth); his plays cater to a very definite taste on the part of audiences, in New York and on the road; his formulas, his technique, and the success they have brought him are therefore clearly a matter of critical interest unless a critic is to limit himself, in sterile purism—to a thoroughly academic conception of "worth-while" drama.

As regards collaboration, we are not primarily concerned, here, in establishing which elements in each play are attributable to Kaufman himself and which to his collaborators. It is often humanly impossible to tell, since in the hurly-burly of rehearsals and last-minute revisions, cuts, and additions, creation becomes a matter of high-pressure collective invention, trial and error, and the hasty adaptation of other people's ideas!

Kaufman's name, therefore, may be taken as a kind of trade mark covering the work of several people, of whom one remains constant, from *Dulcy* to *You Can't Take It With You*. The first period of Kaufman's work can be dated roughly from 1921 to 1926, and called the Connelly period. During this time most of his plays were written with Marc Connelly, and those in which others had a hand or which he wrote alone show clear traces of Connelly's influence. They have a kindliness, a humanity, abundantly evident in Connelly's own plays, such as *The Wisdom Tooth*. They deal for the most part with the trials and tribulations of the "little man," the common American "man in the street" and his family; comedy centers around the follies and absurdities of an individual who is caricatured to the point of being a grotesque. That the pattern did not become mechanical is probably due to Connelly's special quality of humor, which is always touched with compassion.

In strong contrast is Kaufman's later sophisticated and "hard-boiled" vein, developed after he had severed literary connection with Connelly, in the Gershwin-Ryskind musical satires, and the alternate farce and melodrama of his work with Edna Ferber and Moss Hart. His name becomes synonymous with bitter acerbity of wit, brittleness, the surface glitter which comes from a preponderating emphasis on trivia and atmosphere rather than character. Beginning with *The Royal Family* Kaufman and his co-authors depend increasingly on glamorous subject matter (the stage, Hollywood, the world of politics), on sophisticated patter as a substitute for humor of character, and on the tempo and excitement inherent in the background of their plays, to sustain action and interest. The influence of moving-picture and musical-comedy technique is unmistakable. Kaufman was spending as much if not more of his time, in conjuring up those fabulous musical entertainments which set the style for a decade of showmanship—*Strike Up the Band, Animal Crackers, The Band Wagon, Of Thee I Sing*— as in writing legitimate drama, and it shows in the dramatic weakness of his more recent plays.

For years Kaufman showed a keen interest in social problems. This is an aspect of his work which has been too often overlooked. In *Beggar on Horseback* he wrote some of the most biting satire our stage has seen; *The Good Fellow* and *Merrily We Roll Along*, though widely dissimilar, both show concern for what is inconsistent and shoddy in our society, an interest which is never followed through. Most striking of all was a play called, successively, *Hot Pan* and *Eldorado*, which never came in to New York, and which failed as a play precisely because Kaufman was unable, or unwilling, to pursue his observations to their logical social conclusions.

This serious strain hardly seems compatible with Kaufman's reputation for glib and sophisticated comedy. The truth is that the two tendencies have been in perpetual conflict, and the slick and superficial writer in Kaufman has come out on top. There is no doubt that, like S. N. Behrman and Philip Barry and others, he is a casualty of the kind of existence to which a successful playwright is apt to succumb. Deprived of stimulating firsthand experience, varied contacts with a many-sided world, the best satiric talent loses its edge.

I

The first Kaufman-Connelly play was a "hit" of the 1921–22 season. The authors of *Dulcy* frankly acknowledged their indebtedness for their leading character to F. P. A.'s column on the New York Tribune editorial page. Dulcy is a broadly limned caricature of certain traits which have become identified with the feminine sex, chiefly because only a woman comfortably situated in the middle or upper class, who has never had to exert herself on her own behalf, could survive such witlessness. Because she is both energetic and ignorant, her passionate desire to be helpful, coupled with an utter lack of the rudiments of common sense, make her a social menace. Characters and situations alike are of the type best known as "stock"; in no case does motivation or action have the faintest resemblance to reality. As farce *Dulcy* is not unamusing, chiefly because the authors succeeded, to a surprising degree, in extracting humor from a most unlikely source: Dulcy's unfailing dullness. But despite the skill which such a feat attests, the humor of the play, because it is mechanically contrived, belongs essentially to the period in which it was created. Only comedy rooted in character survives the passage of time, and *Dulcy* today is badly dated.

Later in the same season the authors followed their sensational success with yet another, *To the Ladies*, a warmly human play which is not only comic but touching, and not without its fair share of irony at the expense of masculine delusions and complacency. Elsie Beebe has the utmost faith in her thoroughly commonplace husband. But her faith is tempered, unknown to him, by the knowledge that she is indispensable to him. Content to play ostensibly second fiddle, she nevertheless is the force that gives their life together some promise of security and success. From the moment when the curtain goes up and Leonard tussles with the laundry list, through the Kincaids' visit, the piano catastrophe, the struggle over the speech, and the banquet calamity in which Elsie wrests victory out of ruin, the contrast in character is skillfully built up by incidents in themselves dramatic and amusing. In the second-act banquet scene the play goes beyond comedy to furnish a magnificent travesty of American business as exemplified by the pompous paternalism of the small businessman and the vote-catching state senator who peddles his "few appropriate remarks" from one such gathering to another.

What emerges from *To the Ladies*, with all its humanity and charm, is the bounded horizon, the absorption in the minutiae of daily existence, of a class which is sufficiently above the margin of bare existence to be able to think something else. The comedy of the middle-class home reappears in several of Kaufman's plays: *Minick*, *The Good Fellow*, *June Moon*. But only in *Beggar on Horseback*, the work of Kaufman and Connelly, did the authors achieve real satire and enduring significance through understanding expressed in brilliantly imaginative treatment.

Minick, based on a short story of Edna Ferber's, is illuminating because the transformation which the character of old man Minick undergoes from the story to the play throws light on the basis of all Kaufman's comedy during this period of his work. In Miss Ferber's story Minick is an extremely likable old gentleman, with a touch of talkativeness but thoroughly shrewd and keen. Lacking companionship and understanding from his son and daughter-in-law, he makes friends with some old men he meets in the park, all thoroughly alert and intelligent, and eventually makes his home with them in an institution for the elderly. Dramatized, this conception would have made either a serious play or at least a comedy which used its wit to make a serious point, however lightly: the inevitable conflict between two generations, the tragedy of youth and age.

Instead, Kaufman and Miss Ferber demoted Minick to the level of a caricature. He becomes a tiresome old bore, garrulous, meddlesome, lacking all tact. The authors belittle him to the point of making him ridiculous; the play becomes a farce. The authors have missed the point, and consequently have written no more than farce where they might have achieved satire. This tendency to derive comedy from imbecility is the formula on which *Dulcy*, *To the Ladies*, *Merton of the Movies*, *The Butter and Egg Man*, and *June Moon* are all based. The comic emphasis is placed, not on real human weaknesses, or circumstances, or social contradictions, or even character as such, but on certain traits in one character exaggerated to the point of fiction.

A good instance in point is *Merton of the Movies*, the first of a long series of burlesques on Hollywood, of which more recent examples have been *Once in a Lifetime* and *Boy Meets Girl*. The chief theme of the play, however, is not so much the general confusion and folly of picture-making, although several scenes are devoted to a broad burlesque on the movie industry; instead it is the effect of the faked glamour and idealism with which high-powered publicity has invested Hollywood stars, on a high-strung, sentimental boy whose life in a country store is so dull that he transfers all his dreams and ambitions to the magic screen. Here is material for merciless satire; the effect of a false set of romantic ideals, built up to aid the commercial exploitation of a valuable commodity, on a mind which lack of sophistication renders an easy victim, is a theme worthy of Shaw at his best. But the authors throw away their opportunity by too closely following their original—a story by Harry Leon Wilson; they make Merton such a fool that it is impossible to blame his tribulations on anything but his own addlepatedness. He goes to Hollywood determined to crash into stardom, and his fantastic idealizations collide with an even more insane reality; he nearly starves to death, and loses faith in life. He is rescued by the Girl, who turns his delusions to his own and her advantage; Merton is hoaxed into playing in the comedies which he so deeply despises. The play degenerates into farce on the one hand, and sentimentality on the other: the Girl falls in love with Merton while she is taking

advantage of him. In the end he submits to his fate of
being a comedian despite himself, and the Girl's love
enfolds him, making amends for everything: a sadly inconclusive finale to a plot with the elements of penetrating satire.

In *The Good Fellow*, written with Herman Man-
kiewicz, it looked as if Kaufman were going to probe
more deeply into the same material he had skimmed in
To the Ladies. Jim Helton, a Wilkes-Barre real-estate
dealer, is first and foremost a loyal Corsican. Between
meetings, conventions, and the ordinary routine of
"lodge" affairs and sociability, he has little time left
for such minor concerns as his family and his business.
He climaxes his devotion to the order by undertaking to
raise a fund of ten thousand dollars to bring the next
convention of the Corsicans to Wilkes-Barre; he borrows
five thousand dollars on his life insurance, and gets the
other five thousand dollars from his daughter's suitor.
His exasperated family rebel when these dealings come
to light and force him to abjure further brotherly en-
tanglements and accept a business position that Ethel's
young man offers him—a weakly-contrived ending.

The Good Fellow depicts, with surprising veracity,
one aspect of American small-town life, not only its
humors but its less engaging side as well. There is nothing funny in the predicament of Mrs. Helton and Ethel,
condemned to a life of drudgery by the light-minded-
ness of the head of the family. By way of contrast, there
is Mrs. Kent, the Helton's old-maid relative, one of the
most devastating and acidulous of Kaufman's long succession of sardonic commentators. But the play goes no
farther than realism on the one hand and mockery on
the other; it never probes beyond phenomena to dis-

cover their cause. Why do Jim Helton and his cronies shirk their responsibilities for the sake of such fandango? What human instincts are so frustrated or warped by our middle-class life that they drive men to a fantastic game of make-believe ritual, "dressing-up" and a whole artificial set of obligations which bear no conceivable relation to their real lives? Kaufman and Manciewicz show us the ridiculous trappings and procedure of a Corsican gathering; they give us a hint of what Jim Helton is looking for—("Big times, prominence for all," he says, of the convention's coming to Wilkes-Barre). But the canvas is small, the dilemma particular and personal. This is due in good part to the characterization of Helton, a superficial comic character into whose social and psychological reactions as a human being the authors never inquire. He is just another Kaufman sap.

In *Beggar on Horseback*, on the other hand, Kaufman and Connelly produced an outstanding commentary on our civilization. Its theatrical distinction is enhanced by its discerning appraisal of what is commonplace, opportunistic, and shoddy in our culture and in the goals of achievement which a large portion of our society has set itself. The original of the play is a short German comedy, *Hans Sonnenstössers Höllenfahrt*, by Paul Apel; Winthrop Ames saw the possibilities in an adaptation of Apel's play and called in Connelly and Kaufman. They took the original idea, which is no more than a brief skit on the artist's distaste for bourgeois family life, and elaborated it into a wholesale indictment of American materialism.

Neil McRae, a talented young composer, ekes out a bare living by making orchestral arrangements of popular music. His friends Albert Price and Cynthia Mason feel that Neil's only chance of saving his health and doing the work he cares about is to marry Gladys Cady, daughter of a prosperous businessman, who is already angling for him. After a tea party with the Cadys, Neil takes some pills Albert has given him to quiet his over-tautened nerves, and falls heavily asleep. He dreams a fantastic dream: he marries Gladys—a nightmare wedding in a railroad station; he meets the Cadys' relatives and friends at a reception, at which phalanxes of butlers rush in and out; he enters Cady's business, and attends a board of directors' meeting; he goes with Gladys to a restaurant; finally home life with the Cadys harries him to such a point that he murders the entire family. In the second act he stands trial in a court where the Cadys figure as magistrate, witnesses, and attendants; he wants to present as evidence in his own defense the symphony on which he has been working, but Gladys has torn it up and instead he offers the pantomime on which he was working with Cynthia before he married Gladys. Condemned nevertheless, Neil begins to serve a life sentence in the Cady Consolidated Art Factory, where he grinds out popular songs. Only death can free him, he discovers, so he chooses death, and having submitted to an execution, wakes up. His nightmare has resolved his doubts; he breaks with Gladys, and marries Cynthia.

A bare outline of the proceedings can do little justice to *Beggar on Horseback*. It cannot give any idea of the high imaginative level to which stylization of dialogue, movement, costuming, and scenic design raise the entire conception. For satiric effectiveness, there is no comparison between such a treatment and the usual farcical bent to which Kaufman and his collaborators are addicted.

Symbolism is used to show the artist's loss of integrity when he adopts a way of life based, not on achievement, but on material standards of comfort and success:

CADY

You know your sentence, don't you? You've got to work our way till you die.

NEIL (Dully)

Yes. I know.

CADY

We own you now. The family owns you.
(He falls into rhythmic measure)

You take our money and you live our life,
    We own you, we own you.
You take our money and you live our life,
    We own you, we own you.
You take our money and you live our way,
    We pay the piper and we tell him what to play.
You sold your soul and you can't get away,
    We own you, we own you.

But since his sentence is only a life-sentence, Neil can escape by dying.

NEIL

I can die! You can't keep me from it! That's how I can get away from you! Open the door! Open the door! (He shakes the door of his cage. It opens) It was never locked!

The artist is not always the prisoner of circumstance which he imagines himself to be. The loss of integrity is a definite act of choice.

No realistic transcript of the turmoil of a great business office could convey the reality half as effectively as the nonsense Neil hears and encounters as he wanders around the Cady establishment. He tries to get a pencil:

MISS HEY

Of course you've filled out a requisition?

NEIL

No—I haven't. A piece of paper, isn't it?

(*She hands him a tremendous sheet of paper. It is about twenty inches by thirty inches*)

What I want is a pencil. There's a place for that to be put in, I suppose?

MISS HEY (*Wearily*)

Yes—where it says "The undersigned wishes a pencil to do some work with." How old are you?

NEIL

Thirty-two.

MISS HEY (*Taking the paper away*)

That's the wrong form.

(*She gives him another—a blue one this time*)

Parents living?

NEIL

No.

MISS HEY

When did you have your last pencil?

NEIL

I didn't have any.

MISS HEY

Did you have any before that?

NEIL

I don't think I ever had any.
   (*He indicates the form*)
Is that all right?

MISS HEY

It isn't as regular as we like, but I guess it will do.

NEIL

What do I do now? Go to someone else, don't I?

MISS HEY

Oh, yes. Sometimes you travel for days.

NEIL

Are we all crazy?

MISS HEY

Yes.
   (*She resumes typing*)
You might try Room E—right down the corridor.

   (*In another room Neil approaches Miss You, likewise at a typewriter.*)

NEIL

Is this room E?

MISS YOU (*Mechanically*)

Did you have an appointment?

NEIL

No—you don't understand. I'm trying to get a pencil.

MISS YOU

Well, what do you want to see him about?

NEIL (*Handing over the requisition*)

MISS YOU

Oh.

(*Looks at it*)

Mr. Bippy! The man is here to see about getting a pencil or something.

NEIL

It *is* a pencil.

MISS YOU

Did you see Mr. Schlink?

NEIL

Yes.

MISS YOU

Mr. Woodge?

NEIL

Yes.

MISS YOU

Mr. Meglup?

NEIL

Yes.

MISS YOU

What did *they* say?

NEIL

Why, they seemed to think it would be all right.

MISS YOU (*Calls again*)

Oh, Mr. Bippy!

(*To Neil*)

Belong to the Employes' Mutual Mutual?

NEIL

Oh, yes.

MISS YOU

Cady Gold and Building Fund?

NEIL

Yes.

MISS YOU

Well, all right.

(*She stamps the requisition with an elaborate
machine, which rings a bell as it works. She hands
the paper back to Neil*)

NEIL

Oh, thanks. Do I get a pencil now?

MISS YOU

Oh, no! It has to be O.K.'d by the President. All
requisitions have to be O.K.'d by the President.

NEIL

Is he around here some place?

MISS YOU

Oh, no! He's in a big office. Just keep going till
you find a great big office.

NEIL

Where?

MISS YOU

Oh, somewhere in the new building.

(*She calls*)

Mr. Bippy!

Cady, on the telephone (which is strapped to his
chest), in the midst of the reception for the newlyweds,
talks business:

CADY

Yep! Yep! Hullo! Well, I'll tell you what to do!
Sell eighteen holes and buy all the water hazards.
Yep! Yep! Hullo! Well, I'll tell you what to do!
I expect caddies will go up any time now. How's
the eighth hole this morning? Uh-huh. Well, sell
it in three. Yes, sir. That's fine. Yep! Yep! Hullo!
Well, I'll tell you what to do! Buy—

Only the long-drawn-out trial scene falls below the
rest in interest, because it is not related to any immediate
problem that we have seen Neil wrestling with. Its intent is therefore not clear; we do not see just what the
authors are mocking in this scene. By contrast the office,
restaurant, wedding-reception, and factory-prison episodes are crystal clear in their implications. There is no
evading their brilliant irony. Nothing else that Kaufman
has had a hand in can compare with *Beggar on Horseback* for intellectual and imaginative distinction.

II

Kaufman has always had a particular fondness for the
life of the theatre itself; it is a theme which recurs repeatedly in his plays. In *The Butter and Egg Man*, written in 1924, he first began to develop what became a
characteristic technique, combining terrific pace with
the most realistic and minute detail, a combination to
which the show business, with its frantic tempo, pro-
verbial confusion, and the self-conscious and dramatic
theatrical temperament, lends itself very well. *The
Butter and Egg Man* was the first of a highly successful
series of comedies that included *The Royal Family, June
Moon, Once in a Lifetime,* and *Stage Door.*

The Royal Family, written with Edna Ferber in 1927, ushered in the second period of Kaufman's development. From now on the scale of the plays is consistently enlarged; they become panoramic in scope, huge casts populate the stage. The milieu changes from the middle-class home to a background of wealth, modishness, and sensation, the tone becomes more artificial, more cynical. In dramatic structure and in tone, the influence of the musical-comedy gentry makes itself felt. The change, however, is gradual. The Royal Family is still warm and full of gusto. It exemplifies the unfailing spirit and affection with which Kaufman always writes of the stage. The play is a genre study in lunacy; it deals with the tumultuous vagaries of a theatrical family, the Cavendishes, three generations of which are shown in simultaneous and stormy activity. With unequaled dexterity the authors juggle the various threads of action and keep half a dozen characters and situations developing simultaneously, not always in successive scenes but often on the stage at the same time. Climaxes, exits, and entrances, "laugh" lines, off-stage upheavals, are handled with an unfailing knowledge of stagecraft. As an example of playwrighting carefully adjusted to the practical needs of a stage production, The Royal Family has few equals.

Although perhaps outside the boundaries of legitimate drama, Kaufman's contributions in the musical field cannot be overlooked. Among the many shows in which he has had a hand, three at least stand out as landmarks. Strike Up the Band, written with Morrie Ryskind in 1930, was a novel departure in musical comedy because it was written around an idea; although its satire of war was halting and diffuse, it was nevertheless a long step ahead of the inanities previously in vogue. *The Band Wagon*, the joint work of Kaufman and Howard Dietz in 1932, proved that a revue need not confine itself to stupid display and dirty jokes in order to be successful; the wit, irony, and beauty of its sketches and musical numbers inaugurated a new era in musical revues. And *Of Thee I Sing*, again a collaboration with Ryskind, as the first musical satire of the American scene, opened the door to a wealth of new material of which the musical stage was sadly in need.

By present satirical standards *Of Thee I Sing* is not very barbed, and in comparison with *The Cradle Will Rock* it is mere milk toast, but its historical importance cannot be underestimated. It is certainly the forerunner of Blitzstein's savage caricature, and it gave the theatre in general a vigorous shot in the arm. Its ridicule of Supreme Court sanctity, of the witless and undifferentiated idiocy of party conventions and platforms and election campaigns, and the figures of Alexander Throttlebottom and the stuffed-shirt legislators are enduringly comic. In fact, it is a pity that more people do not realize the appalling realism of such episodes as the senatorial debate over Jenny, Paul Revere's horse!

But *Of Thee I Sing* lacks the penetration and grasp of reality which informs such satire as *Beggar on Horseback* before it, or *The Cradle Will Rock* since. The results of such a lack of orientation are even more apparent in the sequel which the authors attempted in *Let 'Em Eat Cake*, in which they leave the rails altogether. *Let 'Em Eat Cake* trod on dangerous ground by trying to get right down to cases: depression, unemployment, revolution and demagogy, and ended up with the authors' making quite as much sport of anyone bent on a thoroughgoing

job of straightening things out as of the fossilized members of the Union League Club. Everybody is a fool but
no one more so than Kruger, the "agitator";

> ——no matter who gets in, my job is to get him out
> of there. And there's only one thing that can ever
> stick me——If I ever get in *myself*—good-night!

Seen in relation to the events it "kidded" and the audience to which it played, *Let 'Em Eat Cake* illuminates
the dilemma in which Kaufman's taste for social questions and his penchant for sacrificing anything for a laugh
place him.

Once in a Lifetime marked the first collaboration between Kaufman and Moss Hart. Kaufman has said that
this uproarious satire on Hollywood is more than two-
thirds Hart's. Whatever the case may be, the authors
have certainly concocted between them one of the most
excruciatingly funny plays of our day. What raises it
high above the level of casual folly is the idea around
which the play centers. They have not only burlesqued
the insanity which is the byword of Hollywood, but have
focused that insanity at a particular moment which furnishes them with an inherently dramatic situation: the
advent of the "talkies." Before the coming of the Vitaphone, nothing counted in Hollywood but looks: an
actor's voice, accent, and vocabulary were irrelevant. But
the Vitaphone destroyed all reputations, all security,
overnight. Stars and extras jittered together; producers'
ideas of what the public wanted and didn't want were
annihilated; all precedents were demolished. As far as
preconceived notions went, the motion-picture industry
had to start again from scratch.

Into this chaos the authors introduce Jerry, May, and

George, with their idea of a school for voice and speech training. In their rise and fall is mirrored the fantastic processes of an industry in which caprice and mood are the governing principles. The trio are taken up by the producer Glogauer—"the man who first turned down Vitaphone, so he buys everything now!" One fine day when everything appears to be going well, they discover that a painter is taking their names off the doors of their office; it is their first intimation that they are fired. Being a congenital moron—he is another typical Kaufman "sap"—George is unable to say anything but the truth; he therefore tells Glogauer candidly what he thinks of him. Glogauer, confronted for the first time with a man who is not afraid to contradict him, declares that George is a genius and puts him in charge of all motion-picture productions on the Glogauer lot. Eventually George is discovered to have made the wrong picture and demoted as suddenly as he was elevated, Glogauer crying: "Never in my life have I known such a thing! After this I make a ruling—every scenario we produce, somebody has got to read it!" However the picture turns out to be the hit of the year, so George and his cronies are restored to favor, only to have their fortunes jeopardized afresh when George heedlessly buys two thousand airplanes. When it turns out that he has created a monopoly and caused a terrific demand for airplane pictures he is again established as a genius, and once more reinstated!

For two insane acts there is hardly a break in the hilarity. The second act probably contains more variegated insanity than was ever compressed into a similar length of time on the stage before. Remembering the plaints of writers who have been imported at enormous salaries from New York and London to write for the pictures, only to spend months in enforced idleness without an assignment, Kaufman and Hart show the convulsive efforts of Lawrence Vail, a successful dramatist fresh from Broadway, to get some attention—above all, some work. For three months he has been drawing a fabulous weekly check; for three months he has been trying without success to see someone in authority. After a final despairing bout with Glogauer's secretary, Miss Leighton, he goes berserk, and rushes out of the room consigning the motion-picture industry to perdition. Thereupon a high-powered lady columnist hurries in to ask whether Miss Leighton knows anything of the whereabouts of a missing author, by the name of Lawrence Vail:

HELEN

From New York. He's supposed to have come here a long time ago, and nothing's been heard of him. He seems to have just disappeared.

MISS LEIGHTON

Why, isn't that terrible! Have you tried Paramount?

HELEN

No, he's not at Paramount. They've lost six playwrights of their own, during the past month. Once they get out of their rooms nobody knows what becomes of them. You'd think they'd lock the doors, wouldn't you?

MISS LEIGHTON

Yes—that's what we do. (*Looks through a stack of cards*) Lawrence Vail. I'm sure he isn't one of our playwrights, because if he was I'd be sure to——

(*Finds the card*) Well, isn't that strange? He *is* one of our playwrights——he came out here on October 18——he was one of a shipment of sixteen playwrights.

HELEN

(*Reading card*) "Dark hair, brown eyes"——

MISS LEIGHTON

Suppose I look in the playwrights' room. Maybe he's there.——Though I hate to go into the play-wrights' room. It always scares me—those padded walls, and the bars over the windows.

If the third act sags below the level of the preceding two, it is because the authors have failed to construct a plot which could maintain the requisite tension and sus-pense for three acts. Farces depend more on incident than on sustained development of a plot; very few suc-ceed in maintaining interest on the outcome of a story as well as on the hilarity of successive episodes up to the final curtain (as did *Three Men on a Horse*).

The charges of superficiality and insincerity which are frequently leveled at Kaufman are based in large part on his attitude towards Hollywood. He has written, his critics point out, three plays—*Merton of the Movies, Once in a Lifetime,* and *Stage Door*—which mercilessly ridicule the motion-picture industry. Kaufman and Moss Hart put a damning indictment into the mouth of Lawrence Vail in *Once in a Lifetime:*

> I think Hollywood and this darling industry of yours is the most God-awful thing I've ever run into. Everybody behaving in the most fantastic fashion— nobody acting like a human being.——Thousands

of dollars thrown away every day. Why do they do that, do you know?——Plenty of good minds come out here. Why aren't they used? Why must everything be dressed up in this goddam hokum?

Yet for all his vituperating, Kaufman continues to reap a substantial income from pictures. Is this, his critics ask, integrity?

The truth is that large numbers of the highly salaried specialists who make their living from Hollywood— writers, actors, and directors—have little more respect for the hand that feeds them than Kaufman. In general, the intelligent man or woman who pursues a career which furnishes them with a substantial living, and which they can also respect, is today an exception rather than the rule. The commercial theatre, journalism, politics, advertising, education, and business are all filled with people who either view their work with outright distaste, or else enjoy it without much conviction of its social or ethical value, and innumerable social critics and writers have seen in such a state of affairs evidence of the moral decay of our civilization. In Kaufman's case, the mockery of Hollywood in *Once in a Lifetime* is only one aspect of a cynicism which manifested itself more clearly in his next two plays.

Nor is the absence of any belief whatever, which emerges from *Dinner at Eight* and *Merrily We Roll Along*, confined to Kaufman alone among our present-day writers. While upper- and middle-class America to a great extent still accept the attainment of wealth, position, and refinement as the be-all and end-all of life, the writer of today—if he is endowed with any degree of insight—has come face to face with the emptiness of the

old symbols of success. If he has no new ones to put
in their place, he is confronted with a terrifying dilemma.
His sense of values prevents him from according any
great degree of pity to the victims of empty self-delu-
sions; on the other hand, his thralldom to a set of standards and ideals which he cannot respect, but which he
has not the courage to abjure nor the vision to transcend,
robs him of any hope. He can only contemplate and
describe, with profound cynicism, a society he is unable
either to respect or to abandon.

Dinner at Eight shows, with complete openness, the
tragedy, the disillusionment, the decadence and vanity
and brutality at work, like blind worms, behind the brilliant façade of wealth and sophistication. Every character with a shred of decency is miserably defeated:
Oliver Jordan, in business, in health, even in his relationship to his family (his marriage is a social conveni-
ence, his child a stranger to him); Paula Jordan in her
love for Renault; Lucy Talbot in her marriage; even
Dora, the little maid, in her bid for happiness. (Cul-
minating irony, Millicent Jordan, whose life is a society
game, is thwarted in her ambition to give a party which
shall be the last word in distinction, according to her
standards, by the Fernsworths' desertion and Renault's
absence.) It is only the Packards, Carlotta Vance, and
Millicent, who emerge unscathed.

The futility, emptiness, and self-interest which go
with a certain degree of social decay and wealth have
never been more damningly depicted. Yet something
is missing from this picture of corruption—a sense of
outrage, a scale of values, a point of view. Ralph Fox,
young English biographer and critic, has written of the
art of fiction (and it applies no less to that of the drama):

"Novel-writing is a philosophical occupation. The great novels of the world: *Don Quixote, Gargantua and Pantagruel, Robinson Crusoe, Jonathan Wilde, Jacques Le fataliste, Le Rouge et Le noir, War and Peace, L'Education sentimentale, Wuthering Heights, The Way of All Flesh,* are great precisely because they have this quality of thought behind them, because they are highly imaginative, inspired—if you like—commentaries on life. It is this quality which distinguishes the first-rate from the second-rate in fiction. It is true that there are philosophers who have lamentably failed to write novels, but no novelist has ever been able to create without that ability for generalization about his characters which is the result of a philosophical attitude to life." [3]

It is precisely this "philosophical attitude to life," this "quality of thought," which is lacking in *Dinner at Eight.* Its melodrama is essentially of the tabloid variety —superficial, sensational, shoddy. The intrigues, the suicide, the love affairs, are calculated to titillate a sensation-hungry audience, not to provoke it to reflection, in the same way that "yellow journalism" provides exclusive society scandal for the dreariest working girl to share and quiver over. The authors are neither shocked at the frivolity and the decadence of the society which they portray, nor particularly concerned with or hopeful of its betterment. They write without anger and without hope; they lack any belief which might give *Dinner at Eight* the *positive* quality which ruthless critics—Fielding, Molière, Ibsen, Tolstoi—have been able to extract from an examination of the most decadent societies.

Merrily We Roll Along, written with Moss Hart, tells its story backwards; beginning at the height of Richard

[3] Ralph Fox, *The Novel and the People,* International Publishers, 1937.

Niles' success and bitter disillusionment, it shows, step
by step, how his professional advance has been won at
the cost of artistic and personal integrity. In the last
scene he stands on the threshold of mature life, an
idealistic college graduate.

As in *Dinner at Eight*, artifice is substituted for analysis. *Merrily We Roll Along* has been brilliantly dis-
sected by John Howard Lawson.[4] He points out that the
method of telling the story backwards, which has been
criticized as a "trick," is actually that best suited to the
authors' purpose, which was to present an ironic retro-
spection over the years since the World War, and the
disintegration of a man. What makes the play inherently false and superficial, according to Lawson, is not
this technique, but the authors' point of view, and consequently the use they make of the technique.

The fault lies in the authors' evasion of real analysis, and their substitution for it of what Lawson calls
"shock." Whenever a scene progresses to the point
where an examination of the causes and forces which
govern the characters might *begin*, they bring down the
curtain by an incident which is in itself effective—the
iodine-throwing, Niles' attack on Crale, the suicide of
Althea's husband—but which cuts short any deeper
understanding of the motivation. The result is irony and
theatricality, but never anything more than the most
superficial melodrama. By sacrificing the fundamental
line of the play, which is character analysis, for incident for its own sake, the authors throw away their
chance of writing a devastating indictment of social decay, and achieve nothing better than cheap sensation.

If we analyze its "tragedy," we find that Kaufman and

4 *Theory and Technique of Playwriting*, G. P. Putnam's Sons, 1936.

Hart are waxing eloquent over the disillusionment of successful mediocrity. The actual degree of Richard Niles' original idealism and talent, which is of extreme importance to the validity of the play, is a matter of hearsay. There is nothing in the play except Jonathan Crale's faith in him, and Julia Glenn's infatuation, to indicate that there was anything unusual about Niles to begin with. As Lawson points out, "We never see Niles express his idealism in conduct, we have no way of knowing what sort of conduct it would involve." It is here that the "backward" method of telling their story serves the authors in good stead, for it effectively masks such an omission, which would be glaringly apparent if the play were written in the usual order of time. The novelty of the treatment covers all gaps, at least for the duration of the performance, and momentarily exempts the authors from the inevitable why? Obviously the reasons lie in Niles' desire for wealth and success, the domination of an opportunistic woman, etc., but to dismiss causation this lightly is to think only in clichés, and this superficiality is clearly reflected in the writing. The dialogue is the merest patter, brittle and meaningless, with the exception of the one scene between Crale and Niles in which Crale calls the playwright to account for his surrender, and which stands out from the rest of the play because the authors have something to say and hence write with fire and style.

III

Merrily We Roll Along was Kaufman's second excursion into serious drama. Since then he has been chiefly concerned with the lighter side of life. Two of his plays are comedies which invoke the charm of irresponsibility;

in both the sole axiom of conduct is, "I like it"; both are far below the level of his earlier brand of hilarity. *First Lady*, written with Katherine Dayton, is a satire on the role of Washington society in national politics. The conception is inferior to Maxwell Anderson's *Both Your Houses*, which indicated the piracy of politics, a sounder idea than reducing it to a parlor game. The humor of *First Lady* arises from Lucy Wayne's engaging habit of saying whatever comes into her head, and getting away with it. In *You Can't Take It With You* the keynote is again irresponsibility; the benign Grandfather Vanderhof and his erratic family turn their backs on the turmoil of life and substitute their own private brand of turmoil and enjoyment in its place. Whenever matters begin to drag (which is not infrequently, because the plot is hackneyed, the situations threadbare and the love scenes long and trite), Kaufman and Hart produce a new eccentricity for some member of the family. Thus the Vanderhofs busy themselves with playwriting, manufacturing fireworks, toe dancing, candymaking, playing the xylophone, painting, printing, dartthrowing, pet snakes, and evading the income tax ("because I don't believe in it").

This latest of Kaufman's plays is also a kind of reversion. It represents an attempt to return to an earlier, kindlier genre—to the humors of domesticity, the kindliness of family relationships—on a comfortable income. What was most noteworthy about *You Can't Take It With You* was the way audiences enjoyed its extraordinary triteness. There is hardly a situation or device which is not a long-tried adjunct of vaudeville humor, and its bromidic philosophy is very nearly incredible, even in jest. Having walked sanely and not unsuccess-

fully along the straight and narrow path of business for
a good many years, Grandpa Vanderhof suddenly decided one morning that it wasn't worth the effort, and
retired to enjoy life on a modest but dependable income.
Says Grandpa:

> The world's not so crazy. It's the people in it. Life's
> pretty simple if you just relax.

KOHLENKOV
How can you relax in times like these?

GRANDPA
Well, if they'd relax there wouldn't be times like
these. That's just my point. Life is simple and kind
of beautiful if you just let it come to you. But the
trouble is, people forget that. I know I did. I was
right in the thick of it—fighting and scratching and
clawing. Regular jungle. One day it just kind of
struck me. I wasn't having any fun.

KOHLENKOV
So you did what?

GRANDPA
Just relaxed. Thirty-five years ago, that was. And
I've been a happy man ever since.

Of course, from one point of view this is sane philosophy—debunking the pursuit of wealth for its own sake,
the insane helter-skelter of business; the same idea is
developed in Meteor and Holiday. On the other hand,
the effect is to identify the "fighting and scratching and
clawing" of "the jungle" with the insensate competition
of high finance alone, to make it something which any
sensible human being who would be content with a

modest income could step out of in a moment if he only had the good sense to. It puts the blame for life's not being "simple and kind of beautiful if you just let it come to you" on the people who foolishly lose sight of that principle, and consequently don't have any "fun." The audience "relaxes" in a delightfully mellow mood —because life is made so simple, and its tragedies are shown to be only errors in good judgment as to what is and what is not the good life. All of which amounts to a gigantic distortion of the difficulties which do eat at the majority of people's lives and keep them from "relaxing."

It must be pointed out how often the humor itself contains implications which are undeniably serious, not to say unfortunate. One cannot keep comedy in a vacuum. Inevitably it is related, in origin and effect, to the social attitudes which an audience brings with it. For instance, one of the craziest and funniest things about the Vanderhofs, according to the authors, is their charmingly egalitarian treatment of their Negro servants; the servants themselves are distinguished by their nonchalance and pertness. Inevitably these qualities become identified with, and serve to reinforce, the ideas prevailing in the minds of the audience regarding the slovenliness and irresponsibility of the Negro race, prejudices which owe their origin, not to any reality, but to an endless succession of slandering caricatures on stage and screen, in literature and song.

Stage Door is a joint reversion, on the part of Mr. Kaufman and Miss Ferber, to their old love, the theatre. Terry Randall perseveres in her ambition to be an actress in the face of every obstacle and discouragement; she refuses dazzling offers of luxury and advancement in Hollywood in order to work six days a week behind a counter at Macy's and tramp around agents' and producers' offices during her lunch hour. The other denizens of the Footlights' Club, where the scene is laid, have their fair share of failure, disappointment, and stark tragedy. *Stage Door* not only shows the less glamorous aspects of theatrical life for young actresses, but is the most appealing human document Kaufman has produced since his days with Marc Connelly.

But because in *Stage Door* Miss Ferber and Mr. Kaufman do occasionally eschew the hard-boiled and the brittle in favor of humanity and compassion, they lay themselves open to further criticism. With only two exceptions—Terry and the girl who kills herself—the dozen and a half girls who come and go throughout the play are the merest stencils. This is most apparent in the cases of the rebels and failures. One and all are drawn with a single purpose—to get laughs. Again, the radical young playwright who "sells out" to Hollywood is an obvious caricature. Kaye Hamilton and Terry are different; they provide the "serious contrast," and have immediacy and poignancy. But Kaye is only one episode of many. Her heartbreaking confession to Terry in their bedroom makes extraordinarily little impression on the latter, and her suicide comes as a climax to Act II, Scene 1, nothing more. Neither Kaye nor her tragic fate is referred to again throughout the play, and structurally they disappear in a welter of exits, entrances, and gags, without lasting impression or significance.

But the most significant weakness of *Stage Door*—and one which perpetuates a widely accepted fallacy—is the distinction which it draws between the stage and the moving pictures. Terry clings to her ideal of a stage

career at any cost because acting in the moving pictures
"isn't acting, it's piece-work. You're not a human being,
you're something in a vacuum.——They put it in a can
—like Campbell's soup. And if you die the next day it
doesn't matter a bit. You don't have to be alive to act
in pictures."

By these standards Beethoven's Violin Concerto
played by Szigeti and the New York Philharmonic on a
gramophone recording is not art, but when heard in
Carnegie Hall it is. The fact that cinema is printed on a
film and preserved from the ravages of time and climate
in a metal container does not affect its quality as art,
any more than a living performance is insured against
being unutterable tripe. The Renaissance painters
painted on canvas with oils; the actor paints with his
voice and body on a sensitized film. The real issue is
cinema as an art versus Hollywood as a business. In the
real-estate and business-ridden Broadway theatre a production like *Yellow Jack* or Maurice Evans' *Richard II*
is not the rule but a triumphant exception. There are
cinematic performances such as those in *The Passion of
Joan of Arc* or *Poil de Carotte*, the poor working class
mother in *Der Kampf* or the Mongol in *Storm over Asia*,
which rank with anything ever done on the stage. And
the cinema has the inestimable advantage of being able
not only to create art but perpetuate it for all time,
whereas the theatre can create at most a legend, such as
Mrs. Siddons, or Burbage, or Duse.

IV

Reference has already been made to a memorable
scene in an otherwise undistinguished play, *Merrily We
Roll Along*. It is a scene which should be stamped on

the memory of every writer and indeed of every creative artist. Jonathan Crale, whose personal integrity extends to his painting, upraids the playwright Richard Niles for the compromises he has made in the name of success; his last play is of a piece with the rest:

CRALE

You know how I feel about those plays. I liked it; I laughed. And by the time I got to Broadway and 45th Street I'd forgotten all about it. It's a carbon copy of the other two you wrote. This year's model.

NILES

(Good humoredly) Well, a lot of people don't agree with you.

CRALE

Oh, I know it's a hit. But what are you going to do? Keep on writing those things? You're better than that, Richard. My God, you wrote a fine play once.

RICHARD

All right, and what happened to it? Two weeks at the Provincetown Playhouse.

CRALE

Yes, and you were better off then with a failure than you are now with a hit, whichever way you look at it.

RICHARD

So, that's the new argument, eh? If it's a hit it isn't a good play. It's wrong to be successful. You've got to starve to death and write plays for a little art theatre that nobody comes to see.

CRALE

I don't mean that. You know what I mean.

NILES

All right. What do you mean?

CRALE

I mean—all this. (*A wave of the hand that takes in all the room*)——The whole life you're leading now. The people around you. It's doing something to you. You're not the same Richard I used to know.

RICHARD

Why? Because I don't eat in those bum restaurants and don't have to worry about where my next dollar's coming from?

CRALE

Yes—among other reasons. You're getting away from the guts of things into a whole mess of polite *nothing.* And that's what your play's about. Why, I used to come into the studio and find you bubbling over with ideas, good juicy ones. And in the past year all I've heard you talk about is how much the play grossed, and what you got for the movie rights, and you met Noel Coward.

NILES

All right—now let me tell you something. I *like* my life the way it is, now. I like meeting Noel Coward and I enjoy being successful. I'm enjoying myself for the first time. I had plenty of the other thing—all those years with Helen. Working in a shoe store all day and writing that fine play at night. And what for? So that you and Julia could tell me how great I was?   I don't see myself writing plays for two people, and being miserable the rest of the time. Why has that got to be part of it? Why do you have to be poor to write a fine play?

CRALE

Because when you're rich you never write it. That's why.

RICHARD

I don't want to be rich, Jonny. But give me a chance. Give me a chance to get a little money in the bank and I'll write you a fine play. I'll write you the finest play that ever closed in a week.

CRALE

No, you won't. The longer you wait the tougher it gets. It's like a man saying he's going to take up reading when he's forty. You start reading at ten or you don't read at all. Besides, the trouble with the plays you're doing is you don't dare stop. You've got to write one a year or they'll forget you ever wrote a line. But you write one good play and they'll always know who you are. If I paint one good picture they'll remember me.

RICHARD

But I'm not like you, Jonny. That's the answer to the whole thing. I'm not like you!

CRALE

But you are, Richard. I know you too well for you to tell me that. You are, but you won't be if you go on living this way, getting in deeper and deeper with these people.——I get my fun in front of an easel, and it's the only fun I'm entitled to. And that's

where you ought to get yours—in front of a typewriter. I don't know whether you ever get any re-
ward for it, but I do know this: you've only got so
many good years, and when they're gone—and that
may come sooner than you think, Richard—if you
haven't made use of them it's very tough. Because
then you've got nothing.

Here for a few moments, Kaufman and Moss Hart are
close to "the guts of things." The dilemma between the
playwright's compulsion, artistic and financial, to write
plays that people will come to see, and the effort to
preserve his integrity in the face of success, is basic, under
our existing system, for every artist. What is important
is that this scene clearly indicates that the tragedy of
Merrily We Roll Along is not the career of Richard
Niles, or of the modern playwright in general, but of
Kaufman himself. Again and again he has posed significant questions, only to swerve away "into a whole mess
of polite nothing." In *Merrily We Roll Along* he points
a finger squarely at himself, and then side-steps, with the
plea—"I like my life—I enjoy being successful—I am
not like the Jonathan Crales of this world." Coming
from the author of *Beggar on Horseback* and *Once in a
Lifetime*, the answer is not good enough. He has given
too much evidence of being capable of the best.

2 GEORGE KELLY

Since 1927, our genre of comedy has been undergoing a change. The emphasis is less and less on character, and increasingly on brilliance of conversation—a flippant dialogue which reveals, not individual character, but the mental clichés of a social class and a generation. We have seen the transformation take place in the work of Sidney Howard and George Kaufman; it is also vividly shown in the contrast between George Kelly, who wrote his last good play in 1928, and the new generation of dramatists as personified in the work of Robert Sherwood, who made his first appearance with *The Road to Rome* in 1928.

Like the earlier Sidney Howard, George Kelly has excelled in the painstaking, often slow-moving study of character, set in a kind of dramatic still life. The action in *The Show-Off* and *Daisy Mayme* is desultory. Instead, the talk is so real, so untheatrical that one seems to be actually listening to the conversation of a typical American family at supper with the fourth wall miraculously removed. The discussion revolves around a box of candy, cigarettes, the playing of a piano, a dusty detour by motor, an item of domestic routine. It is no part of Kelly's technique to condense or imply; his characters indulge in no mental or verbal short cuts. The result is a degree of realism overwhelming in its intensity, achieving its theatrical effect through sheer cumulative reiteration, rarely explicit in its point of view but undeniable in its implications.

Like Sidney Howard, Kelly is interested in the types which people the American scene, usually types which he can satirize by the very ferocity of his realism: Mrs. Pampinello, Aubrey Piper, Mrs. Fenner, and—outstanding example of his method—Harriet Craig. At first glance seemingly exaggerated, we soon recognize in all of them both the generality and the individual. More, they contain within themselves all the frustration and consequent sentimentality, the resentment and pettiness, which boil under the surface of our middle-class life. No other dramatist of his period has caught this phenomenon as consistently as George Kelly.

His first full-length play in 1923, after writing, directing, and playing in a number of one-act plays on the vaudeville circuit, was The Torchbearers, still one of the best-known American comedies. This uproarious farce ridicules the complacence and pretentiousness of a group of amateur actors and their pompous director. Its fun at the expense of their acting is perfectly good-tempered; it is their pretense of doing so much more than just amusing themselves, their avowed mission of carrying the torch of culture among the Philistines, which Kelly satirizes so keenly.

The Torchbearers is essentially an acting play. Much

of the comedy arises from "business" and pantomime which the script can only indicate, both in the farcical rehearsal at Paula Ritter's house and in the backstage view of the performance at the Horicultural Hall ("Hutchy-Kutchy!"). The lines are invariably commonplace; Kelly never obtrudes his own brilliance at the expense of the consistency of his characters, and this alone distinguishes him from such writers as S. N. Behrman and Philip Barry.

Lacking the impetus afforded by the sheer idiocy of the episodes in *The Torchbearers*, *The Show-Off* depends solely on the interest aroused by the character of Aubrey Piper. He is a superb study in pompousness and braggadocio, and because there is no malice in him the playwright is able to enlist the audience's liking so that his vagaries become comic rather than unpleasant; its interest is sustained by sympathy, a fortunate circumstance in view of the play's haphazardness, for of plot there is next to none.

But with *Craig's Wife*, Kelly took off his gloves and wrote one of the most devastating and effective plays of the decade. In it he shows how tragedy inevitably overtakes a woman whose sense of values has become so corrupted that she sacrifices everything to material security. For Harriet Craig the symbol of this security is her home. In a first act which escapes tediousness only because of the dramatist's consummate skill (for there is little action), Harriet's character is revealed through her conflict with her husband's aunt. In the second act her husband himself suddenly (and yet believably) recognizes her sordiness and selfishness, when suspicion of a friend's violent death rests on him for an instant, and Harriet can think only of herself and his reputation. In a brief but overwhelming final act everyone leaves her—husband, niece, aunt, and servants—and she is left alone with the fetish to which she has sacrificed every human relationship—the house.

Craig's Wife is evidence alike of the technical excellence of which our playwrights are capable at their best, as well as the limitation of understanding which robs their work of real stature. Like *Ned McCobb's Daughter* and *The Silver Cord*, *Craig's Wife* is a drama of character in a vacuum, whereas it should treat of character as the result, in good part, of social and psychological influences. The play would then have been, not only the tragedy of a selfish woman, but an evaluation of the social relationships and conditions of life which cast people in so harsh a mold. That Harriet Craig's obsession is not a fortuitous individual phobia is apparent in two scenes in which she expounds her philosophy to her niece. Her passion for tidiness, for possession, are not merely the expression of an acquisitive desire for possessions, but of her need for security in a society where women are still (in the class and milieu to which she belonged ten years ago, and still in many places today) economically dependent on men. This relationship breeds, at one end of the scale, outright prostitution; at the other, the apprehension and trickery and callousness of a Harriet Craig:

> I saw to it that my marriage should be a way toward emancipation for *me*. I had no private fortune like you, Ethel—no special equipment—outside of a few more or less inapplicable college theories. So the only road to independence for *me* that *I* could see, was through the man I married.——It isn't financial independence that I speak of particularly. I knew

that would come—as the result of another kind of independence; and that is the independence of authority—over the man I married. And that doesn't necessarily imply any dishonesty of attitude toward that man, either. I have a full appreciation of Mr. Craig—he's a very good man; but he's my husband —a lord and master—my master. And I married to be independent.

Ellie Dunn in Shaw's *Heartbreak House*, or Marx and Engels in the *Communist Manifesto*, do not expound the theory of the cash nexus as the basis of modern marriage more explicitly than it is voiced here. Its corruption of human emotions and character, of the marriage relationship itself, is the burden of Kelly's play; nevertheless Kelly persists in treating Harriet as a *moral* phenomenon. She is dishonest; she is guilty of marrying a man without love and without trust; she is a pitiless nag. For these enormities she is punished. That she has been trapped, as clearly as Walter Nichols in *Ambush*, by forces beyond her control, is also beyond the dramatist's understanding.

Kelly has not written another play as good as *Craig's Wife*. *Behold the Bridegroom* is a powerful account of the undisciplined, bitter aimlessness of wealth, victim of its own indiscrimination and satiety, whose ending lapses into outright romanticism. Significantly, it was produced the same season as Philip Barry's *Paris Bound*. The following year saw his *Holiday*, Rachel Crothers' *Let Us Be Gay*, Elmer Rice's *Street Scene* and the turbulent Hecht-McArthur *Front Page*. Between Kelly's genre, and the new fashion in tempo, dialogue, and characterization, lies a gulf in taste and technique which he has been unable to cross.

3 RACHEL CROTHERS

Unlike George Kelly, Rachel Crothers has never found herself unable to keep in step with new trends in the theatre. For thirty-one years, with few interruptions, she has been writing commercially successful plays and assimilating new manners and subject matter. Nevertheless, her work during the past two decades does not measure up to the promise of her earlier plays. By comparison with *A Man's World*, *When Ladies Meet* and *Susan and God* are unimpressive. Miss Crothers has come increasingly to sacrifice dramatic force and honesty of thought for sprightliness and well-turned phrases. In doing so she has followed a tendency which, as has been pointed out, is evident in the work of writers of comedy in general. More and more they have abdicated the realm of character development and conflict to toss back and forth ideas and arguments couched in witty speeches.

The measure of Miss Crothers' failure is best seen by examining *A Man's World*, which she wrote in 1909.

While it is structurally a mass of devices which we now condemn as artificial and sentimental, it transcends hokum by the force of its ideas and the reality with which Miss Crothers invested her characters; she outdistanced the conventions of her craft in her thinking, and she embodied it in living human beings. She portrayed—remember, in the year 1909—a group of artists struggling for a precarious livelihood, in itself at that time a novel subject which she handled with directness and understanding, and she made her principal figure a woman bent on leading an independent life hampered by the conventions and gossip of a society which declared that if a woman wrote a good book it could be only because she got her ideas from a man or because she was in love. More important still, Miss Crothers tackled the question of the double standard more unequivocally and intelligently than it had yet been treated by an American dramatist, and—wonder of wonders—carried her thinking through to its logical conclusion despite the fact that it meant forfeiting the traditional reconciliation and happy ending.

A Man's World was followed by He and She, and Ourselves, both provocative pieces of work. Then suddenly came a series of sentimental, charming, and perfectly conventional character comedies: The Heart of Paddy Whack, Old Lady 31, A Little Journey, 39 East, coinciding with the war and postwar years when the general level of drama fell to a deplorable level. There were a few striking exceptions to the general rule—Augustus Thomas' The Copperhead, Jesse Lynch Williams' brilliant comedy, Why Marry?—and in Greenwich Village a young man was writing one-act plays about sea-

men, but the trend was away from realism, and Miss
Crothers conformed.

During the season of 1919–20 came the first gun of a
new dramatic revival: Eugene O'Neill's *Beyond the
Horizon.* The following year there was nothing very
iconoclastic about such offerings as *Rollo's Wild Oat* or
Just Suppose or *The First Year* or *Enter Madame,* but
there were also such novelties as *Miss Lulu Bett* and *The
Emperor Jones* and Miss Crothers' *Nice People,* all radical departures in their several ways. Once again Miss
Crothers was among the innovators.

And yet *Nice People,* by the standards of its time, is
nothing like as forthright a play as *A Man's World* was
in 1909. It is true that once again Miss Crothers has a
significant theme: the conflict between the new moral
standards of a postwar, jazz and booze-intoxicated
younger generation and an older, more rigid code of behavior. She went even further, to examine the older generation's responsibility for the younger's warped sense of
values. For you cannot, as Teddy Gloucester's aunt Margaret Rainsford points out, give a girl eighty dollars to
throw away on one night's party, as well as three cars, a
string of pearls, an allowance of twenty-four thousand
dollars a year, and a small farm, and expect from her any
great degree of self-restraint or seriousness.

But while Miss Crothers thus questions and evaluates
the new standards and social relationships which followed the World War, her ideas are those which are to
limit American comedy for the next decade. At one
bound it has reached its apogee. Take the scene in which
Mrs. Rainsford arraigns Teddy's smart, spoilt coterie of
young people for their sins. One of them, Oliver Com-

stock, is congratulating Teddy on her courage in throwing up her old life and working on a farm instead:

It's a miracle, nothing less, what you've done.

TEDDY
Any of you could have done it if you had to.

MRS. RAINSFORD
Of course. You have more energy and daring and cleverness and intelligence for your age than any set of people in the world.

TREVOR
Mrs. Rainsford, I suspect you.

MRS. RAINSFORD
It's true, in spite of appearances. You have it all and you're throwing most of it away.

TREVOR
Am I included in this?

MRS. RAINSFORD
You haven't the faintest idea of your own importance.

TEDDY
You're not included in that, Trevor.

MRS. RAINSFORD
You're an institution—envied and limited—dreamed of and read about. In every city, every little town, all the way down, there's a set of you—and you might be an absolutely dynamic power for good.

OLIVER
Might be? What are we?

MRS. RAINSFORD
An equally great one for harm.

Miss Crothers is appealing here to the sense of responsibility, of *noblesse oblige*, of a privileged class, doubtless having in mind some such ideal as the British aristocracy and its tradition of "public service." Her inconsistency is that she has also gone to some pains to show that wealth is at the root of the evils she has been depicting—degeneration of values, lack of social responsibility. Such inconsistency recurs repeatedly in plays on the same subject: witness George Kelly's *Behold the Bridegroom*, Philip Barry's *Holiday* and *The Animal Kingdom*, S. N. Behrman's *Meteor* and *End of Summer*. All these writers apparently feel that if only the rich could be somewhat less rich, if along with their wealth they could develop ideals of frugality and abnegation, all would yet be well. They overlook the fact that the impulse towards wealth and the moral deterioration which accompanies it are indissolubly bound up with the primary motives of our social organism—profit, competition, *laissez faire*, and that one cannot distinguish between the end itself and the process which achieves it. It would be surprising if Teddy Gloucester and her friends were impelled by the sense of responsibility with which Mrs. Rainsford tries to imbue them; there is nothing in their background or in that of the parents who have accumulated the fortunes they now lavish on their children, to foster such a sense, excepting a superficial concept of charity and voluntary "social service" which provides a needed cushion of justification and self-righteousness to undue prosperity.

Thus Miss Crothers' social philosophy, and that of the

majority of her contemporaries, amounts to nothing more than a code of breeding and good taste. Further they cannot go, for it would be flying in the face of values and ideals which they still personally accept and hold to be attainable, despite their profound dissatisfaction with certain phenomena which they observe and are totally unable to reconcile with their code of behavior.

In *Mary the Third* Miss Crothers was still dealing, however erratically, with a serious problem: the shifting moral code, specifically the question of divorce. She shows youth profoundly disquieted at the spectacle of its parents, who should provide it with a fixed code of moral values, trooping through the divorce courts. She shows the antagonism between youth experimenting with freedom in the search of more stable relationships, and an older generation trying to conceal its bankruptcy from its children. But her conclusions, even her line of reasoning, are lost in a jumble of bad craftsmanship inexcusable in a dramatist of her caliber and experience. Between 1925 and 1932 Miss Crothers confined herself to a series of comedies in which her talent for straight thinking and pungent characterization were less apparent than ever. Whether the milieu was a prosperous home in a Midwestern town, or New York Greenwich Village, or smart society at play on Long Island, her characters are pallid stencils of one another: the women lovely, alluring, smartly turned out "thoroughbreds," the men upstanding, affable American businessmen. One and all they are charming, commonplace, and completely lacking in individuality. In *When Ladies Meet*, however, we notice a very curious phenomenon. Like so many of her contemporaries, Miss Crothers has been forced to admit the fecklessness and bewilderment which have grown in

certain circles of late years. This eventually leads the erst-
while author of *A Man's World* to an interesting position. Mary Howard is typical of Miss Crothers' latter-
day heroines; she is beautiful, well groomed, and gra-
cious. What interests us is her state of mind. Here is the
successful, popular, intelligent, and *independent* woman
who was the ideal of the first quarter of the century, obsessed with a horror of loneliness, with futility.

> Loneliness is something we can't help. If nothing
> comes that *completes* us—what can we do?——I
> haven't got anything that really *counts*. Nobody
> *belongs* to me—nobody whose very existence de-
> pends on me. I am completely and absolutely alone.

Jimmy Lee's verdict rings like a postscript from the un-
emancipated eighteen-nineties:

> Only a woman for a man—and a man for a woman
> —no matter how much of everything else we've got.
> It's true—and it's hell.

Thus the wheel is coming full circle. The modern
woman who fought for and won the right to work on a
basis of equality with men, the vote, moral as well as
economic equality, a creative existence beyond the confines of her home, finds only dust and ashes now at the
end of her struggle. Having broken her chains, fought
with all her might and main *against being possessed*,
dominated, owned by anything or anybody, she cries out
herself for the possession of another human being, for
someone to "belong" to her, someone "whose very existence depends on her." Here, obviously, is something
different from emotional fulfillment as such. It is, of
course a reversion with reservations. Feminine emancipa-

tion will not be completely discarded. Mary Howard will go on working, writing, no matter what ties she assumes. But this futility which she encounters at the end of her battle is a profoundly significant phenomenon today, and that it should emerge in the plays of that feminist among playwrights, Rachel Crothers, only makes it more so.

Miss Crothers has only twice attempted satire; neither time has she been completely successful, and in each case (fourteen years apart) she has almost duplicated her formula. In *Expressing Willie* (1923) she ridiculed the current fad of seeing "greatness" in the most mediocre individuals and of cultivating the "expression" of that "greatness." Her mockery was delightful, and the device of allowing the sane and suppressed Minnie Whitcomb to triumph over her designing adversary by going her one better at "self-expression" and consequently emerging as a real personality, made for audience sympathy and hence good theatre. Yet *Expressing Willie* falls short of real satire because, unlike *Beggar on Horseback*, produced the same season, it never penetrates to the root of what it is mocking. Moreover, there is a dramatic contradiction in the fact that if it had not been for the ridiculous fad we are laughing at, Minnie Whitcomb would never have asserted herself as she does, and hence the pursuit of "self-expression," if one is colorless and repressed, is apparently not quite as silly as Miss Crothers would have had us think. The dramatist is caught invalidating her own premise.

Precisely the same thing happens in *Susan and God* (1937), and once again lack of penetration blunts her satire. Susan Trexel and her husband are practically separated: Barrie is a drunkard, and Susan flits from one

craze to another. Then she espouses "the new way to
God"—a thinly veiled equivalent of Buchmanism—and
sets about interfering in the lives of all her worldly friends
with a view to reforming them. But her new gospel becomes a boomerang; her drunken husband overhears her
saying that with God's help any man can make a fresh
start. He demands not only God's help but hers, promising her the divorce she wants if he once breaks his word
to stop drinking. Caught in the net of her own professions, she accepts the bargain, albeit unwillingly ("I wish
I'd never heard of God!"). Actually it is affection for
his daughter and the hope of winning back his wife's love
which keep Barrie Trexel going straight until Susan herself realizes the extent of both her love and her obligations to her husband and child.

> I don't think God is something out there—to pray
> to. I think He's *here*—*in* us. And I don't believe
> He helps us one bit—till we dig and dig and *dig*—
> to get the rottenness out of us.

Now this is all very fine, but without her excursion
into misguided piety Susan would in all probability never
have acquired such insight. Yet Miss Crothers also shows
us the less admirable results of "the new way to God"
—hypocrisy, meddling, the evasion of immediate responsibilities for a "more glamorous mission." We are
left of two minds as to whether it is thoroughly pernicious or admirable in its indirect results.

Her satire is further blunted by superficiality. Buchmanism is a spiritual and intellectual manifestation
whose roots go deep into present-day life and whose implications are far-reaching. But Miss Crothers eschews
any inquiry as to why it should take such hold among

certain social groups, or mention of certain arresting recent developments in the movement, such as the endorsement, by some of its leaders, of fascist trends of thought. The only hint of more profound consideration is a remark by one of Susan's worldling friends:

> I don't think it makes much difference what it is as long as it's something to believe in or hang on to.

This is precisely the bankrupt frame of mind which leads, not only to Buchmanism but beyond it to more extreme ideologies, but Miss Crothers ignores or passes over the danger. The problem, as she sees it, is solely one of individual character, an approach which is certainly not that of the satirist, who must probe beyond the particular to the general. This ability Miss Crothers once possessed, and has now apparently lost.

4 PHILIP BARRY

The characteristic cleverness and "brightness" of Philip
Barry's dialogue have tended to obscure the similarity
of pattern of his plays. He deals for the most part with
the individual's revolt against conventional pressure for
social conformity and attempts to force him into a
pattern of behavior to which he is inimical. Most frequently his antagonist is "business" and everything it
stands for: its goal, way of life, its hostility to originality
and individuality. To Barry "big business" represents
everything he abhors in modern life.

The right to do as one pleases and the desire for
leisure are two themes basic in most of his plays. They
are the motives which successively impel Richard Wins-
low in *The Youngest*, Maitland White in *You and I*,
Adrian Terry in *In a Garden*, Johnny Case in *Holiday*,
Tom Collier in *The Animal Kingdom*, the Farley brothers in *The Joyous Season*, and Norman Rose and Tom
Ames in *Hotel Universe* to turn their backs on success

and prosperity and seek a more satisfying existence. Without such freedom—freedom of action outside, freedom of the spirit inside—life is unendurable; this is the principal tenet of Philip Barry's philosophy.

It is obvious that he does not go beyond one particular aspect of the problem of "freedom," that relating to persons whose only fetters are those of habit or acquiescence. As H. T. Parker, the distinguished critic of the Boston Transcript, put it, in a review of Hotel Universe, Barry's characters "need take no thought of the financial morrow, since their balances in bank are renewed like the widow's cruse in Scripture. It is their privilege to rise up and depart, to sit down and linger, the world around, as impulse without obligation may prompt." (Italics mine.) Gail Redman in Tomorrow and Tomorrow and Daisy Sage in The Animal Kingdom are only exceptions to the general rule of trips abroad, ladies' maids and, the "general atmosphere of plenty with the top riveted down on the cornucopia" which constitutes Barry's favorite dramatic milieu.

In other words, though he poses the question of individual redemption from Philistinism, Barry limits himself to the spiritual welfare of a microscopic section of the population which appears to be making an injudicious use of its advantages. Like Miss Crothers, Barry would like to have his financiers and businessmen stop at a certain point in their accumulation of wealth, from natural judicious restraint, and turn to self-cultivation and contemplation. The real problem involved, and therefore the real reason why Edward Seton and Rufus Collier and the Farley brothers lack understanding or warmth, completely escapes him: that self-seeking at the expense of other people's elementary human rights

destroys humanity and ideals no less surely than it increases the size of a bank account.

The limitations of Barry's point of view are clearly
brought out by the people whom he designates as models
of human behavior. There are the Potters, Nick and
Susan, in *Holiday*, of whom Johnny Case remarks—

> It seems to me that they know just about every-
> thing.——Life must be swell, when you have some
> idea of what goes on, the way they do.

Linda Seton's opinion of them is equally rapturous:

> You've always seemed to me the rightest, wisest
> happiest people I've ever known——You're my one
> real hope in the world.

These are big words, all the more revealing when we
hear Linda explaining the reason for her faith in the
Potters: "They get more fun out of nothing than anyone I know." In comparison to Edward Seton and his
daughter Julia, and to their cousins, the Crams, the
Potters are certainly refreshing. At best, however, they
are dilettantes who have made a fine art of living pleas-
urably for themselves, "like the dirty loafers we are," to
quote Nick Potter himself.

Then there is Christina Farley in *The Joyous Season*.
She is one of Barry's finest characterizations, and in her
selflessness, her discrimination and vitality, she represents the highest type of Catholic. But she sees the
degeneration of the Farleys purely in terms of their loss
of adventurousness and joy of living. What they do is
wrong only insofar as it affects them. The rich must be
saved from themselves. Her understanding penetrates
no further, and her weapons against greed and stupidity

are only her religious faith and an ethical code of behavior.

Lastly take the philosophy which Stephen Fields in
Hotel Universe recommends to his daughter's troubled
friends. What goal, what hope, what discipline, does it
offer them? To "accept" life, to "live" it:

> To suffer and rejoice. To gain, to lose. To love,
> and be rejected. To be young and middle-aged and
> old. To know life as it happens, and then to say,
> 'This is it.'

Such an outlook, he suggests, will render them invul-
nerable to bewilderment and discouragement. But his
precepts, noticeably, do not extend to a scale of values,
to a suggestion that their neuroses may arise at least
in part from undue self-absorption, and that psychological dislocations may exist, due primarily to social
causes, which cannot be cured by the Freudian technique
or a return to the faith of one's childhood.

Naturally the milieu to which he confines himself has
determined the type of characters Barry portrays. Probably Barry himself is unaware of how significant is their
unvarying similarity. Like Rachel Crothers when she
came to devote herself to comedy in the higher social
brackets, Barry can only reiterate himself: his men and
women are of an appalling sameness. Lissa Terry, Mary
Hutton, Cecelia Henry, Terry Farley, Ann Field—are
one and all slim, immaculate, exquisite, poised, urbane.
The same with the men: Adrian Terry, Jim Hutton,
Tom Collier, Pat Farley, Gail Redman: they are invariably well set up, likable, straightforward young Americans, with slightly varying degrees of imagination. Even
the few individual types whom Barry has created—

Linda Seton, Johnny Case—talk just like the others. Only occasionally do we find life and feeling—in Christina Farley, in Eve Redman and Nicholas Hay. But the young artist rebels in *The Animal Kingdom* are stuffed caricatures, and in *Bright Star* hardly a single character gives the illusion of life.

Some of this weakness may be traced to Barry's absorption in clever dialogue for its own sake. His characters all talk alike, not the way people really do speak, but in phrases which have become the playwright's own mannerisms. He has no ear for the ordinary colloquial rhythms of speech. Instead, he creates his own, staccato and clipped to the point of stylization. Take a passage from *The Animal Kingdom*, where Tom Collier has told Daisy Sage what he honestly thinks of her painting:

TOM

Daisy, darling—

DAISY

You're cruel, inhuman. You're a brute.

TOM

Oh Daisy—

DAISY

Thanks for being.

TOM

If you mean it—

DAISY

From my heart—(*She looks at him, smiling now*) Oh, you skunk—(*He laughs, relieved*)

TOM

Worse, much worse.

DAISY

(*Serious again*) Who but you, Tom? (*She points her finger at him*) Look: only you and strangers honest with me ever.

Or these lines in *Tomorrow and Tomorrow*, in which Eve finally communicates to Nicholas Hay her decision not to leave her husband for him:

HAY

You've decided?

EVE

Yes.

HAY

You were never not decided.

EVE

I think that's true. I want to think so. Because now I see that even if there weren't Christian—Oh, if I didn't love us—you and me—! (*She concludes, simply*) And I couldn't, then—I simply couldn't.

This is not realism, the inarticulateness of overpowering emotion, but dialogue stylized until it has become a shorthand of emotion, artificial instead of significant, inexpressive rather than heightened in effectiveness.

Its comedy value, which is at times of a high order, lies, not in an epigrammatic gift such as that of S. N. Behrman's, or in speech arising from characterization, as with Sidney Howard at his best, but in a rapid exchange—question and answer, thrust and parry—of witty lines that cap one another. Dramatically Barry's greatest weakness is his habit of imposing a situation or a line of behavior on his characters instead of allowing

both to arise from the nature of the characters themselves. His approach is in fact exactly what he decries
so strongly in life itself: he manipulates, he contrives, he
is arbitrary instead of permitting his characters to develop naturally.

In *Paris Bound* (1927) he struck what was to be his
most successful vein: presenting an essentially serious
idea in an amusing and sprightly fashion. In this case
he contends that divorce for adultery is a much more
serious offense than adultery itself. In the case of really
happy marriage, a transitory affair on the part of the
husband does not infringe on his wife's province. The
question is whether the younger Huttons will duplicate
the tragedy of young Jim's parents. Mary Hutton starts
her married life swearing that she will not be a possessive
wife. Characteristically, Barry then shatters all our ideas
of the kind of person Mary is (quite a different matter
from showing up human inconsistency); hearing of
Jim's affair with one of her ex-wedding attendants (whom
she already knows has a strong attraction for Jim),
Mary decides instantly to divorce him. She is only de-
terred by discovering for herself what Jim has experienced
—a physical attraction for someone else, and the profound difference between such an attraction and her
relationship with her husband. Jim's sudden return from
abroad, his instinctive awareness of what has happened
to her and his refusal to take notice of it stamps both
episodes as irrelevant and carries them over the danger-
point.

Regardless of the merits of such a point of view, we
can see in *Paris Bound* an example of Barry's difficulty
in fusing two dissimilar styles. He creates a charming
relationship between husband and wife, but his tendency

to express tenderness and deep feeling always in light comedy vein presages a time when he will be unable to write in any other. His penchant for underwriting handicaps him in his serious scenes, which are rarely written with sufficient fullness and clarity.

In *Holiday* Barry once again does violence to his characters. The cause of the misunderstanding between Johnny Case and Julia Seton would ordinarily become apparent in their first serious talk after their engagement. Instead, at the playwright's direction, they talk carefully around it until the moment when Barry wishes to precipitate a showdown. If we overlook this piece of hokum, and the limitations of Barry's social point of view, we can accept *Holiday* as his best play and one of the most amusing comedies of the decade. For once he has contrived an engrossing story and some brilliantly witty characterizations, and the figure of Edward Seton, "financier and cotillion-leader," ranks among the best caricatures in our drama.

On his first holiday in all his life at Lake Placid, Johnny Case, a self-made young lawyer who has been working since he was ten, meets Julia Seton and promptly becomes engaged to her. It is not until he comes to call, on the Sunday of their return to town, that he discovers she is one of *the* Setons, and fabulously rich. From the beginning Johnny gives evidence of not being cast in the ordinary mold of get-rich-quick young man; but Julia persists in taking for granted that once safely married and on the way up he will conform to standards: "You'll love it. I know you will. There's no such thrill in the world as making money." He tries to explain to Julia what he is really after; but they are interrupted and somehow he never gets around to it again until just before their engagement is to be announced. He does talk it over with Linda, Julia's younger sister, a kindred spirit who has every sympathy with his desire to take time off while he is young, instead of when he is played out, in order to—

try and find out who I am and what I am and what goes on and what about it.——I want to live every which way, among all kinds of people—and know them—and understand them—and love them——

With growing interest in Johnny Linda watches his struggle against having to make money for its own sake. In the end Johnny relinquishes Julia "because I love feeling free inside even better than I love you, Julia," and Linda breaks with her family and goes after Johnny herself with every promise of success.

Some of Barry's best writing has gone into the portraits of Johnny, Linda, young Ned Seton—fighting a losing battle against boredom and futility, with drink as his only weapon—and of Edward Seton himself—unbelievable and yet true down to the buttons on his spats—pompous, dogged, inhuman, and historic. We get a pretty good idea of the impending Mr. Seton from the catechism through which Ned and Linda put Johnny, whose cause they have already espoused, before the arrival of "big business":

NED
He's a good man, this Case fellow.

LINDA
The point is, there's no moss apparent, nor yet the slightest touch of decay.

NED

I expect Father'll be a job. When do they come to grips?

JULIA

Before luncheon, I suppose.

LINDA

That soon? See here, Case, *I* think you need some coaching.

JOHNNY

I'd be grateful for anything in this trouble.

LINDA

Have you anything at all but your winning way to your credit?

JOHNNY

Not a thing.

JULIA

Oh, hasn't he though!

LINDA

The first thing Father will want to know is, how are you fixed?

JOHNNY

Fixed?

LINDA

(*Firmly*) Fixed.—Are you a man of means, and if so, how much?

JULIA

Linda!

LINDA

Be still, Beauty! (*To Johnny*) I know you wouldn't

expect that of a man in Father's position, but the fact is, money is our god here.

JULIA

Linda, I'll—! Johnny, it isn't true at all.

NED

No?—what is then?

LINDA

Well, young man?

JOHNNY

I have in my pocket now, thirty-four dollars, and a package of Lucky Strikes. Will you have one?

LINDA

Thanks.—But no gilt-edged securities? No rolling woodlands?

JOHNNY

I've got a few shares of common stock tucked away in a warm place.

LINDA

—Common? Don't say the word. I'm afraid it won't do, Julia.—He's a comely boy, but probably just another of the vast army of clock-watchers.

NED

How are you socially?

JOHNNY

Nothing there, either.

LINDA

You mean to say your mother wasn't even a Whoo zis?

JOHNNY

Not even that.

JULIA

Linda, I wish you'd shut up.

NED

Maybe he's got a judge somewhere in the family.

LINDA

Yes, that might help. Old Judge Case's boy. White pillars. Guitars a-strummin'. Evenin', Massa.

NED

You must know some prominent people. Drop a few names.

LINDA

Just casually, you know: "When I was to Mrs. Onderdonk's cock-fight last Tuesday, whom should I see but Mrs. Marble. Well sir, I thought we'd die laughing—"

JULIA

(*To Johnny*) This is a lot of rot, you know.

JOHNNY

I'm having a grand time.

LINDA

"Johnny," she says to me—she calls me 'Johnny'—"

JULIA

Oh, will you be *quiet!* What on earth has set you off this time?

LINDA

But it's dreadful, sister. (*To Johnny*) Just what do

you think you're going to prove with Edward Seton, financier and cotillion-leader?

Holiday is Barry's last attempt at satire. *The Animal Kingdom* bogged down in the old conflict of wife versus mistress; his remaining plays have been serious in outlook despite the bantering tone which predominates in the writing. In fact, one of our best-known comedy writers has not written a real comedy in ten years, if we except *Spring Dance*, his most recent offering and an adolescent reversion which is more charitably ignored.

Instead, he followed *Holiday* with *Hotel Universe*, his most ambitious enterprise in the intellectual sphere. Actually what befuddled critics and audiences was, not its profundity but its inchoateness. For Barry permitted himself to veer from problems of individual psychological adjustment to metaphysical considerations of the human mind abroad in space and time which add nothing to the clarity of the play. Its very obscurity, however, enhanced its apparent significance, and thanks to an uncanny use of theatrical devices and some fine writing *Hotel Universe* held audience attention.

The setting of *Hotel Universe* is particularly effective —a stone terrace overlooking the Mediterranean, at dusk. The terrace itself sets the mood: beyond the low wall at the back and to one side, "Nothing is visible: sea meets sky without a line to mark the meeting. The angle of the terrace is like a wedge into space." One of the characters, bemused like all the rest by the peculiar fascination of the place, remarks—

It's fantastic, this terrace. It just hangs here. Some day it'll float off into space—and anchor there, like an island in time.

With great skill Barry builds up this unreality of atmosphere. As darkness increases, a lighthouse at sea throws its beam across the terrace at regular intervals, "like the finger of God." The characters all sense an eerieness of some kind: they recall the past with the immediacy of the present, they have chills of premonition, moments of acute sadness, and they are haunted by the recollection of a young stranger's suicide that afternoon on the beach—"off for Africa."

The whole action of the play takes place on the terrace, without an intermission; like *Yellow Jack*, *Hotel Universe* depends on carefully created atmosphere sustained without interruption. Six people, the modern sophisticates whom Barry delights in depicting, are on a brief visit to an old friend, Ann Field, who is living in exiled solitude with her invalid father. They are leaving in a few hours, and one by one they reveal to Ann, who loves them dearly and most of all Pat Farley, their profound unhappiness and disillusionment with life. In the words of H. T. P.'s review, already quoted, "Barry deals with the malaise of a time and a breed that lack illusions and want faith.——They have lost illusions and found nothing to replace them. They are at odds, in their own fashion, with living."

Much of the obscurity of *Hotel Universe* derives from Barry's failure to make clear the causes for this frame of mind *in general*. We know that it is not limited to any group of individuals, that it is widely prevalent. Of this there is only a hint.

PAT

There was a great big war and we survived it. We're living on borrowed time.

TOM

Lost: one battalion.

PAT

We're not lost. Our schedule's different, that's all.—What I mean is, we'll have had the works at forty instead of eighty.

Instead of pursuing this line of analysis, Barry sees each case of discontent and maladjustment as a purely *individual* affair—the result of an incident or an emotional experience in childhood or youth. Under the guidance of Ann's father, each of the characters goes through a dramatically compressed course of psychoanalysis which liberates him from his fixations; one by one we see them re-enact the episodes which derailed them, Stephen Field assuming the role of interlocutor. He plays the old Franciscan father to whom Tom Ames goes back to beg for renewed faith, the father whom Lily Malone feared and loved too much, the father of a young English girl who killed herself for the unrequited love of Pat Farley.

Unfortunately the continuity of scenes is so jumbled that we are continually confused. To make matters worse, Barry embellishes Stephen's particular brand of Freudianism with something that resembles most closely the philosophic concept known as "serial time." By way of preface to his psychiatric efforts, Stephen propounds his theory:

I have found out a simple thing: that in existence there are three estates. There is the life of tables and chairs, of getting up and sitting down. There is the life one lives in one's imagining, in which one wishes, dreams, remembers. There is the life past death, which in itself contains the others. The three estates are one. We dwell now in this, now in that —but in whichever we may be, breezes from the other still blow upon us.

To walk back in time is—

. . . A very interesting excursion. You merely lift your foot, place it so, and there you are—or are you? One thinks one is going forward, and one finds instead the remembered touch of water somewhere —the odor of geranium—sight of a blowing curtain —the first sound of snow—the taste of apples. One finds the pattern of his life, traced with the dreadful clarity of dream. Then he knows that all that comes in remains—nothing is lost—all is important.—— Space is an endless sea, and time the waves that swell within it, advancing and retreating. Now and again the waves are still and one may venture anyway one wishes. They seem to be still now—quite still. So which way would you go—where would you travel?

This mixture of two antithetical philosophies deprives *Hotel Universe* of rational meaning and turns it into a pretty piece of sentimental fantasy. Elsewhere, in J. B. Priestley's *Time and the Conways*, for example, we can see more clearly the outcome of the theory of serial time: it leads inevitably to a profound nostalgia on the one hand, and a philosophy of acceptance and resignation on the other. For if life is viewed "in the right perspective—" that is, as a whole, a distasteful present can always be canceled out by a brighter past or future. It leads also to a creed of experience for its own

sake, as we have already seen in Stephen Field's ex-
hortation to Tom Ames. Pursued farther, it lands Philip
Barry side by side with Eugene O'Neill:

TOM

I don't know what I'm here at all for—

STEPHEN

To suffer and to rejoice. To gain, to lose. To love
and be rejected. To be young and middle-aged and
old. To know life as it happens and then to say
"This is it."

TOM

Yes—but what *am I?* And what shall *I* be when
it's over?

STEPHEN

You are the sum of all your possibilities, all your
desires—each faint impression, each small experience—

TOM

But when it's over?

STEPHEN

You will be what your spirit wants and takes of
them. Life is a wish. Wishing is never over.

TOM

Then everything about me *has* a meaning!—Everything I see and feel and do—dream, even!

STEPHEN

Great heaven, yes!

We are struck here not only by the vapourousness of
such a philosophy—notice how the wording resembles

passages in O'Neill—but by its unselectivity and its complete passivity. For Barry, consciously directed action excepting in terms of the "business" he so abhors, does not seem to exist. And the only alternative to despair or "business' that he has to offer is domesticated bucolic bliss. Listen to Pat Farley, freed from his burden of guilt, and his love for Ann assured:

> I want to sit with the wife I love, and read books, and look at maps——and fish trout-streams with my boys, and take my daughter walking——and build a house and mend a fence, and be tired of a good day's work, and sleep——*Good, quiet things.* [Italics mine.]

It is a nice picture, but as the outcome of all the soul storms we have witnessed in the preceding two hours, a distinct letdown. Is this the sum of the vision and understanding vouchsafed to Stephen the seer and through him to his patients? If so, then Barry's excursion into metaphysics has proved little more than a jaunt to a Never-Never Land.

This bankruptcy recurs in one form or another, throughout the remainder of his plays. It is the theme of *Tomorrow and Tomorrow*, *The Joyous Season*, and *Bright Star*. Eve Redman in *Tomorrow and Tomorrow* is another of Barry's "imprisoned" characters. She has a devoted husband and a charming home and plenty of leisure, but she is empty and aimless in spirit:

> I've nothing left to fight for, and I think the only living people are those who fight.

Eve's sole prescription for herself is a child, because then (like Nina Leeds in *Strange Interlude*) she would feel

that she was "living—making—and not slowly dying, a
little more each day." This conception of fulfillment
only in physical reproduction is a curious modern paradox, similar to that of the liberated woman longing for
the bonds of possession in *When Ladies Meet*, or of
Nina Leeds in *Strange Interlude*. Having unleashed the
creative powers of men and women, scientifically
and socially, the view that the creative principle is limited
to the act of birth can only be regarded as retrogressive.
Anthropologists and historians know that the perpetuation of the race has been variously rationalized at different times in different societies: children were destined,
and the mother honored accordingly, to become war-
riors. Later, they were regarded primarily as the means
of carrying on the family line and keeping the family
intact. It remains for our age to see the child chiefly as
the spiritual fulfillment of its mother.

Eve Redman's husband cannot give her a child, nor
does he understand her desolation. But to Nicholas
Hay, visiting professor in the small college town, Eve
is "an artist without an art." He succeeds where Redman
has failed, and then goes away. Fulfilled physically and
spiritually, Eve is happy in her son. But in the third
act we have one of those sudden and unaccountable
derailments of plot to which some of our best dramatic
craftsmen seem prone. The son Christian has been
gravely injured, and Eve calls Hay back to take care of
him. The conflict shifts from Eve's emotional need to
a sick boy off stage, a completely passive figure who has
been only briefly glimpsed. He is the victim of a deeply
sublimated conflict, for Eve has tried subconsciously to
make him Hay's son rather than Redman's. Once the
boy is saved there arises the question, shall he and his

mother go with Hay or stay with Redman? That Eve chooses to stay with her responsibilities rather than follow her own emotional necessity is a satisfactory enough conclusion, but one that bears very little connection with the first two-thirds of the play.

Much of the trouble lies in the vagueness with which Hay is delineated. What is he?—scientist, doctor, psychiatrist, practitioner of some form of mental therapy? We never know, yet his theories and professional practice are fundamental to the course of the action. Vaguely he stands for the dominance of the emotions, while Eve clings to reason, and like Candida, to the man who needs her most. But her own problem of aimlessness and sterility is never properly linked with this duel between reason and feeling, and the play becomes no more important than a nostalgic episode.

By the time he came to write *The Joyous Season* (1935), any feeling Barry had possessed for clear-cut conflict and development had been dissipated; it lacked even the retrospective "action" of the psychoanalytic episodes in *Hotel Universe*. *The Joyous Season* surveys the immobile members of the Farley family, who in one generation have travelled from a country farm to the social eminence of Boston's Beacon Street. This transit represents the loss of a simpler way of living and of ruggedness of spirit and sensitivity to spiritual values, for a mess of potage. In his anxiety to "keep the family together" (which Barry regards as a typically Irish trait but which might just as well be Jewish or Italian) John Farley has been pampering and bolstering up the weaker members of the clan to the point where they have lost all desire to stand alone or adventure on their own.

Christina Farley, who left home under a cloud many

years before to become a nun and who returns for a twenty-four visit, is the catalyst which shatters their lethargy. For two acts she observes her family, and they wait for her to decide whether she wishes to take their old home or their present residence for her holy order, a choice permitted her by her mother's will. She leaves without making a decision, which she puts up to them; and impelled by the new currents she has set in motion they decide to abandon the newer and shoddy life and go back to "Good Ground."

This sudden regeneration is completely unconvincing, as any sunburst finale is apt to be without adequate preparation. The reason for such a conversion ending as well as for its utter uselessness, is that we have never come to know a single character in the play except Christina. And this is inevitable, because to know people you must not only hear them talk but see them act, which is the one thing none of the characters in *The Joyous Season* ever do. They do not act because Barry himself does not know them; he has no idea how they would behave, and therefore cannot launch them into a situation requiring action.

As a matter of fact, each character contains the germ of an implicit conflict, a reservoir of dramatic possibilities, but the dramatist never taps it. Take Terry Farley and her husband Francis. Terry is confused and unhappy, another Eve Redman, or a character carried over from *Hotel Universe*. Her love for her husband, her faith in him, her interest in life, have gone. Why? We never find out. When she and Francis are reconciled at the conclusion of the play, the occurrence is as incomprehensible, as lacking in motivation, as their estrangement was in the first place.

Ross Farley might have been a fascinating character study; there is a wealth of potential conflict in the Catholic turned skeptic and Communist who reverts to the faith of his fathers. John and Martin Farley are typical businessmen. But Martin cherishes a hidden longing for the diplomatic service, and John is in love with his secretary. Less than twenty-four hours after Christina's arrival, Martin is on the verge of leaving for Washington and John of proposing to his secretary. But we never have the vestige of an idea of what either of these men is really like.

This is bad dramaturgy, and its cause is not far to seek. Barry has a knack of picking these disillusioned, bewildered worldlings out of a crowd, of suggesting their distraction in a few lines. But he only sets them into motion among one another. His sphere is the drawing room. Life outside it baffles or bores him, it is hard to tell which. Therefore the *basis* for their disquiet, which must perforce lie in this larger sphere, is arbitrarily ruled out of consideration. His plays take place in an artificial vacuum, where only small, set, secondary motions can take place, and consequently his characters become mere puppets.

This becomes finally clear in *Bright Star*, in which Barry tried to draw a man in close relation to the world of affairs—a "man of action." It is a type he cannot encompass. Quin Hanna, part reformer and idealist, turns into an emotional freak and egoistic introvert. His social conflict is overlaid, and finally displaced, by fantastic emotional complications. For Quin, a man of "too much head and too little heart," marries an angel from heaven who loves him to extinction. Unable to love Hope, he feels that he has wronged her, and his insensate career of political idealism, degenerating to chicanery, is nothing but a flight from self, from love, from guilt, in which he finally destroys himself.

Nothing is believable in *Bright Star*, not Quin Hanna's particular brand of Napoleonism, not his power to attract and hold friendship from the most unlikely people, not his social schemes, nor is Hope's redundant love and self-abnegation any more convincing. Hanna's Utopian dream of reconciling class antagonisms within the confines of one small municipality is a dream which harks back to the brotherly vistas of Robert Owen and Brook Farm. Like Hanna, Barry's attempt to grapple with reality miscarries because he is not equipped for such a venture. He has dwelt elsewhere too long.

5 ROBERT E. SHERWOOD

Like S. N. Behrman and Philip Barry, Robert E. Sherwood tends to repetition in the matter of plots. A man —wise, cynical, and charming—finds the answer to his quest for a meaning in life, in a woman; suddenly he falls in love, no less suddenly his life is wrenched violently from its old pattern, and in three cases out of four he goes gallantly to his death in consequence. The exception is *The Road to Rome*; the other three instances are *Waterloo Bridge*, *The Petrified Forest*, and *Idiot's Delight*.

Another item common to all these plays is a background of war or violence which endangers the lives of the characters. This is Sherwood's device for sustaining tension, a device forced upon him by his inability to construct a play in which suspense will arise from the actions of the characters themselves. The reason for this is, particularly in his more recent plays, because the central character is completely passive, a symbol of futility. And since, as we have seen in Barry's last plays, such immobility makes for a poor brand of theatre, Sherwood falls back on air raids and gangsters to bolster up his plots.

The same cause eventually leads him to the dramatic formula which is becoming so common among our writers of comedy: a room full of contrasting types (the Bar-B-Q in the Arizona desert in *The Petrified Forest*, the hotel lounge in *Idiot's Delight*) who exchange reflections, and comment on Life with a capital L. Such a reiteration of formula and of types can only reflect the mind of the dramatist himself. Our authors are using the stage increasingly as a place where they can exorcise their own doubts, transcend their frustrations, affirm their beliefs, instead of subordinating themselves to the telling of a story in dramatic terms.

Among Sherwood's intellectual comedies with their macabre backgrounds the best is the deftly ironical *Road to Rome*, incidentally his first play. The revival of Shaw's *Caesar and Cleopatra* several seasons before, the fad for historical novels couched in an irreverent modern idiom, had paved the way for a similar development in the theatre of which *The Road to Rome*, in 1927, was the first successful native example. Rome, cowering at the feet of the oncoming Hannibal and his Carthaginians, is saved by the scandalous expedition of Amytis, wife of the pompous dictator Fabius Maximus, to Hannibal's camp. The fact that Amytis is not primarily actuated by a desire to save Rome, which she heartily dislikes, but rather by a desire to learn the secret of Hannibal's power and then destroy it, is typical of Sherwood's unromantic romanticism. The only scene in the play which holds the interest not by the flamboyance of its dialogue ("I wonder what it feels like to be violated?"), but by dramatic contrast and tension, is that in which Amytis gradually breaks down Hannibal's only aim in life, and reveals him to himself:

> I'm trying to find something in you, something great, something noble, something exciting.——I want you to believe that every sacrifice in the name of war is wasted. When you will believe that you will be a great man. I want you to be a great man.

Having asserted her hold on him by all the weapons at her disposal, she eventually convinces him of the futility of his life. He tells his officers he has had a sign from the gods, and marches his legions away from Rome, his irreverent brother Mago remarking parenthetically, "So Hannibal had a portent, did he?" It is characteristic of Sherwood that the resolution of the play should consist in the dissipation of action before words: Hannibal, the man of force and action, is stripped, emasculated, becomes the victim of abstract ideas. Later his heroes become so attenuated that action is foreign even to their past. Hannibal's submission to Amytis is the first step on the road to the futility of Alan Squire and Harry Van.

The best of Sherwood's plays is a complete departure from his usual preoccupations. He prefaced it with an introduction to which we shall return later as a revealing supplement to his plays. *Reunion in Vienna* itself is one of the most brilliantly witty of our comedies in recent years, in which the philosopher and dramatist in Sherwood are briefly fused. The comedy is two-edged, for the writer is mocking, not only the faded glamour of Viennese imperial glory, but the cocksureness of the new psychology, which presumes to weigh human emotion with chemical accuracy, and admits of no incalculabilities. It is Anton Krug's theory that his lovely wife, an ex-Habsburg's ex-mistress, has only to see her former lover again, for the spell which he still maintains over her to be broken for all time. Elena's reaction is unexpected, for as it turns out, her professor husband has miscalculated in one respect: Rudolph Habsburg has triumphed over the ravages of age and exile and is quite as mad and charming as ever.

Nothing could be in greater contrast to the verve and sprightliness of *Reunion in Vienna* than the introduction Sherwood wrote for it. A more somber document has rarely been penned. Of positive belief of any kind he has, he tells us, none whatever. The position of modern man is one of unrelieved tragedy:

Before him is black doubt, punctured by brief flashes of ominous light, whose revelations are not comforting. Behind him is nothing but the ghastly wreckage of burned bridges.——As an alternative to cynicism is the sentimentalism which derives exquisite anguish from an acknowledgment of futility.——Democracy—liberty—equality, fraternity, and the pursuit of happiness. Peace and prosperity! Emancipation by enlightenment! All the distillations of men's maturing intelligence have gone sour.

The future appears to Sherwood only in horrendous light:

. . . the ultimate ant-hill, the triumph of collectivism, with the law of averages strictly and equably

enforced—a prospect of unrelieved dreariness.——
When man accepts the principles of collectivism
he accepts a clearly stated, clearly defined trend in
evolution, the theoretic outcome of which is inescapable. He is enlisting in the great army of uni-
formity, renouncing forever his right to be out of
step as he marches with all the others into that
ideal state where there is no flaw in the gigantic
rhythm of technology, no stalk of wheat too few or
too many, no destructive passion, no waste, no fear,
no provocation to revolt—the ultimate ant-hill.
Man is afraid of communism not because he thinks
it will be a failure but because he suspects it will
be too complete a success.

There is only one hope to buoy up Mr. Sherwood's
spirits, that

> man may not have time to complete the process of
> his own undoing before the unknown cosmic forces
> have combined to burst the bubble of his universe.

Before such sublimity of despair one stands positively
awed. Useless to argue, to point out inconsistencies of
reasoning, errors of observation, fundamental miscon-
ceptions. The wonder is that Mr. Sherwood ever pulled
himself together to crack another joke. And small
wonder indeed that his subsequent plays partake of the
tinge of futility, that his heroes are henceforth men of a
reflective turn of mind who mope at their own desue-
tude, who stand apart from the chaos about them and
deprecate a situation which they decline to regard as
any kind of personal responsibility.

In The Petrified Forest Sherwood celebrated the death

pangs of the age of individualism. Alan Squire regards himself as "a survival of the in-between age," and quotes T. S. Eliot by way of confirmation:

> Brains without purpose. Noise without sound. Shape without substance. Have you read the Hollow Men? Don't. It's discouraging because it's true. It refers to the intellectuals——

By contrast the gangster Mantee is a man of action but, like Squire, an obsolete survival of a dying age. Individualism has petered out in Squire in inertia and parasitism, and run amok in crime in Mantee. Although there is an element of truth in Sherwood's observations on a decaying class as represented by Squire, he is grossly sentimentalized. Squire is the attractive, "appealing" victim of fate. We deprecate far more than we despise him. He dies so that the girl he loves may have the wherewithal (through his insurance) of getting to France to realize her dreams (dreams which Squire has already assured her are illusions which will disappear at the first breath of reality). His death is as false, as romantic, as his living, yet the dramatist glorifies both.

Specifically the play shows the last stage in the wanderings of Alan Squire who is pursuing an aimless path across the Continent "looking for something to believe in—something that's worth living for—and dying for." He arrives at a lonely lunchroom in the Arizona desert, where his search is cut short by the advent of Duke Mantee and his desperadoes, fresh from a hold-up massacre in Oklahoma City. Mantee is glorified even more than Squire. While he and his prisoners wait for Mantee's girl to join them for the getaway to Mexico, Squire continues to reflect on the chaos of human affairs, and its wherefore:

> Do you realize what it is that is causing world chaos? ——It's nature hitting back. Not with the old weapons—floods, plagues, holocausts. She's fighting back with strange instruments called neuroses. She's deliberately afflicting mankind with the jitters. Nature is proving she can't be beaten—not with the likes of us. She's taking the world away from the intellectuals and giving it back to the apes.

The only positive force, according to Squire, is that of love:

> Any woman is worth everything that any man has to give—anguish, ecstasy, faith, jealousy, love, hatred or death. Don't you see—that's the excuse for our existence? It's what makes the whole thing possible, and tolerable.

Then the pursuit arrives, and pausing just long enough to fulfill his contract with Squire—shoot him dead—Mantee and his gang depart. Squire's love, characteristically, can galvanize him from his slough of inertia only enough for a gesture for which someone else must provide the impulse, the finger on the trigger.

To admit the theatricality of Sherwood's conception, the tension which hangs over the temporary inmates of the Bar-B-Q, the comedy of some of the lines, is only to underline the meretriciousness of *The Petrified Forest*. For thus slicked up for popular consumption, Mr. Sherwood has served up one of the most amoral hodgepodges of philosophy that ever rejoiced the hearts of our dramatic critics and fashionable audiences. In fact, the redundance of praise which it evoked from the first-night reviewers has rarely been equalled in its unanimity and lack of discrimination.

Idiot's Delight was a similar success. Here we find the author discussing the problem of war through the mouths of a group of cosmopolitans isolated in a mountain resort in the Italian Alps at the moment of outbreak of the next and presumably last-because-all-destructive slaughter. With the same mixture of "just so far" realism, Sherwood lashes out at the forces which breed wars —jingoism, the accumulated injustice of the Versailles Treaty, and the international munitions racket: "the one real League of Nations—the League of Schneider-Creusot, and Krupp, and Skoda, and Vickers, and Dupont— the League of Death"—and on the other hand extends his bitter cynicism to the potential forces for peace. His enlightened scientist returns to his mother country to offer her his services in the cause of destruction. His revolutionary proletarian, Quillery, mouths phrases in the best stage-revolutionary tradition:

> There is a force more potent than all the bombing planes and submarines and tanks. And that is the mature intelligence of the workers of the world! There is one antidote for war—Revolution! And the cause of Revolution gains steadily in strength!

But to the dramatist Quillery is no more than a heroic fool who succumbs to nationalism at the news of the outbreak of war, screams provocations in the face of the Italian officers, and is promptly shot for his pains. There is no more sense to the whole idea of working-class opposition to war than that, Sherwood implies. And thereupon he presents us, in juxtaposition to the folly of Quillery and the surrender of Dr. Waldersee, with the pleasant, tired skepticism of Harry Van—nonplussed by the spectacle of a world crashing to its annihilation, resentful of such "god-damned bad management," and bent above all on determining the identity of the strange pseudo-Russian princess whom he encounters in the Hotel Monte Gabriele.

What mars *Idiot's Delight*, even more than the confusion of its thinking, is its inexusable cheapness vis-à-vis its given theme. What its audiences will recall, what obviates any necessity for thought on the question of war or peace, is the soothing irrelevance and flippancy of Harry's meeting with Irene, the gyrations of his six chorus girls, the inanities of "*les blondes*," and the absorbing question of which bedroom in which Midwestern hotel was once jointly occupied by Harry and Irene. When Irene's lover, a munitions king, becomes embarrassed by her pacificism, and arranges for her to be detained while he continues on his way to safety, Harry stays behind with her, and they face the prospect of death while an air raid roars overhead, sitting at the piano playing and singing "Onward Christian Soldiers" as the curtain falls.

Dramatically, interest depends on a skillful alternation between wisecracks, and the tension induced by air-raid sirens, off-stage executions, and the imminence of general destruction. Action, in terms of conscious choice, of character determining events, of mind shaping life, is not only absent, but is implicitly denied. Men, being fools, not only submit, but cannot do otherwise because they are fools—"obscene maniacs." Harry Van's philosophy is so muddled in its kindliness as to be inane:

All my life I've been selling phoney goods to people
of meager intelligence and great faith. You'd think
that would make me contemptuous of the human
race, wouldn't you? But—on the contrary, it has
given me Faith. It has made me sure that no
matter how much the meek may be bull-dozed or
gypped they will eventually inherit the earth.

Van is, presumably, killed with Irene in the air raid
which brings down the final curtain. In the light of his
confessed philosophy, what is this supposed to prove?
The irony of life? The futility of directed effort of any
kind, specifically against war? The fecklessness of modern man? What it does convey, of course, is a picture of
Mr. Sherwood's own mind which corresponds at every
point with the self-portrait painted in the introduction
to *Reunion in Venna*. It also furnishes additional proof
that the line between tragedy and comedy on our stage
is growing steadily less palpable. Mr. Sherwood is not
the only alleged writer of comedy who more and more
approximates the perplexity and gravity of our avowedly
serious dramatists. There is little to choose, for real
gaiety, between Anderson and O'Neill on the one hand,
and Behrman, Sherwood, and Philip Barry on the other;
the latter, quite as much as the former, are troubled and
at a loss, and unable to "laugh it off." It is a far cry
from their plays to Meredith's Comic Spirit, whose
"common aspect is one of unsolicitous observation,"
with its "volleys of silvery laughter." Certainly the gaiety
of our stage has notably abated of late, and an ever-in-
creasing proportion of it, such as there is, has come from
a succession of new writers who, after one or two successes, have migrated to Hollywood to coin laughs for

the screen. Comedy is returning to the slapstick farce school, and there is small cause for wonder; to laugh once you have begun to think requires a solid foothold amid chaos—something our dramatists do not, in the main, possess.

VII   The New Realism

1

If we attempt an audit of the fifteen years from 1918 to 1933 in playwriting we are struck by the number of outstanding plays which were written by men and women not regarded as our leading dramatists. One thinks of Susan Glaspell's *Inheritors*, Arthur Richman's *Ambush*, Elmer Rice's *Adding Machine* and *Street Scene*, Sophie Treadwell's *Machinal*, John Howard Lawson's *Processional*, Paul Green's *In Abraham's Bosom*, and John Wexley's *The Last Mile*.

If we add to these the best of the plays considered in the preceding pages—*The Silver Cord*, *Yellow Jack*, *Gods of the Lightning*, *Beggar on Horseback*, *Once in a Lifetime*, *Craig's Wife*, *Anna Christie*, and *S. S. Glencairn*, we have a not inconsiderable list from which, it will be noted, there are certain apparently arbitrary omissions. It does not, for instance, include *Mourning Becomes Electra*, or *Mary of Scotland*, or *Reunion in Vienna*. The reason is, that despite their technical excel-

283

lence and their emotional or entertainment value, they are, in the last analysis, outside the main stream of our dramatic tradition, as *Anthony Adverse* is outside the most significant tradition of the American novel. Our literary tradition, whatever the form, is not in the main one of historical romance; it is rather, as must be that of any nation which has a living literature, one of illumination and criticism of life, either contemporaneously or, infrequently, as a reinterpretation of the past in living terms, such as Maxwell Anderson attempted in *Valley Forge* and Sidney Howard succeeded in evoking in *Yellow Jack*.

From this viewpoint of evaluation and criticism, the best plays of the years between 1918 and 1933 have made valuable contributions. We have the satire, frequently in a highly imaginative form, of certain aspects of modern and characteristically American life, in *Beggar on Horseback*, *The Adding Machine*, *Processional*, and *Machinal*, with their emphasis on the problems of a machine civilization. We have the tragedy of the Negro struggling for betterment in Paul Green's deeply moving play *In Abraham's Bosom* (which ranks far ahead of O'Neill's contribution to the same problem, *All God's Chillun Got Wings*). We have the realistic melodrama of *Street Scene* with its implicit indictment of slums and poverty, and the searing protest against capital punishment and criminal law of *The Last Mile* and *The Criminal Code*.

We also find, on searching through these plays for some kind of common denominator, a complete unanimity in certain respects: 1. they constitute a collection of facts, incidents, items without any reference to the causes which bring them about, and without full consideration of the consequences of those facts, 2. they depict the struggles of individuals pitted against circumstances which, almost invariably, end in tragedy, 3. they show an absence of understanding, for the most part, of the forces and relationships which bring about these tragic impasses and, lacking such understanding, a failure to struggle against catastrophe in terms of conscious effort along a clearly thought out line of action, whether economic, political, or social. The only alternative to the passivity of Mr. Zero in *The Adding Machine* is an individual, unreasoning, and purely instinctive resistance such as that of Walter Nichols in *Ambush* or Abraham McCranie in *In Abraham's Bosom*, or of the trapped criminals in Flavin and Wexley's prison dramas. These dramatists saw no possible course of action open apart from violence or purely ethical endeavor, both arising from an emotional rather than a consciously rational impulse. Above all, what is lacking is any perspective of dynamic social change. Hope of any kind is conspicuous by its absence, with the exception of the early *Inheritors* (1922) and *Yellow Jack*; the general pattern is one of heartbreaking futility and eventual resignation.

In the work of one dramatist in particular during these years we can see the origins of a new trend. John Howard Lawson's influence on the men who are writing in different vein today has been profound, and his work of greater significance, seen in historical perspective, than that of most of his more successful colleagues. Lawson's interest in experimental forms dates from his earliest play; in addition, he is alone among his contemporaries in traveling the path from confused dissatisfaction with the theatre and with society at large to where, his point of view at last solidly integrated, we can expect from him his best work.

From *Roger Bloomer* down through *Gentlewoman* his plays voice the same query. In the character of Roger Bloomer himself we find a passionate expectancy and curiosity about life, adolescent restlessness, revolt against the callow materialism of middle-class life, a turbulent and poetic mysticism. Vaguely Lawson relates emotional confusion to social chaos: money arouses revulsion in Roger, yet it is fundamental; the lack of it corrupts and distorts no less than its possession. Above all, Roger desires "life"—"the real thing"—but what is it? This urgent, unsatisfied longing for an inexpressible desire impels not only the prototype Roger but Sadie Cohen and Dynamite Jim in *Processional*, David and Alise (most distracted and mystical of revolutionaries!) in *The International*, Larry and Annabel in *The Pure in Heart*, the tormented Sol Ginsberg in *Success Story*, Gwyn and Rudy in *Gentlewoman*. The answer to this prolonged Odyssey of the American spirit is already hinted at in *Roger Bloomer*: "The young are marching, marching——far-off the tread of marching people singing a new song." It emerges more and more clearly from play to play. *The International*, for all its grotesquely neurotic revolutionists, traced the pattern of modern psychosis and economic chaos back to the contradictions of imperialist capitalism. Larry in *The Pure in Heart*, trapped in his gangster hideout, envisions a better life:

There must be more to it than that. Maybe some place it's different—I don't know: where they'd keep busy working, digging, plowing, building cities

too, laying one brick on another brick——People
could be happy, people could build things, work
without stealing, love without going crazy——

ANNABEL

You couldn't find a place like that, it would take a
hundred years to find it.

LARRY

You couldn't find it, maybe you could build it.

Gwyn in *Gentlewoman* finally sees clearly.

Our children won't play at life in boudoirs and
offices; they'll face something different whether they
like it or not.——I'm afraid—perhaps I can make
a child who won't be afraid, he'll take sides and
die—but there's always a chance, he might live and
make a new world.

With *Marching Song* in 1937 Lawson broke sharply
with his dramatic past which had nevertheless led him
step by step to this new beginning, and took his place
among the leading playwrights in the new school of
explicit and militant social statement. The importance
of his earlier work lies largely in its influence on the
slowly crystallizing forces of this new trend. The plays
themselves are beautifully written yet lacking in dramatic
clarity, lyric recitatives of emotions, moods, aspirations,
rationalization. They want dynamic development and
action, faults to which Lawson's lyricism, his addiction
to the expressionistic technique and his mystical philosophy all contributed. Yet he succeeded in evolving a
style compounded of vaudeville, slapstick, jazz and burlesque which projected, as did no other, the quality of the
American jazz era, its tragi-comedy, its color and vitality,

and which comes nearer to being a native theatrical genre than anything else created during the same decade.

During the theatrical season of 1931–32 two significant events took place. One was a short-lived play called 1931–, by Paul and Claire Sifton, which, for the first time on Broadway, took notice of the grimmer aspects of the current depression. It completely knocked the wind out of reviewers and audiences and lasted just twelve performances. But it served to herald the advent of a new type of realism and it also marked the fact that in the Group Theatre, which had made its debut only four months previously with Paul Green's *The House of Connelly*, New York had a permanent theatre which was interested in something more than its balance sheets. The second important event was a play by two young authors, George Sklar and Albert Maltz, *Merry-Go-Round*, which attacked machine politics and political skullduggery and struck so close to home that the Walker administration did everything in its power to have the production banned.

There have been other attacks on municipal corruption, and by itself *Merry-Go-Round* would not have been so important. But two years later, in 1933–34, its authors helped to found the Theatre Union, another nonprofit-making organization which planned to present plays with a definite social point of view, at low prices. The new theatre's first offering was a play by these same two authors called *Peace on Earth*, the first antiwar play in the American theatre which attacked war as the inevitable outcome of a social system based on the profit motive.

Another contribution to the growing movement had been made the previous year by Elmer Rice with his

We, the People, a panoramic and sprawling survey of the depression which exercised great influence on young writers. The floodgates were now open. The same season as *Peace on Earth* the Theatre Union presented *Stevedore,* by Paul Peters and George Sklar, in which the theatre of social protest reached its first maturity; that winter also saw John Wexley's uneven but forthright play on the Scottsboro case, *They Shall Not Die,* and Lawson's *Gentlewoman.* In another year the Group Theatre was presenting the first plays by Clifford Odets and newspapers everywhere were featuring articles on "the new Left theatre."

What distinguishes each and everyone of these plays, despite their varying artistic merit, from any that preceded them, is a shift in emphasis from the depiction of tragedy as such to a concern with its *causes*—an analysis which proceeds beyond individual willfulness or ignorance or the workings of chance to fundamental laws of cause and effect, and which leads to struggle based not only on heroism but on an understanding of these principles. The result is on the one hand the labor or antiwar or other type of "militant labor" play, and on the other, the drama of middle-class "awakening" and "conversion." These two elements are to be found in every so-called Left or social play of the past five years, and have led to new problems for dramatists, some of them still unsolved. How, for instance, avoid undue repetitiousness of pattern, degenerating into the formula of the "strike play" or any other particular formula? How, on the other hand, draw the line between one particular theme, and its wider social aspects, a consideration of which leads into chaotic all-inclusiveness such as that found in Rice's *We, the People,* Odets' *Paradise*

Lost, and Lawson's *Marching Song,* which tackle every issue on the calendar of protest today!

Yet despite any crudities or shortcomings, no one can deny that this development has enriched the theatre with a vast new field of subject matter, novel and vital forms (witness the recent development of the "left musical"), and above all has brought to the consideration of social problems a positive and dynamic point of view which, when coupled with first-rate craftsmanship, yields superb theatrical results.

An outstanding example is Clifford Odets' *Waiting for Lefty.* Ideally adapted to amateur productions by the simplicity of its form, its incisiveness, and its brief, episodic character, this play had literally hundreds of productions throughout the country during the space of two years, and was a potent factor in the growth of a popular and workers' theatre movement to which we shall refer again.

The story of how *Waiting for Lefty* came to be written has become legendary. While the Group Theatre was playing a six-weeks engagement in Boston in the fall of 1934, one of its lesser-known players, Clifford Odets, shut himself up in a hotel room during the day to write a play for a one-act social play contest sponsored by the New Theatre League and New Theatre Magazine. *Lefty* was written in three days, won the contest, and was first produced at a special Sunday-night benefit performance by members of the Group. No such sensation had been witnessed in years. After renewed special performances it opened on Broadway along with another hastily written Odets "one-acter," *Till the Day I Die,* dealing with the underground anti-fascist movement in Germany.

Waiting for Lefty takes place at a taxi-drivers' union meeting which dramatizes the struggle between a militant rank and file and a reactionary gangster-ridden leadership intent on blocking strike action at all costs. The audience are the union members, and periodically speakers jump up from orchestra seats and rush up onto the stage to take part in the proceedings. On the stage, bare except for a few chairs, are the strike committee, the union head, and several of his gunmen. The desperate need for a strike is established in a series of short scenes in which, one after another, the members of the rank-and-file committee re-enact the incidents which made them class-conscious workers. In their dramatic economy and the vigorous language in which they are written, some of these scenes are superb. Edna, the wife in the first episode, is a magnificent character: bitter, grim, anguished by the years of struggle to make both ends meet, she flays her husband for his passivity, in the face of the 6 or 7 miserable dollars a week he brings home:

> We're stalled like a flivver in the snow. For five years I've lain awake at night listening to my heart pound.——When in hell will you get wise?

> JOE
> I'm not so dumb as you think! But you're talking like a Red.

> EDNA
> I don't know what that means. But when a man knocks you down you get up and kiss his fist! You gutless piece of baloney!

> JOE
> One man can't—

EDNA

(*With great joy*) I don't say one man! I say a
hundred, a thousand, a whole million, I say. But
start in your own union. Get those hack-boys together! Sweep out those racketeers like a pile of
dirt! Stand up like men and fight for the crying
kids and wives! Goddammit! I'm tired of slavery
and sleepless nights.

Succeeding scenes show a young scientist forced out of
his job for refusing to work on a poison-gas formula, an
actor who cannot find work, a doctor losing his hospital
position because of anti-Semitism. One and all are now
cab drivers, and members of the strike committee. Perhaps the most poignant scene of all is that between the
young hackie Sid and the girl whom he loves and cannot
afford to marry. Her brother warns her to stop seeing
him "for her own good":

Don't get soft with him. Nowadays is no time to be
soft. You gotta be hard as a rock or go under.

Sid has a very clear idea of what they are up against, and
the passage Odets has given him, describing the class
struggle in a colorful vernacular, is extraordinarily brilliant:

We worked like hell to send him to college—my
brother Sam, I mean—and look what he done—
joined the navy! The damn fool don't see that the
cards is stacked for all of us. The money man dealing himself a straight royal flush. Then giving you
and me a phoney hand like a pair of tens or something. Then keep on losin' the pots 'cause the cards
is stacked against you. Then he says—what's the

matter you can't win—no stuff on the ball, he says
to you. And kids like my brother they believe it
'cause they don't know no better. For all their
education they don't know from nothing.

But wait a minute! Don't he come around and say
to you—this millionaire with a jazz band—listen
Sam or Sid or what's-your-name—you're no good but
here's a chance. The whole world'll know who you
are. Yes sir, he says, get up on that ship and fight
those bastards who's making the world a lousy place
to live in. The Japs, the Turks, the Greeks. Take
this gun—kill the slobs like a real American. Be a
hero!

And the guy you're poking at? A real louse, just
like you, 'cause they don't let him catch more than
a pair of tens, too. On that foreign soil he's a guy
like me and Sam, a guy who wants his baby like you
and the hot sun on his face. They'll teach Sam to
point the guns the wrong way, that dumb basket-
ball player!

FLORRIE

I got a lump in my throat, honey.

SID

You and me, we never even had a room to sit in,
somewhere—

FLORRIE

The park was nice—

SID

In winter? The hallways—I'm glad we never got
together. This way we don't know what we missed.

FLORRIE

(*In a burst*) Sid, I'll go with you—we'll get a room
somewhere.

SID

Naw—they're right. If we can't climb higher than
this together we better stay apart.

FLORRIE

I swear to God I wouldn't care.

SID

You would, you would—in a year, two years, you'd
curse the day. I seen it happen.

FLORRIE

Oh, Sid—

SID

Sure, I know. We got the blues, Babe. The 1935
blues. I'm talkin' this way 'cause I love you. If I
didn't I wouldn't care—

Unswervingly Odets pursues the trail of human misery
to its source in the grinding inhumanity and inevitable
contradictions of a profit-seeking economic order. The
cumulative effect of scene piled on scene is terrific. The
episode in which Agate Keller unmasks his brother as a
stool pigeon furnishes welcome comic relief despite its
savagery. That job done, he turns to the audience in an
appeal not to wait for Lefty, the absent leader, but to act:

Tear down the slaughter-house of our lives! Let
freedom really ring. These slick slobs stand here
telling us about bogeymen! But the man who gave
me food in 1932, he called me Comrade! The one
who picked me up where I bled—he called me Com-

rade too! What are we waiting for—don't wait for Lefty! He might never come.

A man dashes down the aisle and up onto the stage.

Boys, they just found Lefty!——Behind the car-barns with a bullet in his head!

Agate Keller dominates the uproar:

Hear it boys, hear it? Hell, listen to me! *Coast to coast! Hello, America, hello! We're stormbirds of the working-class. Workers of the world . . . our bones and blood!* And when we die they'll know what we did to make a new world! Christ, cut us up in little pieces, we'll die for what's right, but fruit-trees where our ashes are! Well, what's the answer?

ALL

Strike!

AGATE

Louder!

ALL

Strike!

AGATE

Again!

ALL

Strike, strike, strike!

Curtain.

Odets' full-length plays are on a different pattern from *Waiting for Lefty.* They display the same realistic and trenchant point of view, but the form, dictated by their content, is dissimilar. Both *Awake and Sing!* and *Para-*

dise Lost are plays of family life, in the curiously un-organized, haphazard style of dramaturgy which has earned Odets the adjective Chekhovian. Answering the charge that he was consciously aping the Russian master, Odets claimed that he had never read Chekhov's plays until after the production of *Paradise Lost.* What is more likely is that the portrayal of social decay, the im-prisonment of the individual in the material contra-dictions of a society that has outlived its validity and usefulness, the bewilderment and fear and dawning hope of the individual thus trapped, led both writers, the master and the younger man, to a similarity—it is no more than that—of technique.

Certainly Odets' style in *Awake and Sing!* is some-thing new and fresh in American drama. Its shortcom-ings are manifold, but at its best it achieves a unique impressionism. The story, such as it is, is nearly sub-merged in the casual chatter and routine of family life. People come and go, wander from room to room, eat, dress, and speak their minds in endless parenthetical allu-sions. Of sustained conversation leading directly up to contrived situations or progressive action there is almost none. Questions go unanswered, reflections die in mid-air, people blurt out their inmost thoughts and then hastily divert the talk yet again. Out of this seeming chaos, however, Odets contrives to build up characteriza-tions, situations, and a deeply moving sense of life in both its tragic and its comic aspects. One is conscious of the same anger and compassion that flare out with such vehemence in *Lefty,* but here they are modulated and controlled.

Nevertheless, the same informing purpose runs through both plays: a desire to portray life as it is, as it is changing, death leading to birth; the awakening class consciousness, out of suffering and confusion, in middle and working class lives. The Bergers in *Awake and Sing!* are that typical American phenomenon, a working-class family with middle-class aspirations. Some of them are aware of the discrepancy between the circumstances against which they are pitted and the dreams they cherish; others cling to the American gospel of success through effort and virtue, or take refuge in the past, or in the passing moment. Barely stated, the story is that of Hennie Berger, who has an illegitimate child, marries an unloved man, and leaves them both for the racketeer who was her first lover; of old Jacob Berger, whom family nagging drives to suicide but who has a vision of a better life which he has succeeded in communicating to his grandson Ralph; and of the latter's awakening at the impact of his grandfather's death to a reality only dimly perceived before.

The plot is obviously without clear direction, and Hennie's flight with Moe Axelrod conveys no meaning beyond the inevitable chaos of moral standards when people are warped into bitter molds by circumstances beyond their control. The significant thing about *Awake and Sing!* is the people who inhabit it and who assume a poignancy and meaning greater than their individual selves because Odets understands so profoundly what they are—not chance aggregations of good and bad qualities but people helplessly and subtly conditioned by their environment, by the laws of the society in which they suffer and struggle, to be as they are. What makes Bessie Berger, the mother who is in reality "the man in the house," so human and so significant is that her very harshness towards her son's first love is born of her pro-

tective instinct, sharpened by years of obstinate battle
to keep her family alive and honest. She wants a golden
future unencumbered by a penniless child bride for her
son Ralph and she will protect him despite himself and
at any cost to his pride or happiness.

What Odets is also intent on pointing out is that the
family, in circumstances of poverty and frustration,
necessarily becomes an instrument of unjust coercion,
even of unmorality, perpetuating false and outworn social values. The dreariness of her life drives Hennie
Berger into an affair which gives her a child. Intent on
respectability at all costs, Bessie marries her to young
Sam Feinschreiber. Only old Jacob is outraged at such
tactics, and quotes Karl Marx: "Abolish such families!"
Inevitably Hennie revolts against Sam, against the child,
against a loveless domesticity. Moe Axelrod offers her a
little glamour, comfort, money, and rides down her
doubts with his realism: "One thing to get another!"
They go away together, a conclusion which has brought
down upon the author the charge that he himself has no
scale of values, and is pointing out such an amoral and
irresponsible conclusion as desirable. Instead, the moral
is the inevitability of such behavior when human beings
are on the one hand pushed to the wall by their circumstances and on the other lack the understanding and the
desire to struggle towards a better kind of world which
we see so clearly in old Jacob and in the awakening
Ralph.

In *Awake and Sing!* Odets has not yet mastered his
own individual style. Motivation is often confused, or
false; the story jerks and hitches. He is writing scenes
and character portraits, often extraordinarily effective in
themselves, but not yet integrated into a play that will

set all these people into complex and simultaneous inter-
action and development. Yet such characterization and
dialogue are not to be found previously in our drama.
His dialogue displays what is little less than genius for
sharp vivid phrasing which is unrealistic while it is still
lifelike and human, a poetizing of speech that is nevertheless more realistic than poetic. When Ralph Berger
says that all he wants is "a chance to get to first base" he
is talking like any American boy. But when he rebels at
sitting around "with the blues and mud in your mouth,"
his cry "We don't want life printed on dollar bills," and
his mother's vigorous and pithy expressions—"You mean
we shouldn't have food in the house but you'll make a
jig on the street-corner," or "You got money and money
talks. But without the dollar who sleeps at night?"—
these are the poet's transformation of a commonplace
idiom into literature.

Coming after *Waiting for Lefty* and *Awake and Sing!*,
Odets' *Paradise Lost* was a disappointment. It represents a retrogression into mysticism, since its revolutionary thesis is overlaid with an involved and at times
invalid symbolism. It is conceivable that if Odets gave
the poetic and symbolic elements of his talent free rein
they might end by leading him into the same morass as
that which threatens Anderson and O'Neill. From this
his grasp of the dialectics of reality should save him, as
evidenced in *Golden Boy*, where, despite the fact that
his conflict is an extremely symbolic one, he succeeded
for the first time in a full-length play in telling a vividly
dramatic story.

The son of an old Italian fruit peddler, possessing a
fine musical talent, young Joe Bonaparte is the victim
of profound social disharmony. Goaded by the emphasis

put upon success and wealth by a materialistic society, he gives up the violin which affords him solace but no future for the career of a boxer which promises him wealth and fame. He wins them, but at the cost of losing his identity as a human being; instead, he becomes a commodity, owned by men who invest their money in his hands and demand a return, who haggle over him and trade shares with complete disregard of him as a person.

His manager, Tom Moody, is a man with fundamentally decent instincts. But he has become no better than the racket of which he is a part and from which he tries to wring his living. When Joe begins to chafe at the terms of his bondage and regret his music, Moody uses his young mistress to hold him to the prize-fighting game. Joe and Lorna Moon fall in love. The triangle is a desperate and insoluble one, for Lorna cannot bear to hurt Moody, who saved her from the gutter and who really loves her, and yet she cannot deny Joe whose need for her, under the pressure of sudden success, inner, confusion and unhappiness, is no less great than Moody's. She tries to stick to Moody but in a big fight Joe accidentally kills his opponent, and goes to pieces: he will not continue in a game which makes him a murderer, even accidentally, but what else can he do? His hands are ruined for music and he has been geared too high to step back into obscurity. He is spoiled, wasted. In desperation he and Lorna go for a ride in the high-powered car which is the symbol of Joe's desire for wealth and his flight from reality, and are killed in a smash-up.

Odets' talent has never been seen to better advantage than in the construction and swift unfolding of *Golden Boy*, or in its long and rich gallery of characterizations:

the old fruit vendor, with his dream of a life of beauty
and quiet contentment for his son, and his anguish at
the brutal game that Joe chooses as his profession; the
sensitive and lonely girl, sprung from a background of
drunkenness and poverty, who rebels at feeling like "a
tramp from Newark"; the ebullient and sagacious young
brother-in-law ("What the hell's so special in bed?");
the philosophic neighbor Mr. Carp; the wise and kindly
trainer; and the two significantly juxtaposed brothers:
the modest labor organizer, also a fighter—for his beliefs
—and Joe himself, driven relentlessly by the virus of ambition and the lust for wealth—"those cars are poison
in my blood"—alternately intoxicated and sickened by
his success, victim of the conflict between his real nature
and the society to which he cannot adapt himself. The
closing scene drives home the bitter lesson with a minimum of words. The idealistic father and the racketeers
who have preyed on Joe's talent face each other across
the stage. Centered between them is the labor organizer,
and his is the last word: "What waste!"

Structurally *Golden Boy* is for the most part as solid
and tight as were the individual scenes in *Waiting for
Lefty*. The characters (with the exception of Fuseli) are
never mere commentators, but always functionally related to the action. There is some unclear symbolism,
such as the significance of Fuseli and his relationship to
Joe, and the latter's own optical affliction (he is cross-
eyed, and a good deal is made of it in the play); the old
fruit peddler's ability to save up twelve hundred dollars
may also be questioned. But the most serious charge
which can be brought against the play is the validity of
Odets' primary assumption—that a boy with the hands of
a fine violinist can be a first-rate boxer as well—and hence

of the choice of symbols for the conflict with which he is concerned. His own justification presumably lies in his desire to present his ideas in as racy and gripping a story form as possible. Whether in so doing he has compromised the integrity of his conception, and if so why, is a question which will be postponed until a final consideration of the problems which confront our dramatists today.

2

The social trend in the theatre today has assumed impressive proportions. Odets, although outstanding, is only part of a great movement. Next to *Waiting for Lefty*, the finest among the earlier militant plays was *Stevedore*, by Paul Peters and George Sklar. The setting is the New Orleans water front and the theme the dawning realization among Negroes and whites that only by fighting together can they triumph over their common foe: the boss; that race prejudice is fostered as a means of splitting the working class, to keep the Negro in check and use black labor, forced to accept a starvation wage, to undercut white labor. But *Stevedore*, far from being an economic theorem, is a thrilling play. Lonnie Thompson, a Negro longshoreman, is accused of rape for no other reason than that he has emerged as a potential leader in the struggle for decent working and living conditions on the docks. Incited by the Oceanic Stevedore Company, which is seriously incommoded by Lonnie's militancy, the lynch mobs go after him, and terrorize the Negro districts of New Orleans. The rest of the play is the story of Lonnie's growing understanding and leadership, his efforts to rouse his people to resistance, and—most moving of all—the rescue of the embattled Negroes, barricaded in an alley and bereft of their leader, by the white members of the longshoremen's union, come to fight shoulder to shoulder with their fellow workers.

What lifts *Stevedore* from an episode to the level of an epic is the truth of its content and the skill of the authors. Never for an instant do the ideas implicit in the material transcend its human and dramatic values; not once do the characters become grotesques or caricatures. The lynchers, those Negroes and workers who are vacillating and ineffectual, the boss Wallcott, are differentiated as individuals and drawn with as much psychological insight and care as Lonnie and Lem Morris, the white union organizer, and the great-hearted Negro woman Binnie. The scene in which Lem Morris tries to show Al Regan how fatal a color line in trade unionism is to his own interests, is dramatically as gripping as those in which the terrified Negroes huddle in Binnie's lunchroom while Lem tries to break down their age-old distrust of the white man, and a lynch mob rages outside. Unforgettable too are the dock episodes, with the stevedores singing at their back-breaking work, and the scene in which Lonnie by sheer magnetism and the force of his arguments converts the wailing of a prayer meeting over a dead man's body into heroic resistance.

Lonnie is a superb characterization, the first instance in our theatre of a Negro conscious of his power and unfaltering in his demand for equality and justice. He is able to lead his people in their first rebellion, and die, and still continue to lead them in death, because he has found the answer to the question his entire race is asking:

What dat mean, good nigger? Dat's just a scared nigger, dat's all. Nigger dat don't see and don't hear and do just what white boss tell him to.——Lawd, when de black man gwine stand up? When he gwine stand up proud like a man?——The lowest animal in the field will fight fo' its home. And all you can think of doing is running away. And supposing you do run way? Whar you gwine go to? Baton Rouge? Mississippi? Is it gwine to be any different thar? Dey gwine treat you better thar? You gwine find jobs? You gwine get yo'self a home? Nassuh. You got black skin. You can't run away from dat. Make no difference whar you are, dey hound you just the same.——Ain't no peace fo' de black man—ain't never gwine to be, till he fight to get it——We try to organize to get ourselves a decent living. And what happen? Dey beat us up, dey arrest us, shoot us, burn down our houses. Why? Why? Why dey do dat? Because dey just plain mean? Because dey want to give you pain? Because dey like to see you dangling from a tree? No. Dat ain't de reason. De reason is dey want to keep de black man down!——Because dey want to use him. Dey want to use him fo' de hardest jobs dey got. Dey want him to work fo' nothing.

Another fine example of the militant labor play is *Let Freedom Ring*, Albert Bein's dramatization of Grace Lumpkin's novel *To Make My Bread*. Here the theme of exploitation and awakening power is enriched by the study of Carolina mountaineer stock lured into the city factories by promises of fabulous wealth, and drawing on its heritage of strength and integrity to resist bondage at

the cost of life itself. The McClures are a magnificent
example of the wealth of dramatic material available to
regional drama in our most native types, and of how
pride and toil and the struggle for a life of dignity and
aspiration are the essence of our national tradition.

On a par with *Waiting for Lefty* among one-act plays
are Paul Green's demoniac picture of the brutality and
degradation of a southern chain gang, in *Hymn to the
Rising Sun*, and Irwin Shaw's *Bury the Dead*, which
aroused nearly as much notice as *Lefty*. In Shaw's fantasy against a bare stage setting, six corpses, victims of
the war "that is to begin tomorrow night," refuse to be
buried. Instead they stand up in their common grave,
in passionate protest against their fate and that of their
unnumbered fellows. The frantic attempts of army, government, and church dignitaries to make them lie quietly
down again, in order to preserve the morale at the front
and at home, are richly satiric. Finally the authorities hit
on the device of using their womenfolk to break down
their resistance. Mother, sister, sweetheart, and wife,
they come one by one to plead with the men who stand,
macabre silhouettes with their backs to the audience, in
the indentation of the orchestra pit. They are obdurate,
and in the end the women themselves take up the cry
against further slaughter. The scene in which Martha
Webster excoriates her dead husband for his ineffectu-
ality in life, and calls society to account for her own
miserable half-life and that of millions of other men and
women, is electric theatre. Unfortunately, Shaw, using
the device of "spotting" successive speakers in a kind of
rapid-fire cinema technique, breaks up the cumulative
impression of the longer episodes; the tension and suspense repeatedly dribble away in interjections by officers,

newspapermen, priests, radio announcers, and others, often mere voices issuing from the darkness, until the action becomes a rat-tat-tat of words and the dramatic intensity is dissipated. The curtain should fall on Martha Webster's last blazing speech, which should bring the corpses out of their grave to rally mankind behind them.

The influence of this new drama has undoubtedly been one of the factors which has led established playwrights such as S. N. Behrman and Sidney Howard to the consideration of problems for which their point of view cannot provide them with a valid interpretation. On the other hand, it has also resulted in a play like Sidney Kingsley's Dead End, an extraordinary study of incipient gangsterism unerringly related to the conditions under which slum children grow up. Forced to play in the streets, nourished by the films and newspapers on gangster exploits, spectators of a struggle for existence in which they are also called on to participate from their earliest years, they know no code but that of violence and self-protection. Dead End drew an unforgettable object lesson from the juxtaposition of a wealthy East River apartment house and a miserable tenement slum, and Kingsley outdid himself in his portrait of the young street gamins. Unfortunately however the play suffers from lopsidedness, since the characters representing the other end of the social scale are caricatures and the love story is weak and irrelevant.

The most recent development in social drama is along the lines of musical satire. Its first example was Parade, originally a collection of biting sketches by George Sklar, Paul Peters, Emanuel Eisenberg, and others, and finally presented by the Theatre Guild to its refined subscription audience in much diluted form. It remained for a trade union, the International Ladies Garment Workers, to present the first full-blown "left revue," *Pins and Needles*, in the characteristic American musical tradition. At the same time, Marc Blitzstein's brilliant satirical operetta of "Steeltown," *The Cradle Will Rock*, opened up new avenues.

The formal unrealistic manner in which this production finally made its appearance throws an interesting light on the whole question of theatrical trappings and presentation. The operetta was prepared for production by the Federal Theatre with a complete array of scenery, lights, orchestra, etc. It was scheduled to open during the summer in which the Steel Workers' Organizing Committee was organizing the open-shop steel industry, but the W.P.A. suffered a sudden attack of cold feet. The producers, John Housman and Orson Welles, refused to submit to a ban on the production, and gave a historical opening performance at the Venice Theatre, with actors standing up in the audience to sing their roles, accompanied by a lone piano in the orchestra pit. Struck by the effectiveness of the proceedings, the producers tried a performance from a bare stage, with the cast seated in rows of chairs facing the audience and coming forward to stand beside the piano to "play" their scenes. Its success was such that the procedure was adopted as the regular mode of presentation, and raised anew the question of the importance of scenery in the theatre.

The development of "sceneryless plays" in conjunction with the newer social drama is no coincidence, and has its source in several factors, of which the economic is the most superficial. The dynamic use of lighting which has followed the discarding of scenery has proved more expensive, although there is no denying that the earliest labor plays were written without scenery because there were no funds for such an outlay. The influence of Continental expressionism, the later Brecht "epic" theatre, and the Russian constructivists also played a part. But the most potent factor lies in the new approach to *content* implicit in such plays as *Waiting for Lefty* and *Bury the Dead*, in which playwrights have begun once more to look beyond the isolated episode, the "story," to a deeper meaning, to the expression of an outlook on life as a whole. There was no place for the trivia of bedroom fittings and wholesale interior decoration in such plays.

On the other hand, while realistic detail can prove meaningless and cumbersome, an absence of scenery and consequent dependence on lighting may actually be more illusory and romantic than a collection of painted operatic backdrops. In the words of Howard Bay, "The job of the designer is to supply an environment in which hypothetical human beings exist and act. Only a positive specific environment will escape an idealistic abstraction. The formalism and mysticism of *Faustus* and *Julius Caesar* [1] is a direct result of the absence of concrete points of contact with reality, and bespeaks a confusion of basic viewpoint." [2] In the same way the absence of scenery and the use of lights in the production of *Our Town* expressed the essentially romantic and mystical content of Thornton Wilder's play. The problem of

[1] Productions by Orson Welles, the first for the Federal Theatre, the second at the Mercury Theatre.

[2] "Scenery or No Scenery? A Symposium," *Theatre Workshop*, April-June, 1938.

"scenery or no scenery" therefore goes back in most cases to the playwright's point of view which must determine the approach of the scene designer unless scenery and text are to be at odds.

But the question of form and presentation is only one aspect of *The Cradle Will Rock*. Blitzstein's work is a unique contribution to our theatre, not only because of the originality and verve with which it projects its ideas but because of the validity of those ideas themselves. Its satiric power derives from the savagery of its attack, and also from the comprehension of reality which underlies that savagery and which is its source. And its humor and tenderness are a lasting refutation of the idea that social drama is careless of human values, that it rejects the personal and individual for "causes" and theories. While some of the earlier plays may have savored too much of the soapbox, such crudity is completely absent in plays of the maturity of *Waiting for Lefty* and *The Cradle Will Rock*. Nor can one find greater gusto and richer humor anywhere among the Broadway school of comedy in recent years than in Ben Bengal's one-act comedy of a sit-down strike in a candy factory, *Plant in the Sun*. The younger militants have brought back laughter, born of human character comedy, to a theatre lately grown dependent on pallid epigrams or horseplay for amusement.

VIII   Conclusion

In Chapter I the playwright's dilemma was considered in some detail. His plays are produced under conditions resembling chaos. He must write primarily for an audience conditioned to accept only half-truths or falsehoods, and which prefers excitement and novelty, or a pleasantly emotional catharsis, to the drama of actuality. With the best will in the world it is difficult for him to avoid compromise or dilution, a tendency reinforced by his experience as a hack in Hollywood, where he sells his intelligence and integrity in six-month or five-year blocks at a good price.

Is this too pessimistic, too static a view, overlooking the forces within the commercial theatre and film industry making for more realistic and progressive plays and films? Has not the Broadway audience shown enthusiasm for *Pins and Needles;* has not Hollywood produced *They Won't Forget* and *Blockade?* It would be inaccurate and disastrous to overlook such manifestations; they deserve ample recognition to insure further progress. But it would be wrong to see in them signs of a possible wholesale reversal of the tendencies inherent in the amusement industry which block an honest portrayal of life. Audience organization can assist in supporting progressive plays on Broadway; trade union organization can impede production of pro-fascist or militaristic pictures. But such possibilities should not obscure the fact that in the last analysis the future of films and theatre alike must lie outside the field of private enterprise.

Where else? The problem of a theatre which can fulfill its function of illumination and appraisal, free, to some degree, of the bondage of second-rate entertainment and intellectual compromise, is one the dramatist cannot escape. Certainly the commercial theatre is not destined to disappear. It will even continue to furnish, as we have seen, occasional opportunity; ever so often a manager will make a courageous experiment. In addition, some valiant efforts at a solution of its contradictions have come from Broadway itself. The question is, what likelihood is there of realizing their promise?

Take the perennial idea of a collective theatre with a subscription audience, a permanent acting company, and a nucleus of playwrights attached, in direct competition with Broadway. This was the ideal, successively, of the Theatre Guild and the Group Theatre. The Guild, after some honoroble contributions to the art of the theatre, went unabashedly commercial. The Group has had a more fruitful history during its seven years' existence. Its avowed aim has been to present plays of social content which deal honestly and forthrightly with American life, to "the widest possible audience." Its plays have ranged in point of view from the uncompromising radicalism of *Waiting for Lefty* to the haphazard colorfulness of *Gold Eagle Guy* and *Casey Jones* and the conventionality of *Men in White*. Because it elects to play on Broadway, it is forced by high-production costs and commercial standards to compromise in its desire to reach a wide audience by charging $3.30 for its orchestra seats, if it wishes not only to make a success of any one production but to store up a reserve for future enterprises. Although this top price is lowered for the benefit audience which the Group has built up, and which is its best guarantee against the vagaries of critical and public opinion, it is nevertheless dependent, in the last analysis, on the sanction and support of an audience considerably narrower than that which, by its own definition, it seeks. It takes a *Men in White* or a *Golden Boy* to keep the Group going. *Waiting for Lefty* added nothing to its economic stability and in addition failed to find the audience it deserved even with a $1.65 top price, which is higher than the general public can afford to pay for an evening's entertainment.

Clifford Odets' *Golden Boy* offers an excellent example of the dilemma that eventually confronts the writers and producers who wish to present social plays to Broadway audiences. In *Golden Boy* Odets presented his ideas in terms of a symbolic conflict which has been widely criticized. The coincidence of a boy being both a gifted violinist and a first-rate boxer, it was held, is spiritually and physically impossible; therefore Odets is guilty of being melodramatic and of using a thoroughly "phoney" device with which to capture the interest and sympathy of his audience. But the weaknesses of *Golden Boy* cannot be dismissed so easily if justice is to be done its author and its own merits. Harold Clurman, director of the Group Theatre and of the play, points out that an early version carried the subtitle, "a *modern allegory*." "An allegory is an extremely simple but boldly outlined tale in which a series of images is used to suggest a meaning of a more general, and usually moral nature.——Whether or not Clifford Odets has chosen the happiest symbols in *Golden Boy*, it is a fact that his intention was to convey such a truth and to convey it in terms that would not only avoid preachment but entertain us by the mere raciness of its presentation." [1]

In addition, Clurman points out the dual significance of Joe Bonaparte's conflict, which is symbolic not only of the dilemma that confronts man in general, but the present-day writer in America in particular:

"So many artists today stand in relation to Hollywood as our hero in relation to his double career.——From this point of view *Golden Boy* might be regarded as Clifford Odets' most subjective play. Yet with this deeply and subtly subjective material Odets has attempted to write his most objective play—a play that would stand on its own feet so to speak, as a good show, a fast-moving story, a popular money-making piece. He has tried, in short, to bridge the gap between his own inner problems and the need he feels, like his hero and all of us in the audience, to make 'fame and fortune'. In his own work he has tried to reconcile the fiddle and the fist; he has tried to yield himself a positive result out of a contradiction that kills his hero. He has done this by making the whole thing into a morality which would instruct and read us

[1] Introduction, *Golden Boy*, by Clifford Odets, Random House, 1938.

all a lesson (himself and his audience) even while it amused."

Clearly the dramatist has attempted something of a tour de force, with the result that he has been criticized for compromising and cheapening his talent. Yet the mere fact that Odets has written a play whose social meaning is inescapable and which is not cast in the more familiar mold of labor or antiwar drama, is important in enrichening our theatre. On the other hand, there is no doubt that in so doing Odets has verged on melodrama in the conflict which he imposes on his hero between the prize ring and the violin, and in his ending, and has relied unduly on the excitement, tempo, and flashiness inherent in the whole life of the boxing ring to sustain his play, thus laying himself open to the charge of superficiality and sensationalism. The measure of the shortcomings of *Golden Boy* is thus the measure of the problem of reconciling controversial ideas with the requisite entertainment content which will yield a measure of subsistence or even a profit, on Broadway. The problem is well-nigh insoluble. As long as the social playwright continues to tackle it, from choice or from the necessity of making a livelihood, he faces the necessity of taking a chance on very scant returns for his work, or compromising to the degree to which Odets compromised in *Golden Boy. Waiting for Lefty* was a finer play than *Golden Boy* (though a simpler technical problem) and was proportionately less successful. *Golden Boy* was a hit, and sold to a picture company for $75,000. It represents approximately the highest point of honesty coincident with prosperity, beyond which a theatre with social ideas cannot go on Broadway.

There have been other attempts in New York, away

from Broadway, to build a theatre which would avoid the pitfalls of commercialism. Eva LeGallienne's Civic Repertory Theatre tried to solve the problem by escaping high theatre rentals on 14th Street and playing repertory to a $1.50 top subscription audience. Miss LeGallienne offered mostly foreign plays and classics, and built up a steady and enthusiastic audience which grew to near-capacity proportions. But repertory costs were too high to balance the budget at the price scale on which she insisted, and her theatre closed when an annual subsidy of $100,000 from private sources was withdrawn.

It is too soon, after only one season, to draw any conclusions about the newly established Mercury Theatre. So far it has a brilliant record with three creative revivals and the sponsorship of *The Cradle Will Rock*. But like other independent theatres which have kept their prices relatively moderate, the Mercury has staked its chances on success. Its price scale automatically debars it from any measure of security against adversity.

The failure of the Theatre Union's attempt to present social plays at prices ranging from $1.65 to 55¢, a failure which only overtook it after three and a half years of courageous effort, was actually a signpost towards a new American theatre. The Theatre Union based itself directly on the labor audience, whom it reached through trade unions and fraternal organizations. The initial response was such as to leave no doubts in anyone's mind that an enormous practically untapped theatre audience existed in the American working and white-collar class. Benefits were sold twelve weeks in advance for the first three Theatre Union productions: *Peace on Earth*, *Stevedore*, and *Sailors of Cattaro*. Thereafter, serious errors in policy aggravated the difficulties caused by a succession of poor plays. No nest egg was laid aside after the first two productions (both of which had made a small surplus), with the result that ensuing productions ran into the red (tiny deficits of a thousand to fifteen hundred dollars apiece, compared to that of the average Broadway "flop"!) and accounted in the end for an indebtedness of approximately $15,000, which was all that closed the Theatre Union. In addition, it ran aground on a sectarian policy as regards plays which should serve as a lesson to any further attempts along the same lines. Its audiences tired of the reiteration of formula which, at that stage of development of Left dramaturgy, was a widespread failing. Moreover, such plays as *Mother* and *Bitter Stream*, in addition to being repetitious, were dramatically inferior to the plays that preceded them. But the failure of the Theatre Union only showed the rich possibilities awaiting the theatre which would root itself in the trade-union audience and combine a flexibility of program with good business judgment.

In the final chapter of his excellent book on the Soviet theatre, Norris Houghton points out the fatal contradictions of our own theatre, and considers some alternatives.[2] He weights the potentialities of the Little Theatre movement outside New York, at one time considered the white hope of our drama, and dismisses it because of its tendency, with a few honorable exceptions, to dilettanteism[3] Mr. Houghton goes on to point out the diffi-

---

[2] Norris Houghton, Moscow *Rehearsals*, Harcourt Brace & Co., 1936.
[3] As far as a demand for more honest and provocative plays than those on Broadway is concerned. The trouble lies in the similarity of both audiences, since the patrons of the little theatres correspond in general to those on whom the box-office tills of the commercial theatre depend.

culties that confront a "collective" enterprise if it tries
to swim in commercial waters, and he makes the even
more fundamental point that the American public is
today far more "movie" than theatre-minded. A govern-
ment-subsidized theatre as a possible escape from the
evils of the "show business," must wait, he feels, on audience demand; at the moment it would be more logical,
from the point of view of popular demand, if the government moved into Hollywood and nationalized the
film studios!

What Mr. Houghton overlooked, even at the time of
his writing,[4] was the uncovering, by the Federal Theatre
Project, of an amazing degree of interest in the theatre
whenever and wherever it was made available. This
latent interest has now been shown to exist throughout
the length and breadth of the United States.[5] It dates
back several decades ago, prior to the theatrical trusts
when the moving pictures and other factors strangled
the theatre and drove it into a tiny area in the city of
New York, to the time when every city of any size
boasted its own stock company, and touring companies
ranged from coast to coast. It is this reservoir which constitutes the hope of the theatre today; so far only the
Federal Theatre and a few labor theatres have tapped
even a fraction of it.

During the 1938 session of the Seventy-Fifth Congress, a bill was framed which would establish a Bureau
of Fine Arts, to continue the work of the present art
projects on a permanent nonrelief basis.[6] The Federal

[4] 1936.
[5] Willson Whitman, *Bread and Circuses,* Oxford University
Press, 1937.
[6] The original bill, sponsored by Congressman Coffee, contained

Arts Bill presents a feasible and immediate means of amending the conditions which have hampered and endangered the work of the Arts Projects to date, such as red tape, bureaucracy, control by administrators whose knowledge of the arts involved was negligible, and insecurity of tenure, none of which are inherent in the conception of a government financed theatre. Those who protest that theatre and politics do not mix should consider the unquestionably nonpolitical administration of such institutions as the Health Service, the Geodetic Survey, and the Bureau of Standards; in addition, it should by now be abundantly evident that art and business do not mix any too well either.

Even without the immeasurable improvements contained in a structure such as that designed by the Federal Arts Bill, the Federal Theatre as it has existed thus far has made noteworthy contributions. I refer not only to the extraordinary number of spectators to which it has played or the number of productions made in one year, but to the novel dramatic form evolved by the Living Newspaper, the scope permitted the creative talent of a producer such as Orson Welles, and the Negro acting company which presented Macbeth, and Haiti, and to a number of other productions which measured up to the best of the commercial theatre.

The audience which flocked to the Federal Theatre at prices ranging from 15¢ to 55¢ can be reached in still another way. Since 1930 an amateur workers' theatre

the historic admission that "it is the obligation of the Government to recognize that culture as represented by the arts is a social necessity consistent with democracy and also to recognize that such culture must be encouraged and developed in the interest of the general welfare."

movement has been underway in America, and steadily developing. For all its crudities and shortcomings, and the fact that its individual groups have frequently had a brief existence, it has been a powerful force. It has exerted a considerable effect on the professional theatre since organizations such the Group Theatre, the Theatre Union, and, more recently, the Federal Theatre have drawn personnel and stimulus from different workers' and "new theatre" groups. Organization and leadership for this movement on a national scale have emanated from the New Theatre League, and for four years the most advanced and creative thought in our theatre found expression in the pages of New Theatre magazine. It was for contests sponsored by the League and the magazine jointly that *Waiting for Lefty*, *Bury the Dead*, *The Cradle Will Rock*, and *Plant in the Sun* were written.

The further potentialities of this movement, especially when seen in conjunction with the growth of organized labor, are enormous. One can easily envisage a cultural organization connected with, say, the C.I.O., in much the same way as the Maison de la Culture, with its variegated activities, is the outgrowth of the Popular Front in France.[7] Labor Stage, dramatic section of the

[7] At its annual convention at Atlantic City in October, 1937, the C.I.O. passed the following resolutions:

Workers Education and Federal Arts
Whereas, the extension of education and culture is of vital concern to the progressive labor movement, and essential to the realization of its aims, and
Whereas, for the first time in the history of the country, as a result of the Federal Arts Projects, millions of workers and their families throughout the land have received the benefits of cultural enlightenment beyond an elementary education, and

cultural department of the International Ladies' Garment Workers' Union, which produced the successful musical review *Pins and Needles*, is an instance of what can be done along these lines. Undoubtedly other forward looking trade unions will follow its example, since their membership assures them an audience of large proportions and steadily increasing interest and understanding in social problems. Moreover there is no reason why this cultural work should remain on an amateur or semiprofessional basis, with actors recruited solely from their own ranks, as was the case with the cast of *Pins and Needles*. Professional companies, paid at regular theatrical trade-union wage scales (this naturally excludes exaggerated salaries for stars or featured players), are·a perfectly possible development, and one which, along with the development of regional theatres envisaged in the Federal Arts Bill, might take up much of the present slack in employment in the theatre professions.

The same argument may be raised against both of these possibilities; that they draw the dramatist into a large organization beyond his individual control in which he may be subjected to the rigors and indignities of bureaucratic control, mismanagement, and censorship. This is a very definite danger which must be recognized. Censorship, discreetly veiled, was exercised in

Whereas, it is consistent with democratic government to assure the benefits of education and cultural enlightenment to all, and

Whereas, the temporary and limited nature of the present program means that it is in danger of being entirely liquidated, and that its benefits may be lost, therefore be it

Resolved, that this conference declares the need for legislation by the Congress of the United States appropriating funds to create a permanent and expanded Workers Education and Federal Arts Program.

the case of several Federal Theatre productions, such
as the first Living Newspaper, *Ethiopia*, a projected
script by the same unit on lynching, and against *The
Cradle Will Rock*. In the case of a reactionary trade-
union leadership similar action would not be incon-
ceivable.

But such a possibility cannot rule out the need and
value of a government- or trade-union-supported theatre,
It merely dramatizes the fact that the playwright, like
every other artist and craftsman, has a high stake in the
leadership and administration of his government or the
organization which affords him a market for his work,
that he is deeply involved in the same political and
economic issues as his fellow men. Is this any less true
when the production of his plays depends on such a
chaotic situation as now exists in our theatre as regards
capital, management, and audience approval? Is not
the dramatist at the mercy of the threat of war, of
Fascism, of cyclic economic depressions, unless he,
along with workers of every other category, organizes
effectively against them? The day of the writer safe in
his ivory tower (safe and bored!), if indeed it ever
existed, is clearly past; wishful thinking will not bring
it back. At every point his interests drive him into
shouldering the social responsibility and leadership that
his talent and position impose upon him. Realization of
this fact explains why so many writers, actors, and artists are in the forefront of the struggle for the Federal
Arts Bill, have formed organizations such as the Theatre Arts Committee in New York and the Anti-Nazi
League in Hollywood to help democratic Spain and
China, and fight censorship and limitation of free speech
in America. It explains the growing interest in progres-

sive leadership among the membership of the different artist unions—Actors' Equity, the Screen Writers' and Screen Actors' Guilds, the Dramatists' Guild, and the increasing rank and file pressure to swing these groups into direct participation with the progressive trade-union movement as a whole. Above all, it explains the trend towards explicit and outspoken social drama, and its effect on even the playwrights who have not taken part in it but who are unable wholly to avoid its influence.

There is another criticism which will be voiced against a labor- or government-supported theatre: that while it may not take over the same taboos as those now in force in the commercial theatre, it will develop its own, which will be no less absolute, with which the dramatist will be forced to comply at the same price to his integrity as a craftsman and a thinker that he now pays on Broadway and in Hollywood. He will be restricted to a narrow field of subject matter, because a predominantly labor audience will demand only strike plays, militant and propaganda dramas; and because it will reject much of the drama at present being written for the commercial theatre.

It is necessary to restrain the temptation to answer "So what?" to this last, since it involves the basic question what plays will such an audience ask for and accept? What, by its standards, will be a good play, and how much freedom will it permit its writers? Norris Houghton has aptly written: "Freedom in the arts really means one of two things, either the unrestricted right of the artist to comment on life as he sees it, or else his right to withdraw from life altogether and escape into his art." [8] It is true that the audience of a

[8] Houghton, *Moscow Rehearsals.*

genuine people's theatre would not, in all likelihood, countenance the latter to anything like the extent that it is now tolerated by an audience which is itself eager to escape from certain menacing aspects of life that threaten its hitherto unchallenged immunities. Nor will an audience which is becoming more and more realistic in its attitude towards present-day social and political problems as well as steadily more conscious of its own power, countenance anything like the distortions and evasions of certain facts of life in which the Broadway carriage trade rejoices.

It may be contended that this new "popular" audience coincides to a great extent with the regular movie-going public, which has not yet shown itself so critical of the films in matters pertaining to its experience. But as the moving-picture companies have found to their sorrow in several instances, this audience is beginning to question and reject some of the more obvious distortions perpetrated by the studios, and there are signs that, working through trade unions and other community and cultural organizations, it will make its opinion increasingly felt. The formation of such an organization as Associated Film Audiences which furnishes its members with forthright criticism of reactionary and antilabor trends in moving pictures is a significant symptom.

Far from restricting its demands to a narrow formula of labor play, a people's audience given the opportunity, would develop a wide catholicity of taste—a possibility the Theatre Union overlooked to its own undoing. It would delight in the robustness and high spirits of a production like the Mercury Theatre's *Shoemaker's Holiday*, and would probably uproariously approve a

farce like *Three Men on a Horse*. It would enjoy
Shakespeare, particularly modern interpretive revivals
such as the Mercury's *Julius Caesar*. The playbills of
the Federal Theatre have ranged from "Molière in North
Carolina to Paul Green in Seattle, Noel Coward in
Georgia, Ernst Toller in Indiana and Gilbert and Sul-
livan in Ohio." [9] In fact, such an audience would be
likely to accept at the start very nearly anything at all,
as the above passage makes abundantly clear, since it
is starved for theatre and its critical faculties are still
dulled by dependence on Hollywood products. But as
the moving pictures themselves have learned, through
pictures like *Zola* and *The Good Earth*, and as the radio
has discovered, through its broadcasts of the Metropoli-
tan Opera and Toscanini, the long-suffering American
public will take as much of the best as it can get, *and
afford*. Reached at their most highly developed level,
through their unions and schools and clubs, these people
will shortly begin to demand realism and honesty where
matters of their own experience are concerned, as well
as a high level of imagination and originality. The
playwright who sets out to write for such a nation-wide
audience need not be afraid of being restricted. He is
more apt to escape from what is really cliché—the drawing-room comedy or bedroom-farce formula, the glitter-
ing puerilities of salon and bar—to material that is
vital and exciting and, above all, dramatic. He will come
at last into his real heritage of American life.

We have the possibility of building in America a
theatre which will offer the playwright a great field of
endeavor. Its success—for a theatre cannot exist without plays—and his own fate involve a definite choice on

[9] Whitman, *Bread and Circuses*.

his part: for which theatre, which audience will he write? There is no escape from the inevitability and the finality of this choice as it confronts every dramatist today, a choice in which the problem of earning a living can often be resolved, as has been pointed out, by the question, "What *kind* of a living?" The men and women who continue to write for Broadway and Hollywood are in danger of being trapped in the same way that the composer in *Beggar on Horseback* found that he was trapped:

> *You take our money and you live our life.*
> *We own you, we own you.*

But the composer turned the handle of his jail cell and discovered that it had been open all the time, and he walked out, a free man. The American theatre is waiting for the playwrights who will do likewise.

THE END

Index

327

About the author

Eleanor Flexner was born in New York City and has lived there all her life with the exception of two winters abroad, one in France and one in England. She went through the Lincoln School in New York, graduated from Swarthmore College, and studied for an additional year at Somerville College, Oxford. After a year's volunteer publicity work for a large social agency she began a varied experience in the theatre with a winter in the Apprentice Group at the Civic Repertory Theatre, where she acted as assistant stage manager in several of Miss LeGallienne's productions. Then followed a season with an enterprising young group which tried to establish a permanent acting company—and failed!—a year in a theatrical press office, and two years on the staff of *New Theatre*. In the intervals she has written and translated plays, and read, stage-managed, and reviewed them.